"Persuasive, imaginat:

That's how James Grant, in the introduction to "The Floating Kilogram," describes the 130 editorials on the dollar crisis that make up this volume from The New York Sun. "They constitute . . . a unique record of America's monetary struggles — and of the world's — in the first part of the 21$^{st}$ century."

The Sun was the first newspaper to raise an alarm when, in December 2005, the value of the dollar collapsed to under a 500$^{th}$ of an ounce of gold. It issued an editorial called "The Bush Dollar" and warned that the gold price was a portent. The politicians plunged ahead, and all too soon, the Great Recession was upon us.

Eventually the value of the dollar collapsed to less than an 1,800$^{th}$ of an ounce of gold. That, the Sun said, would have "floored the Founders." For it turns out that George Washington, Alexander Hamilton, Thomas Jefferson, and James Madison knew what they were doing when they made the dollar our constitutional money.

Now that the economy is inching its way out of the long recession, the value of the dollar has recovered somewhat — but to nowhere near where it was as recently at the start of the crisis. So the issue is starting to percolate in the Congress, to which the Constitution grants the monetary powers.

"The position of the Sun is that there are three circumstances when it makes sense to move to a system of sound money. One is when a currency is collapsing. Two is when it is steady. And three is when it is appreciating. What one really wants, at any point, is the confidence that the dollar will remain exchangeable for gold over a long period and that people will have trust in that."

— From "The Moment for Gold"

"There was a time, back during the Bush Boom, when the rise in the gold price was being attributed to the boom itself, to the need for gold in manufacturing. To what is the rise in the gold price — pardon, the collapse in the value of the dollar — being attributed now? The one thing that seems clear is this: None dare call it inflation."

— From "None Dare Call It Inflation"

"For Mr. Bernanke to appear before Congress in a week in which the value of the dollar plunged to the lowest point in its history, meaning a week in which the price of an ounce of gold has risen to its highest nominal price in history, and assert that consumers don't want to buy gold, well, it's just breath-taking. Marie Antoinette, *telephonez votre bureau.*"

— From "The Eclipse of Ben Bernanke"

*Mirror, mirror on the wall*
*Who makes us so un-equal?*
*Answer, thee, this white-haired head:*
*Could it be our very Fed?*

— From "Janet Yellen's Halloween"

"One of our favorite japes is about the group of scientists who figure out the secret to life — a way to make a human being from nothing but dirt. When they've worked it all out, they are so excited they go directly to God to announce their discovery that He is no longer necessary. He appears a bit surprised, but they offer to demonstrate. He nods. One of the scientists bends down and scoops up a fistful of dirt.

'Oh, no,' God exclaims. 'You've got to make your own dirt.'

This is how we feel about bitcoins . . . "

— From "God and Bitcoins"

# Seth Lipsky

# 'The Floating Kilogram'

## . . . And Other Editorials on Money From The New York Sun

—

Foreword by
## James Grant

New York Sun Books

Published at New York City

"The Floating Kilogram
... And Other Editorials on Money
From the New York Sun"

Inquiries: books@nysun.com.

The New York Sun and the drawing of Liberty and Justice with
the slogan "It Shines for All" are registered trademarks used by
permission of The New York Sun.
The an earlier edition of this anthology,
containing 47 editorials, was issued in 2011
under the title "It Shines for All,
The Gold Standard Editorials of
The New York Sun."

ISBN-13:
978-0996123204
(New York Sun Books)

ISBN-10:
0996123202

*10 9 8 7 6 5 4 3 2 1*

www.nysun.com

# Contents

# Foreword

From Alexander Hamilton's time to Abraham Lincoln's, and from Rutherford B. Hayes's presidency to Richard Nixon's, the dollar was as good as gold. It was convertible into gold or an equivalent value of silver, on demand. The coin itself, went plunked down on a counter, made a pleasing, substantial sound. To restore the dollar to that very condition of soundness is the editorial mission of The New York Sun.

One hundred and thirty editorials on this great monetary question are collected here. This is more than double the number included in the original edition of this anthology, which was issued in 2011 under the title "It Shines for All." Individually, the editorials are persuasive, imaginative, and unfailingly entertaining. Together, they constitute more than even the sum of those delectable parts — a unique record of America's (and the world) monetary struggles in the first decades of the 21$^{st}$century.

Most of these editorials are the work of the Sun's editor, Seth Lipsky, an American journalistic original. Having been graduated from Harvard in 1968, he willingly served in Vietnam, a road less traveled if there ever was one. For nearly 20 years, he wrote for the Wall Street Journal, covering, among other assignments, the hearings in 1981 of the United States Gold Commission. Eventually he founded the English-language Jewish Forward and, latterly, the Sun, which for seven years between 2002 and 2008 smudged the fingers of its avid New York readers but is now issued online.

Others in Lipsky's craft might style themselves "journalists." Lipsky, defiantly, remains a "newspaperman." He does not "post" his writings online (where the Sun has appeared since it folded its print edition on September 30, 2008) but rather "files" them. Electronic messages are, in his lexicon, not e-mails but "wires" or "cables." In his journalistic virtuosity, Lipsky calls to mind the great A.J. Liebling of the New Yorker, who boasted, "I write better than anyone who writes faster, and faster than anyone who writes better." In 2014, Lipsky fills that bill if anyone does.

My friend would blanch at being called a constitutional scholar, but facts are facts. His monetary principles come straight from the American Founders, whose handiwork he described and delineated in "The Citizen's Constitution: An Annotated Guide" (Basic Books, 2009). The Founders' devotion to sound money is, for Lipsky, a fact still more relevant to the monetary discussion than the Federal Reserve's best guess for the 2012 inflation rate or the growth of the bank credit. The very idea of an unanchored dollar, he writes in these pages, "would have floored the Founders, who granted the Congress the power to coin money and regulate its value in the same sentence in which they also granted the Congress the power to fix the standard of the other weights and measures. . . ."

New York may be the financial capital of the world, but the crusade for the restoration of sound money is the Sun's scoop. Its campaign is the first in the five boroughs since the peerless Henry Hazlitt was ousted by the New York Times some 65 years ago for his opposition to the Keynes-inspired Bretton Woods arrangements. A few years after Hazlitt's departure, the old Sun — the one that Lipsky and his investors resurrected — had thrown in the towel. "Throughout its career," the editors signed off in the final, page-one editorial in 1950, "[this newspaper] has supported Constitutional government, sound money . . . and has upheld all the finer American traditions."

Cunningly, the editor of this collection has selected "The Floating Kilogram" as the opening essay. In it, Lipsky picks up on news reports that the official kilogram, as kept under a locked dome by the International Bureau of Weights and Measures, has been discovered to have lost some atoms of mass, so its integrity has been called into question. Let me not give away the plot here, save to say that after savoring the opening essay, no reader will willingly put down the book.

In monetary matters, as Lipsky observes, America is busily going backwards: from the gold standard to the PhD standard, and from central banking to a kind of new-age central planning. With scarcely a peep from Congress (the party of one from Texas, Ron Paul, excepted, until he retired) the Federal Reserve has imposed a zero percent money-market interest rate that simultaneously staves the savers and fattens the speculators. The Fed has shouldered the work of manipulating the markets in equities and mortgages, work that the Founders almost certainly never dreamt that any branch of government would presume to undertake.

The Founders did foresee the growth of a free press, however, and the Fed and the Congress proceed in these cockeyed experiments under the fierce, yet scintillating, gaze of the Sun. Lipsky's mentor on the Wall Street Journal, Robert L. Bartley, once quipped, "It takes 75 editorials to pass a law." He was dealing with mere tax reform. With 130 gold-standard editorials already in print, though, Lipsky is fast approaching the point of policy crystallization. May his fingers fly over the keyboard.

— James Grant
New York City

*"You're trying to behave as though
one could stand right outside
our economic system.
But one can't.
One's got to change the system,
or one changes nothing."*

George Orwell,
*"Keep the Aspidistra Flying"*

# The Floating Kilogram

A 'new urgency' is how the New York Times, in a marvelous editorial this week, describes the rush to redefine the official kilogram. That famous weight and measure turns out to be what the newspaper describes as a cylinder of platinum and iridium maintained by the International Bureau of Weights and Measures. It is kept there under three glass domes accessible by three separate keys. It is, the Times notes, more than 130 years old and is what the paper calls the "only remaining international standard in the metric system that is still a man-made object." The "new urgency" comes from the discovery that the official cylinder may be losing mass, which, the Times says, "defeats its only purpose: constancy."

Of course, we could let the confounded kilogram just float. After all, we let the dollar just float, its creation and status as legal tender a matter of fiat, its value adjusted by the mandarins at the Federal Reserve depending on such variables as they from time to time share, or not, with the rest of the world and, in any event, as would have floored the Founders, who granted the Congress the power to coin money and regulate its value and did so in the same sentence in which they also granted the Congress the power to fix the standard of the other weights and measures, like, say, the aforementioned kilogram.

The Founders, many of whom promptly went into the Congress, turned around and regulated the value of the dollar at 371 ¼ grains of pure silver. The law through which they did that, the Coinage Act of 1792, noted that the amount of silver they were regulating for the dollar was the same as in a coin then in widespread use, known as the Spanish milled dollar. And they said a dollar could also be the free-market equivalent in gold. They never expected the value of the dollar to be changed any more than the persons who locked away that cylinder of platinum and iridium expected the cylinder to start losing its mass.

Here in the modern age, though, the members of the Federal Reserve Board don't worry about how many grains of silver or gold are behind the dollar. They couldn't care less. When the value of a dollar plunges at a dizzying rate, the chairman of Federal Reserve, Ben Bernanke, goes up to Capitol Hill and, in testimony before the House, declares merely that he is "puzzled." No "new urgency" to redefine the dollar for him. The fact is that we've long since ceased to define the dollar, and it can float not only against other currencies but against the 371 ¼ grains of pure silver.

So why not the kilogram? After all, when you go into the grocery to buy a pound of hamburger, why should you worry about how much hamburger you get — so long as it's a pound's worth. A pound is supposed to be .45359237 of a kilogram. But if the Congress can permit Mr. Bernanke to use his judgment in deciding what a dollar is worth, why shouldn't he — or some other PhD from Massachusetts Institute of Technology — be able to decide from day to day what a kilogram is worth? Why, not to put too fine a point on it, is the New York Times so concerned about the consarned constancy?

No doubt some will cavil that the fact that the dollar floats makes it all the more reason for the kilogram to be constant. But we would say, what's so special about the kilogram. Maybe they should both float. If the fiat dollar floats, one has no idea what it will be worth when it comes time to spend it. If the kilogram — that basic unit of weight of all that we buy by weight — also floats, it will be twice as hard to figure out what whatever we're buying will be worth. So what if, when we unwrap our hamburger, the missus has to throw a little more sawdust in the meatloaf.

To those who would say that would be unfair, if not completely deconstructionist, let us compromise. Let's go to a fiat kilogram, that is, permit the kilogram float, but apply the new urgency to fixing the dollar at a specified number of grains of — and we might as well pick something essentially inert — gold. To those who say it would be ridiculous to fix the dollar but let the butcher hand you whatever amount of hamburger he wants for a kilogram or a pound of the stuff, we say, what's the difference as to whether it's the measure of money that floats or the measure of weight.

For that matter, one could go whole hog and fix the value of both the kilogram and the dollar but float the value of time. You say you want to be paid $100 an hour. That's fine by your boss. But he gets to decide how many minutes in the hour. Or how long the minute is. You know you'll get a kilogram of meat for the price a kilogram of meat costs. But you won't know how long you have to work to earn the money. It strikes us as a risky deal. But speaking here for The New York Sun, we say if people are going to insist that the whole point of the kilogram is its constancy, then we're going to say that there's no point to it without, as well, a constant dollar.

— February 11, 2011

# The Bush Dollar

If we were President Bush — a stretch, to be sure, but all the greater the honor — the thing that we'd be worried about these days is less the war than the dollar. For every senator and editorial writer wringing his hands over the war, it is possible to find someone sending in an encouraging report from the theater. But when it comes to the greenback, the president's policies, or America's (take your pick), don't seem to be getting much respect. James Grant, writing on these pages last week, pointed out that over the course of Mr. Bush's presidency, the value of the dollar has plunged 46% in terms of the metal that is the greatest store of value. And if it keeps going in this direction, as our Dan Dorfman reports this morning that several experts reckon it will, Mr. Bush will leave his presidency with America's currency a shadow of what it was when he first took the constitutional oath.

Now it is true the greenback has been holding its value against the Euro and the Japanese Yen and, for that matter, the Communist Chinese scrip. But that's not much of a compliment. The Red Chinese are fixing to a basket of currencies that includes the dollar, and the economies of Japan and Europe, meaning, in the latter case, principally the Germans, are textbook weaklings. And it is also true that it was not to the president that the Founders of America delegated the power to fix the value of the dollar. That power was, in Article 1, delegated to the Congress, which has long since abdicated by delegating the management of the currency to the Federal Reserve. And it is also true that Mr. Bush would be far from the first war-time president who saw the value of the dollar decline on his watch. Franklin Delano Roosevelt gave up control of the dollar, as did, notoriously, President Nixon.

All that notwithstanding, the value that has moved from the dollar to gold cannot be good for Mr. Bush's reputation. It may be, as some suggest, that the dollar, at about a 265th of an ounce of gold, was, when he took office, over-valued. It's not a concept that sits comfortably with us, but there is a school of thought that reckons a good place for the dollar to have been managed would have been at something close to a 350th of an ounce of gold. Even if one accepts such a view, a dollar that is worth less than a 500th of an ounce of gold is something Mr. Bush is going to have a hard time explaining to his grandchildren - not to mention the rest of us. With three years left to go in Mr. Bush's presidency and the gold value of the dollar collapsing, something, as Mr. Dorfman writes, "certainly seems out of whack."

Mr. Dorfman quotes Frank Holmes of U.S. Global Securities as pointing out that whenever inflation, as measured by the Consumer Price Index, is greater than the Federal Funds rate — which Mr. Dorfman notes is currently the case — the price of gold tends to rise because of the negative return on cash. It wouldn't surprise us were Mr. Bush to understand this. He picked, in Ben Bernanke, a Federal Reserve chairman who has a record of understanding the importance of constraining changes in the values of a currency. Mr. Bernanke has supported a regime of monetary management known as inflation targeting. Inflation targeting tends to be about domestic goals, that is, how much prices go up in a certain time frame. We'd like to think at some point he will want to, or have to, pay attention to the gold price.

— December 5, 2005

# The Golden Why

As the price of gold pushes toward $550 an ounce, Wall Street asks, "Why?" We would ask, "Why not?" The dollar is a piece of paper of no intrinsic value. It costs next to nothing to produce. It is ubiquitous, especially in the vaults of America's Asian creditors. Gold is costly to produce and hard to find - easy on the eyes, too. In the day, gold was money itself. It was the collateral behind the paper. If you didn't trust the dollar - or the pound, the yen or the various European currencies now rolled up into the euro - you could exchange the paper for the specified, lawful weight of bullion.

The full-strength gold standard died in World War I. An eviscerated gold-based monetary system was instituted in the 1920s. A still less rigorous regime was set in place at the end of World War II. And this second pale shadow of the real McCoy — it was called Bretton Woods — ended with President Nixon's 1971 decision to sever the final connection between gold and the dollar. At the time, an ounce of gold was the equivalent of $35. A great inflation followed.

As a monetary asset, gold is unsurpassed. You can conjure up all the dollars you want, if you happen to be the American government, but gold occurs in the earth in only three to five parts per billion. Once found and mined, it is indestructible. The world's supply of gold therefore grows slowly but steadily. A given year's output (or shortfall in output) makes no great difference in the size of the global hoard.

In two weeks, Ben S. Bernanke is expected to relieve Alan Greenspan at the helm of the Federal Reserve. Mr. Bernanke, a former Princeton economics professor with a weakness for the vivid heuristic metaphor, once incautiously boasted that the Fed could, if it wanted, drop dollar bills out of helicopter doors. This was in 2002, when the Fed, of which Mr. Bernanke was then a governor, was on a campaign to prop up the rate of inflation. "Deflation" was monetary enemy No.

1, or so said the central bank.

"Like gold, U.S. dollars have value only to the extent they are strictly limited in supply," said Mr. Bernanke in the heat of this campaign to whip deflation, of which there was none. "But the U.S. government has a technology, called a printing press (or, today, its electronic equivalent), that allows it to produce as many U.S. dollars as it wishes at essentially no cost. . . . We conclude that, under a paper-money system, a determined government can always generate higher spending and hence positive inflation."

Gold, though beautiful to behold, pays no interest. Then, again, interest rates the world over are the lowest they have been in generations. In Japan, they are virtually zero. Dollars yield more than euros - on money market deposits, 4% rather than 2% — but the yield is not so much higher than the rate of inflation. By choosing to buy gold, a saver pays no great penalty in foregone interest income.

Nowadays, the dollar is faith-based. So is every other national currency. All owe their value to the words "legal tender," or their non-English equivalent, and to the people's confidence in the judgment and probity of the men and women whose hands crank the printing press, or tap the computer keys. No doubt, Mr. Bernanke means to do well by his country. But he has made it plain that he will not countenance a rate of inflation too close to the zero mark. The dollar, he has said, should depreciate by 2% or 3% a year, no more and no less.

We are not sure which part of the chairman-in-waiting's prescription is more concerning: his expressed belief in the necessity of debasement of the currency or his cool confidence that the Fed can exactly bring it about. Central bankers are not seers, not miracle workers. They are government employees. Why, then, is the gold price going up? We'd be surprised if it weren't.

— January 13, 2006

# The Pelosi

The Wall Street Journal's editorial in respect of the weakening dollar yesterday — "The dollar's fate is very much in our own hands," was its point — reminded us of an encounter we had some years ago with Senator Moynihan. It occurred when the senator stopped by to visit with the editors of the Forward. The senator, who was then chairman of the Finance Committee, was asked about the responsibility of the Congress, under Article I of the Constitution, to fix the value of the dollar (and the other weights and measures). We were startled to hear Moynihan declare that controlling the dollar was, because of the great size of the private capital markets by that stage in history, beyond the power of the Congress to control. It was such a stunning, incorrect assertion that, though we loved Moynihan, we went out that November and cast our vote for Bernadette Castro.

The Founding Fathers of America were so clear in respect of their understanding of where they intended to lay responsibility for the dollar that the world knows where to look. So the fact that the imminent accession of the Democrats in the Congress has been met with an a round of currency jitters is a signal to watch. Not that the Republicans were any great role models. The dollar on their watch collapsed to the point that today one is lucky if a greenback will purchase one 637th of an ounce of gold, not even close to half what it would have purchased when, say, President Bush took office. All the greater the impact of the latest flight from the American currency. Some will insist blame attaches to Chairman Greenspan & Co. But it was Congress that created the Federal Reserve. Hence the attention to the Democratic accession.

These columns are not indifferent to the exchange rate of the dollar in terms of foreign scrip, like the Euro or the Communist Chinese currency. The Wall Street Journal noted yesterday that it is heartening to hear Secretary Paulson asserting that a strong dollar is "clearly in our nation's interest," a remark the Journal reported Mr. Paulson making to reporters traveling with him in London. Rather than a "strong" dollar, which strikes us as a relative term, we prefer "sound dollar," which strikes us as making a reference to the dollar's definition against something real. The other day a federal judge actually issued a ruling saying our currency was illegal because all denominations were printed in a size undistinguishable by a person who is blind. But how is even a sighted person, once he has a dollar in his hand, able to predict what, under American law, it's going to be worth a few months hence?

So we'd have preferred to be hearing, from either Secretary Paulson or Chairman Bernanke or the Congress, some reference to a connection between the dollar and something real — gold, say, or even to a price rule. In the months ahead, after all, people are going to be charting the dollar and watching where it stands, not only against other currencies but also against gold. Between now and 2008, we will be in a period in which, if the dollar begins to fall, the blame is not going to attach to the Republicans, who will no longer control the Congress, but to Democrats. If the dollar goes down further from here, it might as well be renamed the Pelosi. Going into a transitional election with a falling dollar is not something the Democrats will want to do. It wasn't all so long after Moynihan rejected the notion that the Congress could live up to its responsibility for the dollar that the voters revoked the party's mandate on the Hill.

— November 30, 2006

# The Greenspan

The Federal Reserve Open Market Committee is scheduled to vote tomorrow on whether to lower interest rates to prevent a housing market contagion from bringing down the rest of the economy, but it would be appropriate to start the meeting by renaming the greenback the Greenspan. This would be in honor — if that is the word — of the former Fed chairman, Alan Greenspan, who is out this morning with his long-awaited memoir.

It turns out, as our Nicholas Wapshott reports, He-of-the-Ever-Furrowed-Brow blames President Bush and Vice President Cheney for the ills of an economy the central measuring device of which is the dollar that it was Mr. Greenspan's job to maintain in sound condition. Yet Mr. Greenspan left the greenback very much weakened and worth but a fraction of what it was worth at the start of Mr. Bush's term of office. To which one can only say, wait until Mr. Bush sits down to write his assessment of Mr. Greenspan. The truth is that the collapse of the gold value of the dollar in recent years is a great scandal. We wrote about it in "The Bush Dollar," an editorial issued on December 5, 2005, pointing out that a dollar that was worth a 265th of an ounce of gold when Mr. Bush took office had plunged in value to less than a 500th of an ounce of gold. A year later, in an editorial issued on November 30, 2006, and called "The Pelosi," we remarked that a new nervousness seemed to be driving down the value of the greenback as the Democrats were preparing to accede to the leadership in the Congress.

At the time of "The Pelosi," the dollar was worth a 637th of an ounce of gold, not even close to half of its value when Mr. Bush took office. At the time we noted that some would insist that the blame attach to Chairman Greenspan & Co. We noted that the Founders of America made it clear that it was to the Congress that they were delegating the power to regulate the value of the dollar and fix the standard of the other weights and measures. We also noted that it was the Congress that created the Federal Reserve.

As we plowed through Mr. Greenspan's book blaming everyone else but the family dog for the problems of the economy, it began to dawn on us that "the Greenspan" has a nice ring to it. It's not a lurch away from "the greenback." It's just a subtle shift in phrasing. Mr. Greenspan admits that he has harbored a nostalgia for the gold standard, but tells us that the value of the dollar is protected by other arrangements. Just not, it seems, the gold value of the dollar, which is the measure of its soundness. Today the dollar is worth less than one 700th of an ounce of gold.

It's become the government's practice to decorate the dollar with pictures of the presidents, and we wouldn't want to push them aside to accommodate the visage of Mr. Greenspan on the currency that would carry his name. We would suggest redesigning the scrip to have two pyramids — one a large pyramid made of gold ingots and the other a tiny little pyramid, also made of gold ingots. And the famous eye atop the tiny pyramid could be glimpsed through an etching of Mr. Greenspan's spectacles. We'd like to think that in the conversations at the Fed about renaming the greenback "the Greenspan" there might be found the beginnings of, if not wisdom, at least humility.

— September 17, 2007

# Ron Paul's Prescience

Congressman Ron Paul: "It just looks like we may well come to a '79, '80. Do you anticipate that there's a possibility that we'll face a crisis of the dollar such as we had in '79 and 1980?"

Chairman Bernanke: "The Federal Reserve is committed to maintaining low and stable inflation, and I'm very confident we'll be able to do that."

Dr. Paul: "You're not answering whether or not you anticipate a problem."

Mr. Bernanke: "I'm not anticipating a problem like '79, '80. No."

* * *

That exchange, between Congressman Ron Paul and the chairman of the Federal Reserve board, Ben Bernanke, took place on July 18 in a hearing of the Joint Economic Committee. It can be viewed on YouTube.com – and has been by tens of thousands. The London fix on gold that day put the value of a dollar a bit less than a 666th of an ounce of gold, according to the Kitco charts. Four months after Mr. Bernanke said he was not anticipating a crisis like that of 1980, when the dollar collapsed to 1/850th of an ounce of gold, the dollar has reached just such a crisis, with the greenback trading Friday at less than 1/837th of an ounce. So much for Mr. Bernanke's anticipatory powers.

Now it will be said that the crises of 1980 and 2007 are not the same. In 1980, the inflation rate calculated from the Consumer Price Index averaged more than 13%, according to a chart at inflationdata.com; the average this year has been but 3.23%. But the dollar crisis comes at a most inconvenient time for the Fed because it comes amid a credit crisis as well. So far, Mr. Paul is looking a lot more prescient in respect of monetary policy than Mr. Bernanke. The Wall Street Journal, in an editorial last week, reached back 30 years to one of its famous editorials from 1978 to warn of a crisis over the dollar. It reckoned another such crisis wasn't inevitable, but that at least we're getting "a reminder of what such a thing looks like, and it isn't pretty."

Our own view is that Mr. Paul's prescience on the dollar is one of the reasons he's showing what the pundits are calling surprising strength on the hustings. The New York Times attributes it to the way the Internet is impacting the campaign. But we're of the view that it relates to the substance. We have a lot of differences with Mr. Paul, but on monetary matters, we've been covering him since his days, in the early 1980s, as a member of the United States Gold Commission, when he coauthored, with New York's own Lewis Lehrman, a minority report favoring a return to a version of the gold standard. What can be said about Mr. Paul is that he's not only ahead of Mr. Bernanke but also of his fellow Republicans, and he will eat into their standing until they address the question of the soundness of our currency.

— November 12, 2007

# $1,000 Gold

No doubt there are going to be a surfeit of newspaper editorial writers and politicians who ignore the news that the dollar fell, as it did yesterday, below a thousandth of an ounce of gold. But it strikes us as a milestone to mark. It was only little more than two years ago, on December 5, 2005, that we issued an editorial called "The Bush Dollar," charting the collapse of the greenback to barely a 500th of an ounce of gold from the 265th of an ounce of gold that it was worth when President Bush acceded.

At the time, Mr. Bush had just named Benjamin Bernanke to chair the board of governors of the Federal Reserve. Value continued to drain from the dollar at an astonishing rate. In mid-September of 2006, we issued an editorial called "The Greenspan," proposing to rename the greenback after the Fed chairman who'd just written a book that gave short shrift to the value of the dollar in terms of what has been called the barbaric relic.

When Congress took a pass, we issued, on November 30, 2006, another editorial, "The Pelosi," focusing on the fact that is was to the Congress that the Founders of America delegated responsibility for regulating the value of the dollar. But, despite the efforts of Congressman Ron Paul, the Congress didn't do anything more about the dollar under Mrs. Pelosi than it had under Dennis Hastert, and the dollar continued its collapse.

So on October 19 of last year, we put out an editorial called "The Bernanke," saying we were well enough into the years when "blame for the dollar's decline" would belong to the new chairman and his colleagues "and the Congress to which he explains his policies." We called the pace at which the dollar was falling "scandalous" and noted that our taxpayers are being forced to help underwrite the salaries of one staff at the International Monetary Fund to tell us that it's overvalued and another staff at the Federal Reserve to puzzle over the fact that the "core inflation" rate remains steady.

That editorial quoted the only member of Congress who seems even to notice the collapse of the dollar, Ron Paul. "Economic law dictates reform at some point," Mr. Paul had written in the fall of 2006. "But should we wait until the dollar is 1/1,000 of an ounce of gold or 1/2,000 of an ounce of gold? The longer we wait, the more people suffer and the more difficult reforms become." He warned that "runaway inflation inevitably leads to political chaos" and declared that the time for action is now.

Since he wrote that warning, we've begun to reap the sub-prime credit crisis, the crisis in insurance, the collapse of the real estate markets. In recent weeks, a growing number of commentators have begun to see that the story is one of inflation — that is, of a collapse of the dollar. It's story with financial, political, and geopolitical import, a fact that was recognized by Lawrence Kudlow in a column these pages carried. The Federal Reserve has been maneuvering frantically to find a way to solve the credit crisis without igniting inflation, putting, as our Julie Satow reports on the business page this week, something on the order of $200 billion in liquidity into the banks via new approaches.

\* \* \*

All this has amounted to the Fed changing its business model, bringing onto its books not only obligations of the United States treasury, which had been its main asset in recent years, but various collateral that once was held by commercial banks. Some of that collateral is extraordinarily complex, including, according to the Fed's own Web site, collateralized debt obligations, also known as CDOs; residential mortgage-backed securities, a.k.a. RMBS; and commercial mortgage-backed securities, i.e., CMBS — in other words, mortgages refashioned into bonds of varying degrees of creditworthiness and complexity. The Fed denies it is putting itself at any additional risk, because it can reject such mortgage securities as it deems unfit. But these securities are uncommonly hard to analyze. Our friends at Grant's Interest Rate Observer tell us that they looked at CDOs of such complexity that 150,000 pages of legal documentation is necessary to describe them.

This strategy has come at a time when the Democrats control Congress and are resisting calls to extend the Bush tax cuts and are abjuring other supply-side fiscal measures of the kind that created the incentives for growth under President Reagan. Those were incentives that powered a boom that continued through the Clinton years and rolled on into the 21st century. The thing to take from the years that Reagan was president and Paul Volcker was chairing the Fed is that it is not impossible to have a strengthening dollar and economic growth. Not only not impossible, we'd argue. It's even necessary to have a sound dollar. Once the Democrats have their nominee, it'll be the moment for Mr. McCain to confront them with the fact that the Congress they have controlled has given us a dollar worth but a thousandth of an ounce of gold and warn of its further collapse without the right leadership.

— March 14, 2008

# A Golden Rent

W hen we ran out a front-page article on the news that the price of Manhattan apartments as measured in gold was declining, it prompted quite a complaint from the real estate industry. But as a case recently decided by the judges who ride the Sixth Circuit shows, looking at real estate values in terms of gold was once a common practice — and the landlord who bet on it has just won big.

The case, 216 Jamaica Avenue LLC v. S & R Playhouse Realty LLC, involves a 99-year lease signed in 1912 on a piece of land in downtown Cleveland, Ohio. The rent escalated to $35,000 a year, but it contained a "gold clause" providing that "said rents shall be paid in gold coin of the United States of the present standard of weight and fineness."

As the opinion by Judges Harold Ackerman, Damon Keith, and Jeffrey Sutton recounts, "In the early 1930s, as part of a series of measures designed to implement the Roosevelt Administration's overhaul of American monetary policy, Congress withdrew gold from circulation and banned nearly all private ownership of it. ... And in 1933, Congress passed a Joint Resolution that declared gold clauses to be 'against public policy,' barred their inclusion in any future contract and suspended the operation of existing gold clauses by allowing all contract obligations to be paid in paper currency instead."

However, the opinion goes on, "Four decades later, Congress changed course. It repealed the ban on private ownership of gold in 1975. And in 1977, it amended the 1933 Joint Resolution, providing that the resolution 'shall not apply to obligations issued on or after' the amendment's date of enactment. ... In an effort to clarify the matter, Congress passed a law in 1996 saying that owners could enforce pre-1977 gold clauses only if the parties to a new obligation issued after 1977 'specifically agree[d] to include a gold clause' in their new agreement."

The case at hand, which was covered in these pages in

June under the headline "Count Those Square Feet in Gold" and which Brownstoner.com has linked to an article on the Web site of the Cleveland Plain Dealer, involves two companies with New York City ties. The landlord, Stuart Venner, is a New York-based real estate investor. The renter is an arm of Forest City Enterprises, which is behind the big effort to develop Atlantic Yards in Brooklyn and bring the Nets to play basketball there. If the gold clause is to be enforceable, Forest City's rent would escalate to about $1.4 million a year from $35,000 a year. The judges, in an opinion issued last week, found that the clause was indeed enforceable.

The landlord who wrote the contract back in 1912 was wise to protect himself against the possibility that a dollar in 2008 would be worth a fraction of what it was in 1912, as measured against gold. Unfortunately, even with Congress's changes to the law, America's monetary system, thanks to decisions by the Federal Reserve Bank or the Treasury, at the moment leaves ordinary investors and wage-earners not as well protected against the chance that the dollar will plunge. Recent months have seen a strengthening of the dollar against gold, but not such a strengthening as to close the rent gap between $35,000 and $1.4 million.

Senator Helms, who championed the 1970s legislation, has passed away, but Rep. Ron Paul is still around. Finding some way to assure that the rest of us who don't have gold clauses in our contracts can be assured of the value of our dollars would be a constructive role for the congressman to play. With this decision, the Sixth Circuit has done what it can, but the real responsibility lies with Congress.

— September 3, 2008

# Golden Opportunity

The big question following Secretary Geithner's admission that monetary policy was in error during much of the Bush administration is whether the Congress is going to step up to its responsibilities in respect of the national currency. Mr. Geithner's comments were made last week in response to a question from Charlie Rose about what mistakes he would see looking back. One the secretary cited was that, as he put it, "monetary policy around the world was too loose too long." That, he said, "created this just huge boom in asset prices, money chasing risk. People trying to get a higher return."

Mr. Geithner's concession was put up in lights this morning by the Wall Street Journal. It chided him for laying too much of the blame on foreigners but praised him for making "a break with the steadfast refusal of Fed Chairmen Alan Greenspan and Ben Bernanke to admit any responsibility. They prefer to blame bankers and what they call the 'global savings glut,' as if the Fed had nothing to do with creating that glut." It reckoned his remarks are a sign of "intellectual progress" and called for the role of Fed Policy in our current troubles to be put the center of hearings being planned in the house by the speaker, Nancy Pelosi.

That put us in mind of an editorial called "The Pelosi," issued by the Sun in November of 2006 and focusing on the failure of the Congress, which oversees the Fed, to carry out its constitutional responsibilities in respect of the currency. At the time the value of the dollar had plunged to be a 637th of an ounce of gold. "If the dollar goes down further from here," the editorial said, "it might as well be renamed the Pelosi."

Not that our criticism of monetary policy was partisan. We'd started with an editorial called "The Bush Dollar," issued in December 2005. At the time the dollar had plunged something like 46% on Mr. Bush's watch, at the start of which the dollar had been worth a 265th of an ounce of gold. We'd gone on to suggest renaming the scrip "The Greenspan," issued in September 2007, when the dollar had collapsed to less than a 700th of an ounce of gold. Eventually, when the value of the dollar was dwindling toward an 800th of an ounce of gold, we suggested renaming the greenback "The Bernanke."

In November of 2007, we observed that the only candidate for president focusing on the collapse of the currency was Congressman Ron Paul. We have our differences with him, but he was w-a-a-a-a-y out ahead of the other candidates on this question. The editorial, "Ron Paul's Prescience," quoted an exchange between the congressman and Mr. Bernanke when the latter was testifying before the Joint Economic Committee and the Fed chairman reassured the Congress that he did not expect a crisis of the dollar like happened in 1979 and 1980, when, in the waning months of the Carter years, the dollar collapsed to below an 800th of an ounce of gold.

Within a few months, the value of our national currency fell, albeit briefly, below 1,000th of an ounce of gold, a milestone we marked, in March 2008, with an editorial called "$1,000 Gold," which observed that the "thing to take from the years that Reagan was president and Paul Volcker was chairing the Fed is that it is not impossible to have a strengthening dollar and economic growth. Not only not impossible, we'd argue. It's even necessary to have a sound dollar." That is the thing to remember as the Congress gets ready to hold the hearings being prepared by Mrs. Pelosi, lest we get to the point where the dollar will have to be renamed "The Obama."

— May 12, 2010

# Reckoning with Ron Paul

No sooner did Congressman Ron Paul emerge in one of latest opinion polls as neck-and-neck with President Obama in 2012 than he came in for a new round of critical postings on the internet. One of them is quoted by Powerline's John Hinderaker, who writes that he detects something "off" about the physician, who is a Republican from Texas. Mr. Hinderaker quotes an email from one of his readers who had heard Dr. Paul speak at a Tea Party event and concluded that he "is a nut, out of touch with reality seemingly."

Our own view of Dr. Paul, however, is different. It has been formed in the process of covering his campaign for sound money on and off for nearly 30 years, starting with his membership on the United States Gold Commission at the start of the Reagan presidency. We clearly have differences with Dr. Paul in respect of foreign policy and, in recent years, the current war. He has, however, earned our abiding respect for the clarity and commitment with which he has pressed the case for a constitutional approach to money, which in our view is one of the fundamental issues facing the country.

We don't by any means dismiss the critical coverage of Dr. Paul by such journalists as James Kirchick, who started at The New York Sun and has become a real voice on the reportorial right and who, in a widely read piece in the New Republic, reported on how Ron Paul's newsletter was infected with pieces hostile to minorities. Dr. Paul has tried to repudiate those articles and their sentiments, while saying he bears a moral responsibility for them because of his failure of oversight of the newsletter in which they appeared.

Also, we are aware that Ron Paul has spoken ill of the pro-Israel lobby, bought into conspiracy theories involving neo-conservatives and Iraq, and voted against a resolution condemning Hezbollah. These are part, although not all, of the differences we have with him that we would characterize as profound. But in the dozen or so conversations we've had with

Dr. Paul over nearly 30 years, he has never voiced views that we would call racist or anti-Semitic. On the contrary, we have heard a tone altogether different.

It gives us the sense that he has the potential to play a leading role in disentangling the sound money movement from unsavory elements. There is no doubt that it has been entangled. The entanglement has roots in our history, in that the most famous form of American paper money, the greenback, was brought in by Lincoln to help the Union pay for the Civil War. So those who opposed Lincoln for all the wrong reasons got entangled with those who opposed paper money for all the right reasons. This disentangling is an important part of the fight for sound money.

Where are Ron Paul's critics in that fight? It is one thing for Dr. Paul's critics to keep a lookout for signs of bigotry. It is another for high-minded critics to go missing in the fight for sound money, which, after all, is another moral issue. We are now in a period in which the dollar has collapsed to less than 1,000th of an ounce of gold, but a quarter of what it was worth at the start of, say, George W. Bush's presidency and but half of what it was worth when, say, the Democrats acceded to their latest leadership of the Congress. It is a catastrophe that hurts all Americans, of all races, and imperils our civil society.

The thing we like about Ron Paul is that he understands the monetary powers and disabilities in our Constitution. He knows that neither the Constitution nor the government created the dollar. He comprehends what the Founders understood a dollar to be, and he understands the implications of the fact that, in 1792, they codified it as 416 grains of standard silver. He has been a steady watcher of the price of gold. So he understood that an economic crisis was on the horizon before any other member of Congress. And he understands the dollar has to be made sound before we will solve the economic crisis.

\* \* \*

Is the fact that such savvy writers as Mr. Hinderaker reckon Ron Paul has something "off" about him the reason that the Texan has been unable to translate his appeal into a major office? That's something for Dr. Paul to think about. Is the fact that Dr. Paul is out front on the monetary issue related to the fact that he has emerged with such strong poll numbers? That is something for his critics to think about. Our sense of it is that the American people are ahead of the political elites in respect of the dollar. As the federal government has debased its own fiat currency, there are already stirrings at the state level to use the constitutional power of the states to make gold and silver coins legal tender. When all the drama in respect of, say, Goldman Sachs has come and gone, Ron Paul will still be correct that at the bottom of the trouble lies the fact that we didn't have sound money able to transmit the accurate price signals that are needed for a free economy.

— April 18, 2010

# The Obama Dollar

The collapse of the dollar to less than a 1,200th of an ounce of gold is emerging as one of the astonishing stories of our time. Yet even more astonishing is the lack of focus on that story by the intelligentsia in our press and politics. It is a silence on which these columns have remarked a number of times of late, including on March 14, 2008, right after the value of the greenback toppled below a thousandth of an ounce of gold. At the time we suggested that, once the Democrats had their nominee, it would be up to Senator McCain to confront them with the fact that the Congress they've controlled since 2006 has resulted in the dollar falling below a thousandth of an ounce of gold and to warn of its further collapse without the right leadership.

Now the default that has followed has been bi-partisan. It was less than five years ago that we issued, on December 5, 2005, an editorial called "The Bush Dollar." It charted the collapse of the greenback to barely a 500th of an ounce of gold from the 265th of an ounce of gold that it was worth when President Bush acceded to the office where the buck — or, to use the phrase that our contributing editor Larry Parks likes, the "paper ticket" that passes for a buck — stops. At the time we issued that editorial, Mr. Bush had just named Benjamin Bernanke to chair the board of governors of the Federal Reserve. We noted that the dollar had continued to lose value at what we called an "astonishing rate."

So on the eve of the election that gave the Democrats the control of Congress, we issued an editorial proposing the dollar be renamed "The Greenspan," in honor, or dishonor, of the Fed chairman who'd just written a book that gave short shrift to the whole idea of measuring a dollar in gold. When it didn't happen, we issued, on November 30, 2006, another editorial, "The Pelosi," focusing on the fact that is was to the Congress that the Founders of America delegated power to coin money and regulate the value of it. Despite the efforts of

Congressman Ron Paul to return to the idea of constitutional money, it rapidly became clear that the Congress wasn't going to do anything more about the dollar under Mrs. Pelosi than it had under Dennis Hastert.

So in 2007 we proposed renaming the dollar "The Bernanke." It called the pace at which the dollar was falling "scandalous." It also quoted Congressman Ron Paul as having, in 2006, written, prophetically it looks like: "Economic law dictates reform at some point," Mr. Paul had written in the fall of 2006. "But should we wait until the dollar is 1/1,000 of an ounce of gold or 1/2,000 of an ounce of gold? The longer we wait, the more people suffer and the more difficult reforms become." We quoted Dr. Paul as warning that "runaway inflation inevitably leads to political chaos" and declared that the time for action is now.

It happens that after the dollar fell below a thousandth of an ounce of gold, we went into a few months of sharp deflation. One can speculate that this was a panic on the part of the Fed. As reported by American Thinker, Professor Robert Mundell, the famed Nobel Laureate at Columbia, recently gave, at the Heritage Foundation, a speech blaming that sudden deflation of the dollar in mid-2008 for triggering the current crisis. He called it "one of the biggest mistakes in the history of the Fed. " And we are not so centered on gold that we don't pay attention to Mr. Mundell's warning.

But we also know that when supply-side measures such as tax cuts and de-regulation are combined with tight money we can have a strengthening dollar and a booming economy. President Reagan and Chairman Volcker proved it. President Obama, however, has chosen demand-side measures, and the Federal Reserve obliged, precipitating the dollar yet again into a long downward slide. So here we are, well into the second year of his administration with a dollar that will associate Mr. Obama's name with faltering scrip.

\* \* \*

This is a time when we need a national conversation about the dollar. What is it? What did the Founding Fathers think it was? When they used the word "dollars" twice in the Constitution but did not deem it necessary to provide a definition, what did that tell us? In fact, the historical record is clear. The constitutional dollar was — and is — 416 grains of standard silver, or 371 ¼ grains of pure silver, the same amount of silver as is in a coin known then, and now, as the Spanish Milled Dollar. What were the Founders thinking when they decided to use, in granting to Congress the power to "coin money and regulate its value," the same sentence in which they also granted Congress the power to fix the weights and measures?

How are we going to get back to a constitutional framework for our national unit of account? And, most ominously, what will happen if we fail to do so? It is too much to hope that this national conversation might be ignited by Mr. Obama himself. The Wall Street Journal editorial page is doing a heroic job among the newspapers, including a piece in tomorrow's paper calling for taking another look at the gold standard, and Larry Kudlow among columnists, his latest being here. We hold out hope that some politician will pick up the issue of the dollar. So far the only one who has gone out on the stump to mark its collapse against gold is Sarah Palin. Come to think of it we're long overdue for having the face of the greenback engraved with a woman.

— May 6, 2010

# Toward a Fed Audit

It is tempting to express disappointment at the watering down the Senate did to Congressman Ron Paul's vision of how to audit the Federal Reserve. Dr. Paul himself is, in an interview with the Sun this morning, characterizing the Senate's bill as only "slightly better than nothing." He is even warning, "It does political harm," in that it gives the Fed "cover — and people can hide from it." The bill that cleared the Senate is aimed at finding out merely what the Fed did during the recent bailouts but not what it is doing, say, at the discount window or in the way of loans to other central banks and governments and international financial institutions. It may lead to an auditing merely of procedures and not of numbers. The right move in the House-Senate conference is a pursuit of a wide audit that would open the Fed to daylight.

In the longer scheme of things, however, it's possible to see a more encouraging side to this story, at least for those of us who came in to the campaign for monetary reform in the 1970s, after President Nixon closed the gold window in 1971 and brought Bretton Woods to its bang-less, whimpering end. A decade later Congress established the United States Gold Commission. The commission backed the current system. But it produced Dr. Paul's famous minority report, in which the congressman from Texas was joined by another member of the commission, Lewis Lehrman, a New York businessman and intellectual. Now here we are, albeit 30 years later, and a version of what Dr. Paul has been asking for, even if a watered down version, has passed the Senate 96 to zero, and Dr. Paul ranks nearly even in the polls with the sitting president.

Everywhere one goes, moreover, there is a growing recognition, among both Americans of average means and the high and mighty, that something is off. We noted, in a story yesterday, that a group of the most distinguished judges on the federal bench is so upset about the decision of the Congress to rescind a promised cost-of-living adjustment in their pay that they are appealing to the Supreme Court. How can judges sue over their own pay? It turns out that judges are a special case, because it is flatly unconstitutional to diminish the pay of a federal judge while the judge continues in office. So our story covers the possibility that their own lawsuit will eventually confront the judges with the need to do something about the fact that a dollar that only a decade ago was worth a 265th of an ounce of gold is today worth less than a 1,200th of an ounce of gold.

No one perceives this vast unease more clearly than the Fed itself, which has been fighting the idea of an audit on Capitol Hill and, if an audit does emerge from the Congress, can be expected to fight it in court. The Fed may win the battle in the short run, dodging the kind of wide and full audit that Dr. Paul wants. We're not immune to the thought that the coalition that is pressing for an audit includes figures on the left, and even far left (the Nation magazine's report starts with an expression of support from the Vermont socialist Bernard Sanders), not normally associated with open government and free market capitalism. But at bottom the shift that is taking place is encouraging. Partisans of fiat money are now on the defensive. Countries, like Greece, are collapsing because they have been pursuing a socialistic course, and millions of Americans are demanding to look under the hood of the Fed to see what is being lent out in the way of our money. The step in the Senate is best seen as but a beginning.

— May 12, 2010

# Paul Ryan's Question

Chairman Bernanke's testimony before the House Budget Committee this week has set the Web buzzing over the fact that he is, as the Wall Street Journal's Jon Hilsenrath put it, "puzzled" by the surging gold price. When one gets a Fed chairman averring that he doesn't "fully understand the movements in the gold price," it's certainly news. But the story from the hearing that caught our ear was the emergence of the congressman who asked the headline question, Paul Ryan of Wisconsin, as a point man on what we see as the issue of the hour — fiat money.

This came 31 minutes into C-Span's video of the hearing, when Mr. Ryan noted that on Tuesday "gold hit an all-time high," or, as we like to put it, the value of the dollar fell to an all-time low. Mr. Ryan suggested that most people would view the development "as a vote of no confidence against fiat currencies." What he asked the chairman was "what does that price signal tell you and what is your view of the long-term repercussions with respect to weak currency policies?" He said he supposed one could argue that we don't have a weak dollar because everyone else is weaker, but asked about the implications for a the "strength and stability of our currency."

"Well," Mr. Bernanke replied, "the signal that gold is sending is in some ways very different from what other asset prices are sending. For example, the spread between nominal and inflation index bonds remains quite low, suggesting just 2% inflation over the next 10 years. Other commodity prices have fallen recently quite severely including oil prices and food prices. So gold is out there doing something different from the rest of the commodity group. I don't fully understand the movements in the gold price, but I do think there's a great deal of uncertainty and anxiety in financial markets right now and some people believe that holding gold will be a hedge against the fact that they view many other investments as being risky and hard to predict at this point."

The chairman's answer strikes us as a classic. One doesn't go into gold because, as the be-puzzled Mr. Bernanke seems to suggest, one lacks confidence in, say, "other investments," soybeans, say, or iron ore. One goes into gold because one lacks confidence in the fiat currencies. So Mr. Ryan has opened the way for the next hearing to come right back at Mr. Bernanke with a question in respect of the Founders — Washington, Madison, Jefferson, Hamilton — and their warnings about paper money. It strikes us that Mr. Ryan has touched on the makings of a terrific presidential plank.

It was they, after all, who used the constitutional authority to coin money to pass Coinage Act of 1792, which adopted the dollar as our unit of account and defined it as 416 grains of standard, or 371 ¼ grains of pure, silver and established the constitutionality of a monetary role for gold (and which, not incidentally, prescribed the death penalty for anyone who would knowingly debase that dollar). It is hard to imagine that the collapse of our currency does not reflect the fact that monetary policy is being conducted without so much as a how-do-you-do to this slab of American bedrock. What an encouraging thing to see one of the bright lights in the Republican Party start to broach these questions with the chairman of the bank that is issuing the notes in which the world is losing confidence.

— June 11, 2010

# The Magma Chart

The Web is heating up over the way the Federal Reserve's volcanic expansion is illustrated in what is being called "The Magma Chart." Ira Stoll, who has been noting the story at Futureofcapitalism.com, has coverage and a piece up at Pajamas Media. Mr. Stoll picked up on a blog post by the New York Times' Catherine Rampell, who provided, in addition to her comments, a link to the chart as produced by the Cleveland Fed. It shows the various elements of the Fed's balance sheet and how they exploded in the last quarter of 2008. Toward the beginning of 2009, they hit a peak of nearly 3,000,000 millions of dollars, or $3 trillion, and more recently have leveled off, at least for the moment, at $2 trillion.

What catches our attention about this chart, aside from its graphic illustration — Mr. Stoll notes that it calls to mind a wall of magma, or lava, flowing down hill — is that the "dollars" in which the Fed's balance sheet is denominated aren't actually dollars. This is a point made over and over again by such partisans of constitutional money as Larry Parks of the Foundation for the Advancement of Monetary Education. The Fed uses the word dollars, and what it calls dollars have been credited as legal tender by the Supreme Court. But such dollars are not dollars under any definition consonant with that understood by the Founders of America when they twice used the world "dollars" in the Constitution. By a dollar they meant 371 ¼ grains of pure silver or the free market equivalent in gold. The constitutional dollar was codified in Coinage Act of 1792, which adopted the dollar — something that already existed — as the new nation's unit of account.

So while the chart is displaying an enormous expansion of the Fed's balance sheet, it is not displaying a relation between the magma of the various balance sheet items and something real. This, in our opinion, is where the Fed and the Congress are vulnerable. Even as we write this, the Drudge Report and the Huffington Post are leading with dispatches, here and here, about the latest warning by the president of the Federal Reserve Bank of Kansas City, Thos. Hoenig, who has been dissenting for months from the Fed's ultra-low-interest rate policies. His warning is that low interest rates themselves are part of the problem. More fundamental, in our view, is the fact that the idea of a group of officials of the Fed deciding rates by fiat, without targeting the constitutional definition of our money, is coming to be seen as itself the most important part of the problem.

As this crisis grows, the idea of the Fed itself is going to increasingly come into question, and calls will grow for replacing the magma building up on the Fed's balance sheet with the concept of constitutional money, which is silver and its free market equivalent in gold. It is well to remember that the movement to audit the Federal Reserve, which has come to encompass a solid majority of the Congress, was launched by a congressman, Ron Paul, who doesn't believe the Fed should exist at all and who, according to one recent poll, was running even with President Obama. Those facts don't a monetary reform make, but they certainly suggest which way the wind is blowing.

— August 14, 2010

# California and the Constitution

One of the points these columns have been pressing is that our country's politics are in such extremes right now that we are getting down to the bedrock of the Constitution. For an example of what we mean by that, feature the email that came in, out of the blue, from one of the smartest politicians in the country. He writes about the prospect that California will be issuing more IOUs to pay its obligations and asks how it all squares with Section 10 of Article One of the Constitution.

What he's asking about is the section of the Constitution that lays restrictions on the States. Article One grants, or with-holds, various powers in three successive sections. Section 8 enumerates what the United States Congress can do, such as, among others, laying and collecting taxes and declaring war. Section 9 prohibits the Congress from doing certain things — granting a title of nobility, say, or suspending the writ of habeas corpus. Then Section 10 lists the things the states are prohibited from doing, such as making a treaty or entering into a confederation, say, or coining money, or emitting bills of credit.

The prohibition on emitting bills of credit blocks states from issuing a bill that is designed to circulate as money on the credit of the state. Justice Story, in his commentary on this part of the constitution, wrote of the "evils attendant upon the issue of paper money by the states." He wrote of the events after what he called "the peace of 1783" that ended the Revolutionary War. Public as well as private credit was "utterly prostrated" and the "fortunes of many individuals were destroyed" and the fortunes of all persons "were greatly impaired by the rapid and unparalleled depreciation of the paper currency."

Story wrote of how, as far back as 1775, Congress directed what he called an "emission" of paper money that had a declaration right on the front that the bearer was entitled to receive a specified number of Spanish milled dollars "or the value thereof in gold or silver." The scrip depreciated because Congress was without funds to redeem them, he noted. So Congress "endeavored to give them additional credit by declaring, that they ought to be a tender in payment of all private and public debts; and that a refusal to receive the tender ought to be an extinguishment of the debt, and recommending the states to pass such tender laws."

Congress went even further, Story relates, declaring that "whoever should refuse to receive this paper in exchange for any property, as gold and silver, should be deemed 'an enemy to the liberties of these United States.'" Story called this a "course of violence and terror" that "so far from aiding the circulation of the paper, led on to still farther depreciation." By 1779, the whole "emission" was more than $160 million. Congress declared that it would not exceed $200 million and, in Story's words, "still held out to the public the delusive hope of an ultimate redemption of the whole at par."

Various schemes were tried, with Story summing up this way: "At last the continental bills became of so little value, that they ceased to circulate; and in the course of the year 1780, they quietly died in the hands of their possessors. Thus were redeemed the solemn pledges of the national government! Thus, was a paper currency, which was declared to be equal to gold and silver, suffered to perish in the hands of persons compelled to take it; and the very enormity of the wrong made the ground of an abandonment of every attempt to redress it!"*

We offer that as a bit of background to underscore the emotion that paper money ignited in our sages. They just detested it. They did not forbid the states from going into debt. The question was emitting bills of credit designed to circulate as money. Here's how Story put the debt question "... as it might become necessary for the states to borrow money, the prohibition could not be intended to prevent such an exercise of power, on giving to the lender a certificate of the amount borrowed, and a promise to repay it."

So the real question about the California IOUs is whether they are designed to circulate as money. If so, they are forbidden. If not, they are not forbidden. How does one know whether they are designed to circulate as money? One clue would be whether they were in small denominations. Another would be whether the IOUs are redeemable by the bearer. If they're designed to serve as money, they're just not permitted. And under no circumstances can California require anyone to accept one of its IOUs as tender in satisfaction of a debt. In actuality, the California IOUs look more like a check. But mark the point. Because the scrip loosed between the Revolutionary War and the Constitutional Convention engendered what Story called "the most enormous evils," "grievances," "oppressions," and "chicanery," the one thing California, or any other state, absolutely cannot do is require someone to accept in tender of a debt something other than gold or silver coins.

— August 24, 2010

————

\* The manual of style of The New York Sun prohibits the quotation of material containing slammers (exclamation points), but an exception is made here for Justice Story, who, after all, cannot, at this stage, defend himself and was, clearly, carried away with emotion.

# The Gold Audit

Congressman Ron Paul is in the news again, this time for calling for an audit of America's gold reserves. He issued the call in an interview with a news service run by a gold dealer, Kitco News, which reported that the congressman intends to introduce legislation calling for such an audit of what we hold at Fort Knox and other sites, such as the New York Federal Reserve Bank in lower Manhattan. It's the kind of thing people tend to laugh at, the way they once did when Dr. Paul launched his legislative campaign to audit the United States Federal Reserve. Yet after years of persistence by the Texas Republican, Congress finally passed a law requiring an audit of the Fed. It passed the mandate by a wide margin and a bi-partisan vote. So whatever snickering there will be over Dr. Paul's proposal for an audit of the gold holdings, it will be more muted.

We are not in the camp that believes a vast conspiracy has stolen America's gold. But neither are we in the camp that sees any harm to an audit. As Dr. Paul put it to Kitco News: "If there was no question about the gold being there, you think they would be anxious to prove gold is there." He has been pressing the point, on and off, since the early 1980s, when he was a member of the United States Gold Commission. He reminded the interviewer from Kitco that his recommendation back then that Congress audit the gold reserve was rejected by 15 of the Gold Commission's 17 members. It strikes us that it would not be a bad thing were an audit to keep our national mind focused on our gold holdings — particularly at a time when the value of the dollar has collapsed to less than a 1,200th of an ounce of gold.

If that weren't enough of a warning, the Bloomberg wire reports that "gold's most-accurate forecasters" are predicting that the value of the dollar may fall to but a 1,500th of an ounce of gold. It reports that what it calls the most widely held option on gold futures in New York is for the dollar to fall to but a 1,500th of an ounce of gold by December. The lowest value to which the dollar has plummeted so far is a 1,266.50th of an ounce of gold, which was the value of the dollar recorded on June 21. Bloomberg reports that holdings through what it calls "bullion-backed exchange-traded products" are within a 10th of a percent of the all-time high of 2,075 metric tons. It quotes one Deutsche Bank analyst, Dan Brebner — whom it calls "the most accurate forecaster so far this year — as predicting the value of the dollar may drop to a 1,550th of an ounce of gold.

Suddenly the question to ask is not why in the world is Dr. Paul asking for this audit but why is he the only member of Congress making our gold holdings an issue. It was only a decade ago, at the start of the presidency of George W. Bush, that a dollar was worth nearly a 250th of an ounce of gold. As it started dropping, these columns warned repeatedly that it was a signal to be heeded, starting with "The Bush Dollar," which was issued in December, 2005, and carrying on up through "The Pelosi," "The Greenspan," "The Bernanke," "Ron Paul's Prescience," "$1,000 Gold," "The Obama Dollar," "Golden Opportunity," and "Paul Ryan's Question," just to name but a few of the editorials of the Sun that have touched on this topic.

By our lights a weak dollar policy is a strategic mistake for America. We felt that when President Carter and his treasury secretary at the time, W. Michael Blumenthal, were running a weak dollar. We've never credited the idea that one cannot have a strengthening dollar and a growing economy, an idea that should have been thoroughly discredited during the Reagan years and the Clinton years. One could say that a strong dollar is a good idea that is bi-partisan in pedigree. But what good can come of a weak dollar policy, such as the one being pursued by Messrs. Obama, Geithner, Bernanke, Mrs. Pelosi and the others who have various levels of constitutional — or, in the case of Mr. Bernanke, non-constitutional — authority over policy in respect of America's money? As the value of the dollar evaporates, why in the world wouldn't ordinary Americans want to have the gold holdings they've been told about for so many years given a full and independent audit?

— August 31, 2010

# None Dare Call it Inflation

"What about inflation?" is the question that Paul Krugman puts in the middle of a column this week run out under the headline "The Real Story." The column is an attempt to debunk those who have been warning that President Obama's massive stimulus spending and other government rescue packages will lead to inflation and ruin — and a call for the president to do something big when, next week, he proposes what Mr. Krugman characterizes as new measures to boost the economy.

"Amid the inflation hysteria of early 2009," Mr. Krugman writes in answer to his question about inflation, "the inadequate-stimulus critics pointed out that inflation always falls during sustained periods of high unemployment, and that this time should be no different. Sure enough, key measures of inflation have fallen from more than 2 percent before the economic crisis to 1 percent or less now, and Japanese-style deflation is looking like a real possibility."

To which these columns would reply — what about gold? The price of the barbarous relic has now topped $1,200 an ounce. Or, as we prefer to put it, the value of the dollar has plunged to below 1,200th of an ounce of gold. Its collapse since 2001, when it had a value of a 265th of an ounce of gold, has been astonishing. These columns began writing about it in 2005, during the Bush presidency, but it is a bi-partisan question. The scrip being issued by our government has lost a quarter of its value in the first 20 months of the Obama presidency alone.

Not that we'd make too much of the presidents' responsibilities. It's our view that because the coining of money, and the regulating of its value, is an enumerated power granted to the Congress in Article 1, Section 8 of the Constitution, it's a responsibility of Congress. But what is this rise in the price of gold? What is it signaling? There was a time, back during the Bush Boom, when the rise in the gold price was being attributed to the boom itself, to the need for gold in manufacturing. To what is the rise in the gold price — pardon, the collapse in the value of the dollar — being attributed now?

The one thing that seems clear is this: None dare call it inflation. Not Mr. Krugman, not Mr. Bernanke, not the president, not the Congress, not the newspaper editors. When they talk about inflation they talk about the consumer price index and too much money chasing too few goods. But could it be that the value of the dollar is falling even while the prices of ordinary goods, expressed in scrip, is steady, because no one wants to buy any goods? And that what passes for a dollar is being inflated anyhow by a Congress that has long since forgotten the constitutional definition of a dollar, which is as 371 ¼ grains of pure silver or its equivalent in gold?

— September 4, 2010

# Greenspan's Warning

Alan Greenspan spoke at the Council on Foreign Relations earlier today, and what was his advice? That central bankers should be doing what these columns, among others, have been rattling on about, namely that they should be paying attention to gold. "Fiat money has no place to go but gold," the former Fed chairman said at the Council, according to economist David Malpass, who, in one of his emails on the political economy, quotes Mr. Greenspan. Mr. Malpass writes that the former chairman of the Federal Reserve's board of governors was responding to a question in respect of why gold was hitting new highs.

Mr. Greenspan replied that he'd thought a lot about gold prices over the years and decided the supply and demand explanations treating gold like other commodities "simply don't pan out," as Mr. Malpass characterized Mr. Greenspan. "He'd concluded that gold is simply different," Mr. Malpass wrote. At one point Mr. Greenspan spoke of how, during World War II, the Allies going into North Africa found gold was insisted on in the payment of bribes.* Said the former Fed chairman: "If all currencies are moving up or down together, the question is: relative to what? Gold is the canary in the coal mine. It signals problems with respect to currency markets. Central banks should pay attention to it."

To which, forgive us, one can only say, "Now he tells us." The fact is that if Mr. Greenspan governed the Fed with an eye on gold, it wasn't a particularly steady eye. He might argue that when he left the chairmanship of the Fed, in January 2006, he left a dollar worth a 400th of an ounce of gold, slightly more valuable than the 461st of an ounce of gold that it was worth when he came in nearly 20 years before. But in the first five years of the 21$^{st}$ century, when he was in the last quarter of his years as chairman, the value of the dollar started its long collapse, plunging from the 282nd of an ounce of gold that it was worth on January 4, 2000. In the years since, it has cratered to record lows once imagined only by such sages as Ron Paul.

Mr. Greenspan's remarks at the council were not the first time he gave us a glimpse of his views on gold. He discusses gold on several pages of his memoir, "The Age of Turbulence," reminding that he once told a Congressional committee that "monetary policy should make even a fiat money economy behave 'as though anchored by gold.'" He wrote that he had "always harbored a nostalgia for the gold standard's inherent price stability." But he confesses that he's "long since acquiesced in the fact that the gold standard does not readily accommodate the widely accepted current view of the appropriate functions of government — in particular the need for government to provide a social safety net."

The American people, he asserted in his book, have for the most part "tolerated the inflation bias as an acceptable cost of the modern welfare state." And he claimed, "There is no support for the gold standard today, and I see no likelihood of its return." We'll hazard a guess that the statement makes him a man more of the past than of the future. But at least some politicians are hearkening to his advice about the price of gold. They're people like Congressman Ron Paul and his son, Rand, who may yet be a senator, and Governor Palin, who was one of the first to warn about the gold price, and Congressman Paul Ryan, who asked Mr. Greenspan's successor, Ben Bernanke about gold.

And, by the way, a few journalists, like Glenn Beck, who are students of history and just can't believe their eyes that the dollar has plunged to the level it has with so few people raising an alarm. We are in a period when gold is more than a canary — to cite Mr. Greenspan's bird of choice — it's a full-throated rooster, cock-a-doodling at the top of its lungs. It was nice to see Mr. Greenspan mark the point at the Council. Would that he'd taken more of his own advice. And nice to see Mr. Malpass mark the Greenspan comments so prominently in his letter to his economic clients. He is more for a gold price rule in monetary policy than a gold standard, but we hope he makes another run for high office at the first chance, and presses the principle for all its worth. It's what we need in the national debate, and none too soon.

— September 15, 2010

---

\* Not just in World War II did the special role of gold come into focus. Covering the fall of free Saigon for the Wall Street Journal in April 1975, your editor witnessed a bank run in which panicked Vietnamese citizens, in the streets outside the financial institutions, bought, when they could, gold that had been pressed into sheets the size and approximate thickness of cigarette paper.

# The Congress and Your Gold

What an astonishing set of issues has been opened up with the announcement yesterday by Congressman Anthony Weiner that he will hold a hearing on what he calls "TV Gold Dealers." The congressman put out on his Web site yesterday a statement that makes the hearing seem like it will prepare a Weinerian form of a bill of attainder against Goldline International and Glenn Beck. Goldline is a dealer that Mr. Weiner characterized as using "conservative spokespeople like Fox News' Glenn Beck to sell overpriced gold coins."

It seems that one of the advantages perceived in respect of gold coins, as opposed to bullion, is that they would be less likely to be confiscated were the government to try in the current economic crisis, when the value of the dollar has collapsed to less than a 1,200th of an ounce of gold, to confiscate gold the way another Democratic administration, FDR's, did during the Great Depression. Mr. Weiner seems to think that worrying about another Great Depression should be illegal.

One of the things Mr. Weiner's bill would seek to do is prevent gold companies from hiding behind "false promises of profitability." The measure would require what Mr. Weiner calls "companies like Goldline" to "disclose the reasonable resale value of items being sold." To which Ira Stoll, on the Web site Futureofcapitalism.com, retorts: "Are Mr. Weiner and Chairman Bernanke also going to agree to print on every dollar the reasonable expectation that its value will be eroded by inflation?"

As Mr. Weiner was putting the announcement of his gold hearing up on his Web site, the former chairman of the Federal Reserve Board, Alan Greenspan, was over at the Council on Foreign Relations warning that "fiat money has no place to go but gold." Our editorial yesterday quoted Mr. Greenspan: "If all currencies are moving up or down together, the question is: relative to what? Gold is the canary in the coal mine. It signals problems with respect to currency markets. Central banks should pay attention to it."

\* \* \*

And so should the Congress. In this sense there is buried in Mr. Weiner's campaign to scare people away from gold at least the glint of constitutional bedrock. For one of the basic enumerated powers of the Congress is "To coin Money, regulate the Value thereof, and of foreign Coin . . ." The Congress has been in default in respect of this responsibility for decades now. The institution to which it has delegated its powers, the Federal Reserve, is issuing scrip in which people are losing confidence. With the value of the dollar at below a 1,200th of an ounce of gold, no wonder there is a clamor for a new monetary system — and, in some quarters, even for the states to use their constitutional power to make gold and silver coin legal tender. The thing to remember about this story as it unfolds is that it's not about Goldline's marketing techniques or Glenn Beck's responsibilities. It's about Congress's responsibilities under the most fundamental law of our land.

— September 17, 2010

# No Place to Go

Only days after the former Federal Reserve chairman Alan Greenspan warned that "fiat money has no place to go but gold," the dollar has collapsed to a new low. The remarks of the former Fed Chairman were made a week ago at the Council on Foreign Relations, causing a flurry of excitement on the Internet. The dollar shed value, dropping to a record low yesterday, within minutes of the Federal Reserve declaring that it was, as characterized by Reuters, "ready to provide more support for the economy and expressing concerns about low inflation."

It's amazing to us that this doesn't seem to be raising an alarm in either the halls of Congress, the administration, or the newsrooms. Kitco News, which is published by the gold dealer, reported the reaction this way: "Around 3:30 p.m. EDT (1930 GMT), spot gold was up $6.90 to $1,285.40 an ounce, compared to $1,272 about 10 minutes ahead of the Fed statement. December gold on the Comex division of the New York Mercantile Exchange was $6.90 higher at $1,287.70, compared to $1,273.30 ahead of time. In after-hours trading following the Fed statement, the December futures went on to a high of $1,290.40; that is a fresh record for a most-active Comex contract."

Regular readers of these columns know that we prefer not to speak of the "price of gold" but rather of the "value of the dollar." Kitco's reporter quoted the managing director of Trend/Max Futures, Zachary Oxman, as saying the Fed "all but confirmed" quantitative easing and predicting that the value of the dollar would fall below a 1,300th of an ounce of gold by the end of this week and to between a 1,400th of an ounce and a 1,500th of an ounce of gold by the end of the year. That would mean that the dollar would have dropped from a 271st of an ounce on January 1, 2001.

Is Matt Drudge the only editor of a general interest publication who understands the front-page nature of this collapse? This is not about a sudden failure of the mines. Or a sudden manufacturing need. This is about a failure of the Congress to carry out its responsibilities under the Constitution. To suggest that the trend is reversible with an adjustment of interest rates does not address the issue we see. The issue is that there is neither a law or a policy being enforced or followed that references gold or silver as a matter of principle in the way that the Founders of the country understood — and, in the founding Congresses, wrote into law.

We have one recent Fed chairman, Mr. Greenspan, who seems to understand the importance of gold — it, he said at the Council on Foreign Relations, "is the canary in the coal mine. It signals problems with respect to currency markets." Now we have another Fed chairman who, in Mr. Bernanke, is prepared to testify before Congress that he doesn't "fully understand the movements in the gold price," though he does acknowledge that "there's a great deal of uncertainty and anxiety in financial markets right now and some people believe that holding gold will be a hedge against the fact that they view many other investments as being risky and hard to predict at this point."

* * *

When we wrote about that testimony in the spring, we called Mr. Bernanke's answer a classic. "One doesn't go into gold because, as the be-puzzled Mr. Bernanke seems to suggest, one lacks confidence in, say, 'other investments,' soybeans, say, or iron ore," we suggested. "One goes into gold because one lacks confidence in the fiat currencies." That's the point Mr. Greenspan spoke of at the Council. The Congressman who put Mr. Bernanke on the spot then was Paul Ryan of Wisconsin.

We suggested at the time that when they next get the chairman back on the Hill they press him about the Founders and their understanding of money, their fear of paper money, their warnings to future generations, and the laws and definitions of the dollar that they put into the national currency. The Founders on the dollar are worth an entire hearing, and by our lights it can't come too soon.

— September 22, 2010

# Nightmare of Congress

Fear that we are in the midst of a slow motion run against the government of the United States is what emerged yesterday as the nightmare animating the Congressional hearings into private purchases of gold coins. Ostensibly the hearings, held by a congressman of New York, were about the marketing practices of a dealer called Goldline and its advertising on conservative talk shows on radio and television. But the deeper issue quickly emerged as the prospect that people are buying gold coins because they fear the government could confiscate private holdings of bullion the way an earlier Democratic administration, FDR's, did during the Great Depression.

At one point, according to a report on yesterday's hearings issued by Politico.com, the congressman chairing the hearings, Anthony Weiner, "grew red-faced" as he railed at an executive of Goldline. The Congressman spoke after "months of fulminating from afar," Politico.com reported. Mr. Weiner had issued a report in May accusing Goldline of having formed an "unholy alliance with conservative pundits to drive a false narrative" that the United States is "destined for hyperinflation with Barack Obama as president." At the hearing the Goldline executive, Scott Carter, insisted that the company gives its customers enough information to make informed decisions about the gold they buy.

It turns out that part of the information Goldline has been giving its customers is background on the executive order President Roosevelt issued in 1933 confiscating private holdings of gold. The reason Goldline and Mr. Weiner are focusing on gold coins is that the Gold Reserve Act of 1934, which codified Roosevelt's confiscations of private gold holdings, had exempted certain coins of numismatic value. The point is lost on neither Mr. Weiner nor Goldline. "These are uncertain economic times," Goldline's Mr. Carter was quoted by Politico.com as telling the hearing. "Our training is that if the executive order were reenacted as it was in '33, that coins with collector value were excluded from confiscation."

Mr. Weiner became slightly unhinged at this line of argument and "lambasted" Mr. Carter for promoting fear of the federal government, according to the report on Politico.com. "The fundamental question," it quoted Mr. Weiner as saying, "is this: Should you be doing this? Should you be exploiting people this way? Should you be implying to people that a confiscation order is in place that hasn't been in place since my father was born?" It strikes us as a formulation as slippery as that the congressman is attributing to Goldline. It is true that the executive order of FDR was in place for only a short while, but the ban on private gold holding lasted decades. It wasn't until the end of 1974, when Mr. Weiner was a 10-year-old child, that the ban was lifted.

Mr. Weiner, moreover, has just introduced a bill that would impose draconian disclosure requirements not just on corporate gold dealers like Goldline but any person who sells, or even offers to sell, for investment purposes any coins or bullion of gold or other precious metals. And one of the things they would have to disclose is the coin or bullion's "reasonable resale value." That sets an awfully broad trap for the public — and, by an extension of logic, for the government, a point that was made by Ira Stoll of Futureofcapitalism.com, in the first dispatch on this contretemps. Should the government, for example, have disclosed that the value of the one-dollar Federal Reserve Notes it has been issuing would plunge to less than 1,290th of an ounce of gold from a 271st of an ounce of gold in the past ten years?

\* \* \*

Our sense of it is that the people are not as easy to fool as Mr. Weiner thinks they are. Or at least they have a better sense of history. Congressman Ron Paul, one of the leaders on the monetary issue within the Congress, wasn't at Mr. Weiner's hearings. He is not suggesting that Congress or the government is getting ready to confiscate gold. But he told us yesterday that Americans are very much alert to the history of gold confiscation. "I get asked that question all the time," he said. It is important, he said, "to keep warning people that they've done it before." Adds he: "Think of where we would have been if we had not had gold ownership legalized in the 1970s." Or, as we would put it, the problem today is not the gold dealers and the conservative talk show hosts but the Federal Reserve, the United States Treasury and, most importantly, the Congress itself.

— September 24, 2010

# Kennedy and Nixon on the Brink

This week marks the jubilee of the Kennedy-Nixon debates. It was on September 26, 1960, that the two future presidents took the stage in the first of their four rounds. It struck us, as we watched them over the weekend, as it struck us when we watched them originally, that they were conducted on a remarkably high plane. The transcript runs to something like 44,000 words, the length of a modest book, and the sloganeering was, in both camps, kept to a minimum. History, however, shows us that they failed to see the monetary catastrophe that lay ahead, a sobering thought in the current crisis.

It turns out the topic is struck upon in the third debate. It was the 16th year of Bretton Woods, which had set up a kind of gold standard, and the dollar was under pressure. Charles Van Fremd of CBS News put the question to Nixon, by noting that in the past three years there had been "an exodus of more than four billion dollars of gold* from the United States . . ." Von Fremd attributed the outflow to the fact that "exports have slumped and haven't covered imports" and to "increased American investments abroad." He asked Nixon, "how would you go about stopping this departure of gold from our shores?"

"The first thing we have to do is to continue to keep confidence abroad in the American dollar," was how Nixon began his reply. That meant, he said, that "we must continue to have a balanced budget here at home in every possible circumstance that we can, because the moment that we have loss of confidence in our own fiscal policies at home, it results in gold flowing out." He also called for an increase in exports. And he declared that America "must get more help from our allies abroad in this great venture in which all free men are involved of winning the battle for freedom."

"The United States cannot continue to carry the major share of this burden by itself," Nixon declared. "We can [carry] a big share of it, but we've got to have more help from our friends abroad; and these three factors, I think, will be very helpful in reversing the gold flow which you spoke about."

"The difficulty, of course," Kennedy responded, "is that we do have heavy obligations abroad, that we therefore have to maintain not only a favorable balance of trade but also send a good deal of our dollars overseas to pay our troops, maintain our bases, and sustain other economies. In other words, if we're going to continue to maintain our position in the sixties, we have to maintain a sound monetary and fiscal policy. We have to have control over inflation, and we also have to have a favorable balance of trade."

The senator from Massachusetts also warned against protectionism abroad. "Many of the countries around the world still keep restrictions against our goods, going all the way back to the days when there was a dollar shortage. " He said we would have to "persuade these other countries not to restrict our goods coming in, not to act as if there was a dollar gap," and to "assume some of the responsibilities that up till now we've maintained, to assist underdeveloped countries in Africa, Latin America and Asia make an economic breakthrough on their own."

In the event, Kennedy won the election, and his intentions in respect of gold were a question throughout his administration. At his 39th press conference, in July 1962, he had vowed to maintain the value of the dollar. "We are not going to devalue," he said. He warned that America had put $50 billion into Europe alone since 1945 and wasn't asking the Europeans "to do anything but meet their responsibilities for their own defense."

Quoth he: "This country is a very solvent country. So I feel it requires a cooperative effort by all of those involved in order to maintain this free currency, the dollar, upon which so much of Western prosperity is built. I have confidence in it, and I think if others examine the wealth of this country, and its determination to bring its balance of payments into order, which it will do, I think that they will feel that the dollar is a good investment and as good as gold." But the behind the scenes there was pressure, and the Internet gives us some glimpses of him conferring with his advisers about gold.

After Kennedy was assassinated, Lyndon Johnson acceded to the presidency and, in 1965, signed the first legislation of retreat — the Coinage Act of 1965. It superseded at least some aspects of the Coinage Act of 1792, in which the Second United States Congress had defined the dollar as 371 ¼ grains of pure silver, the same as was in a coin then current called the Spanish milled dollar.

President Lyndon Johnson, at the signing of the 1965 act, issued this warning: "If anybody has any idea of hoarding our silver coins, let me say this. Treasury has a lot of silver on hand, and it can be, and it will be used to keep the price of silver in line with its value in our present silver coin." At the time, the price of silver was almost precisely the same as it was in 1792, or $1.29 an ounce. Today silver is worth $21 an ounce, having risen sharply since the first of the year.

It was President Nixon who, in 1971, closed the gold window and began the end of the Bretton Woods system. It had taken but 11 years from the debate and all the fine words, of both candidates, for the system to come apart and for the great inflation for the 1970s to be unleashed. They were years that remind that the policy errors involved both Republicans and Democrats, who failed to think about money and the enumerated monetary powers and disabilities of the Congress in the terms in which the Founders thought about them.

— September 26, 2010

---

* With gold at $35 an ounce, that was the equivalent of 114,285,714 ounces of the metal. At today's prices, that would mean the outflow over three years of $147 billion worth of gold.

# $4,000 Gold?

The story that sticks in our mind this week is the prediction by John Paulson that gold could hit $4,000. We first read of his comments on a Web site called Goldalert.com, which reported that the hedge fund multibillionaire had recently told a luncheon group at private club in New York that he reckoned gold, which at the time was a few dollars below $1,300, "could hit $2,400 based only on monetary expansion," as Goldalert paraphrased him, "and as high as $4,000 per ounce based on a projected overshoot." Goldalert said that Mr. Paulson noted that 80% of his assets are denominated in gold. Robert Lenzner of Forbes, who first reported Mr. Paulson's remarks, said Mr. Paulson told "a standing room only crowd" at the University Club that, in Mr. Lenzner's wording, "double-digit inflation is about to rear its ugly head by 2012, killing the bond market, and restoring strength to equities and gold."

No doubt what riveted the town about Mr. Paulson's reported remarks is the implication for investment strategy. An investor is what he is, after all, and based on his record, he's a man worth paying attention to. What interests these columns, however, is less the investment advice (though we're plenty interested in that) than the drama of political economy. It was only three years ago, in July 2007, that Congressman Ron Paul had his famous exchange with the Federal Reserve chairman, Ben Bernanke. In that exchange, Mr. Paul asked whether the chairman could foresee a crisis over the dollar like the one in 1979 and 1980? That season the value of one of the Federal Reserve notes that Mr. Bernanke was issuing in the name of the United States had plunged to an 850th of an ounce gold.

"I'm not anticipating a problem like '79, '80. No," Mr. Bernanke had responded. At the time Mr. Paul popped that question, in July 2007, the dollar was worth a 666th of an ounce of gold. By November, when we wrote an editorial about the exchange, its value had evaporated further, to the levels it had sunk in early 1980. We had a new Speaker in Congress, and we had a presidential campaign heating up, and yet no major figure in either party — save for Dr. Paul — was addressing the collapse in the value of the national currency. Now here we are only three years later, the value of a dollar has plunged to less than a 1,300th of an ounce of gold, and the talk in the heart of Manhattan is not just $2,000 gold but $4,000 gold. It's not coming from gold bugs and flat earth types but from one of our most successful investors in the land.

It's amazing to us that this story is rarely put up on the front pages of our general interest press, though some of the shrewdest editors on the Web have begun fronting the gold story (Matt Drudge sometimes changes headlines several times a day as the dollar sinks).

It is true that Dr. Paul tried to make this an issue in the 2008 campaign, and failed to prosper. And it is true that if interest rates start to move up, we could see gold start to come down. But the question that vexes us is to what degree is the lack of a constitutional dollar that is defined the way the writers of the Constitution expected it to be defined — as a specified number* of grains of silver — responsible for, or contributing to, our economic troubles to begin with.

* * *

And who is going to pick up this issue in the political arena? Governor Palin is one of the few politicians to voice concern about the plunging value of the dollar, which she did when she visited Hong Kong. In June, Congressman Paul Ryan pressed Chairman Bernanke about the gold value of the dollar, to which Mr. Bernanke replied, "I don't fully understand the movements in the gold price." It is Congress that is the body that is constitutionally responsible for coining money and regulating its value. There is at least the possibility that in a matter of weeks control of the House and maybe even the Senate is going be revoked from the Democrats and returned to the Republicans. Will the fact that serious people are warning about $4,000 gold be enough to shock the new Congress into looking at repairing a monetary system as a first step toward returning our economy to the path of stable growth?

— September 30, 2010

---

* 371 1/4, according to the Coinage Act of 1792.

# The Boehner

'*In the months ahead, after all, people are going to be charting the dollar and watching where it stands, not only against other currencies but also against gold. Between now and 2008, we will be in a period in which, if the dollar begins to fall, the blame is not going to attach to the Republicans, who will no longer control the Congress, but to Democrats. If the dollar goes down further from here, it might as well be renamed the Pelosi. Going into a transitional election with a falling dollar is not something the Democrats will want to do.*'

\* \* \*

Those were the words with which, almost exactly four years ago, we greeted the Democrats' accession to the leadership of the Congress. Now, as control of the House is returned to the Republicans, it is the point that we predict will prove most pressing for Speaker Boehner. For it is to the Congress — in contradistinction to the president and the courts — that the Constitution, in Article 1, Section 8, delegates the power to coin money, regulate the Value thereof, and of foreign coin, and to fix the standard of weights and measures. On Mrs. Pelosi's watch, the value of the dollar made an astonishing plunge, collapsing to less than half of the 637th of an ounce of gold it was worth when Mrs. Pelosi's Democrats were given their mandate.

That is history now, and in a matter of weeks we might as well start referring to the greenback as the Boehner. Monetary policy will be by no means the only element of the Congress's responsibility in respect of the economy. There will be fiscal matters, for surely the election was nothing if not a rejection of the Democrats' intention to allow the largest tax increase in the history of the country to go into effect as the country is struggling to pull out of what will come to be known — depending on what the next Congress does — as either the Great Recession or the Obama Recession. But no question will confront the next speaker more urgently than the dollar.

Indeed, the votes were still being cast in what became the Republican landslide in the House when the Bloomberg news wire issued a story yesterday suggesting that the chairman of the Federal Reserve, Ben Bernanke, would be facing more scrutiny from Congress after the Republican election gains. It noted the likely accession to the Senate of Rand Paul, who would, the wire noted, join Senator DeMint, as an advocate for what Bloomberg characterized as "Tea Party candidates who backed an unsuccessful bill to subject the Fed's monetary policy to congressional audits." Rand Paul is now senator elect.

Bloomberg noted that Darrell Issa, now set to become chairman of the House Oversight and Government Reform Committee, "has the Fed in his sights" and quoted Mr. Issa as having declared in an interview last month that Congress must "look in-depth behind the curtain, rather than simply have the Fed chairman come up and lecture us." The wire service quoted the man who is now the new senator from Kentucky as having said in July, "It wasn't that the home builder was stupid, or the mortgage broker was stupid. It was that they got the wrong signal from the monetary policy of the government."

\* \* \*

If the Republican accession to leadership in the House really means that the cause of monetary reform is stirring — and that's how it looks to us — this couldn't be better news. The world waits for a leader who gives evidence that he understands the monetary powers and disabilities established in our system. What is being called a dollar today is so far from the constitutional dollar envisioned by the Founders of America that it is going to be hard to work back to honest money. Hard, but not impossible, and this is one of the things these columns will be watching in the new congress. There are those — Wisconsin's Paul Ryan, say, and, most famously,

Congressman Ron Paul — who have been pressing the Federal Reserve in respect of gold. The issue went right past the Democrats. They led the Congress for four years with nary a how-do-you-do to the crisis of the dollar. Now is the chance for the Republicans to seize the day and establish sound and constitutional money as a principle that goes with Republican leadership.

— November 3, 2010

# Gold and the World Bank

A long career watching the World Bank only increases the delight with which your editor notes the dispatch in the Financial Times by the institution's current president, Robert Zoellick, in respect of the restoration of some kind of gold standard. The piece runs under the headline "The G20 must look beyond Bretton Woods." His reference is to the 19 advanced and emerging nations and the European Union that make up the Group of 20 that was established in 1999. Mr. Zoellick wants what he calls parallel agendas of structural reform and a growth recovery program, to be complemented with "a plan to build a co-operative monetary system that reflects emerging economic conditions."

Mr. Zoellick reckons such a new system is going to need to "involve the dollar, the euro, the yen, the pound" and what he calls "a renminbi that moves towards internationalisation and then an open capital account." Quoth he: "The system should also consider employing gold as an international reference point of market expectations about inflation, deflation and future currency values. Although textbooks may view gold as the old money, markets are using gold as an alternative monetary asset today." He ends his piece by suggesting that the package of reforms he proposes could "get governments ahead of problems instead of reacting to economic, political and social storms."

Much as we're happy to read of this kind of thing coming from such an institution as the World Bank, which is in the business of steering credit where the markets wouldn't normally take it, our own reaction to Mr. Zoellick is that the political storm has already gotten w-a-a-a-a-y ahead of where he's at. It's not just Sarah Palin's challenge to Chairman Bernanke, of which we wrote about earlier; it's a whole raft of new or rising congressmen and women to are onto this issue — including, to name but a few, Michelle Bachman of Minnesota, now bidding for a position in the House leadership, Congressman Ron Paul, his son, Senator-elect Paul, and Congressman Ryan.

And the debate is moving way past the idea of simply "considering employing gold" as an "international reference point." The kinds of reformers now rising in the Congress are talking about a return to the idea of constitutional money, an abhorrence of the idea of paper money. Some are even for moving to a system in which prices are stated not in dollars at all but in ounces of gold or silver, the two types of money countenanced in the Constitution. These reformers are concerned less with the international problem than with the national problem — the monetary powers and disabilities of the Constitution itself.

Such reformers understand that Congress has defaulted on the exercise of one of the most important of its enumerated powers — to coin money and regulate the value thereof and of foreign coin and to fix the standard of weights and measures (it's all in the same sentence). The World Bank, though it's nice to see it headed by a figure who is open to ideas, is the least of it. The reformers advancing on the Hill are taking a look at the Fed itself, at whether Congress erred in delegating to the Fed too much power. They are going to seek the audit the Fed has been trying to deny to Congress (and to the rest of us). We have the sense that at the end of the day gold will be less an international reference point than the starting place of a new system.

— November 8, 2010

# Palin v. Bernanke

One of the questions in respect of 2012 is how it has happened that the only major Republican figure, aside from Congressman Ron Paul, to stand up and be counted on the dollar is Sarah Palin. She is supposed to be an ex-beauty queen without a lot of sophistication. Yet she is reportedly scheduled to be in Phoenix today delivering a major address challenging the plan of the chairman of the Federal Reserve, Ben Bernanke, to inflate the dollar. Snippets of her text were put up Sunday on the National Review Online and began immediately rocketing around the globe, no doubt in part because of the Palinesque phrasing, in which she called on Mr. Bernanke to "cease and desist."

Now we don't mind saying that the Sun has been looking forward to the Alaskan breaking out on this issue. In October 2009, we issued an editorial called "Palin and Paul." We noted that those waiting for a politician to pick up on the monetary issue were perking up to a posting on Mrs. Palin's Facebook page. In it she had noted that the Gulf oil states were reported to be negotiating with Russia about abandoning the dollar as a unit of pricing, observed that an official of the United Nations had called for a new world reserve currency, and, most importantly, warned that the value of the dollar was collapsing in terms of gold. Her posting, we wrote, suggested that she was ahead of the rest of the undeclared contenders for 2012.

At the time, the value of a dollar had slid to just less than a 1,000th of an ounce of gold. Today it has plunged to barely better than a 1,400th of an ounce of gold. In other words, in the year since Mrs. Palin took up this issue, the Bernanke Dollar — or the Obama Dollar, or the Pelosi, as we've sometimes called it — has lost a third of its value. The chairman of the Federal Reserve is now on an announced plan to try to inflate it further. So far the Congress that has oversight of the Federal Reserve has been largely mute, though there have been some notable exceptions (Congressman Paul

Ryan, for example, and Dr. Ron Paul, of course; among the big newspapers, only the editorial page of the Wall Street Journal has been in front of this issue).

We were struck, reading the Robert Costa's National Review advance on Mrs. Palin's speech, with the reach of her warning. She attacked QE2, as the second quantitative easing of monetary policy is called, head on. "The Fed hopes doing this may buy us a little temporary economic growth by supplying banks with extra cash which they could then lend out to businesses. But it's far from certain this will even work. After all, the problem isn't that banks don't have enough cash on hand – it's that they don't want to lend it out, because they don't trust the current economic climate. And if it doesn't work, what do we do then? Print even more money? What's the end game here?"

Mrs. Palin is looking over the horizon: "Do we have any guarantees that QE2 won't be followed by QE3, 4, and 5, until eventually — inevitably — no one will want to buy our debt anymore? What happens if the Fed becomes not just the buyer of last resort, but the buyer of only resort?" She comprehends how it is going to get to the voters she'll be courting. "[E]veryone who ever goes out shopping for groceries knows that prices have risen significantly over the past year or so. Pump priming would push them even higher. And it's not just groceries. Oil recently hit a six month high, at more than $87 a barrel. The weak dollar — a direct result of the Fed's decision to dump more dollars onto the market — is pushing oil prices upwards. That's like an extra tax on earnings."

The worst part of it, in Mrs. Palin's warning, is that "because the Obama White House refuses to open up our offshore and onshore oil reserves for exploration, most of that money will go directly to foreign regimes who don't have America's best interests at heart." In other words, she is reasoning out a coherent economic and geopolitical argument that she and her party — Tea, if not the mainstream GOP — can take to the voters. She is moving effortlessly from her Facebook page, which has more than 2.3 million friends, to our intellectual journals. So as we asked at the outset of this editorial, how has it happened that she is the first to brand this issue?

Was it her time running a state whose economy is tied to oil, which often tracks gold? Is it that she can see Russia from her door? Is she just smarter than the other candidates? Is it her savvy, and her husband's, at running a fishing business? Is it her journalistic instinct? Or does she read more papers than Katie Couric? No matter, she is now out in front of yet another issue as there is about to convene a new Congress of the United States in which she has a brace of allies indebted to her for her help in getting elected. Mr. Bernanke seems to have blithely ignored his other critics, but it will be more dangerous to ignore the Mamma Grizzly.

— November 8, 2010

# Sarah Palin's Seoul

President Obama will be returning from Seoul with his tail between his legs. "Obama's Economic View Is Rejected on the World Stage," is the way it is being bruited at the top of page one in today's New York Times. "European and Asian powers have had it with being lectured* by the U.S," is the way it was put in the Daily Beast, which reported that the president's letter to his foreign counterparts was fated to "make things worse." Mr. Obama couldn't even fetch a free trade agreement with, in Free Korea, a host country that has been running newspaper ads thanking America for 60 years of support. The kind of outreach on which Mr. Obama campaigned for president doesn't, in the event, seem to produce.

So, just as a thought experiment here, let's consider what might have happened had America been represented at the Group of 20 Summit not by a former community organizer but by a certain former governor of a state that, like South Korea itself, feels like it can almost see Russia from its door — and, in Free Korea's case, Communist China, too. The big news on the eve of the G20 was how upset our friends overseas are with the plan for a second round of money printing by the Federal Reserve. Mr. Obama took time out from his Asian travels to defend the weak-dollar policy. It turns out that the politician who challenged Mr. Bernanke most pointedly, and substantively, as the G20 was getting set for its meeting, was none other than Sarah Palin.

So one can speculate that had a President Palin been leading our delegation to Seoul, the monetary tensions would have been dissipated. The whole issue of a currency war — a competition over who can keep their currencies low and thus promote their own exports — would have been defanged. No doubt that had Mrs. Palin been leading our delegation in Seoul, her departure would have been preceded by a wave of warnings in the liberal press about our country's trade deficit.

The conceit is that we need to devalue the dollar in order to make it more attractive for foreigners to buy American products.

Mrs. Palin, however, has a plank in her political campaign that would address the trade deficit in a way that neither Mr. Obama, nor any other Democrat, has been prepared to endorse. She wants to move to domestic energy production, opening up the Arctic National Wildlife Refuge and close-in (and safer to drill in) coastal regions for production. Mrs. Palin has a hard-earned canniness about the energy sector that can be matched by few other politicians in the country. She knows that our oil imports are a major part of our trade deficit. So while pursuing a sound-dollar policy that, at least in theory, could hurt our exports, she'd pursue a domestic oil policy that would help our trade deficit.

And — en passant — also dramatically strengthen our hand throughout the Middle East. Had Mrs. Palin been representing us at Seoul, there would, presumably, have been no announcement from Indonesia of the kind Mr. Obama made carping about Israel's housing construction in its own capital. Mrs. Palin has already declared that the housing question is a matter for the Israelis to decide. More strategically she would be less beholden to the Arab oil producing stages, and they would be feeling the chill of competition from her strategic shift on energy production. They would be wondering how long they can sustain the arrogant position that our ban on developing so much of our own petroleum has helped them finance.

* * *

This is only a matter of speculation, of course, but one can imagine that, had it been Mrs. Palin in Seoul, the other members of the Group of 20 would have received a different letter from the one that Mr. Obama sent them and that they found so irritating. One can imagine Mrs. Palin sending a note about the philosophical roots of her policy, the idea she has been pressing about constitutional conservatism. She might have talked to the G20 about how the Founders of

America thought about money and the warnings they made against paper money and the horror they felt about inflation. She might have talked with them about how she intended to work with the new Congress on fundamental monetary reform, crafting a new system that would constrain an independent board, like that of the Federal Reserve, from debasing the dollar. She might tell them that if they would like to participate she'd be happy to talk it over at a meeting to be known as the Wasilla Summit. Laugh at such a prospect, if you will, but then look at the headlines that are greeting one of the most signal failures of summitry of any recent American president. It's not hard to imagine that our foreign friends and allies would react well to a president who had a clear and savvy world view and knew where he, or she, was going.

— November 12, 2010

---

* According to one count, Mr. Obama's letter to the G-20 leaders used the words "must" or "should" 11 times.

# The Surprise Witness

One place President Obama, Speaker-To-Be John Boehner, Congressman Paul Ryan, or Governor Palin could turn to for wisdom on the current dollar crisis is the editorials of the New York Times. Not the editorials of today, but those that were issued during the mid-1940s, when the nations about to become victorious in World War II were meeting at Bretton Woods, New Hampshire, to lay the groundwork for a post-war monetary system. The Times issued editorial after editorial critical of the Bretton Woods negotiations and their architect, John Maynard Keynes. It turns out that the editorials were the work of a single, prophetic editorial writer, Henry Hazlitt.

Hazlitt warned that what was being set up at Bretton Woods was an inflation trap. He turned out to be correct, and the system unraveled in 1971, when President Nixon closed the gold window. Bretton Woods unraveled over what, in retrospect, seems a modest drop in the value of a dollar — something like 10% — to a 38th of an ounce of gold from the 35$^{th}$ that obtained under Bretton Woods. This ushered monetary arrangements that, under the leadership of President Reagan and the Fed chairman at the time, Paul Volcker, proved serviceable for a while but are turning out to be inadequate in an era of lesser leaders.

No doubt Hazlitt, had he lived, would have said the failure was inevitable. His warnings in the New York Times stand as one of the great scoops in all of newspapering. The oeuvre is anthologized in a book that Hazlitt himself put together called "From Bretton Woods To World Inflation." Issued in 1984, it contains more than 20 of his editorials from the Times, most of them from the 1940s, but starting with one from the 1934, called "The Return to Gold," which contains a warning that could not be more relevant to today's debate when the G20 is feuding over the prospect of competitive devaluations:

"There is no more a 'natural value' for an irredeemable currency than there is for a promissory note of a person of uncertain intentions to pay for an undisclosed sum at an unspecified date. Finally, it has been learned that competitive depreciation, unlike competitive armaments, is a game that no Government is too poor or too weak to play, and that it can lead to nothing but general demoralization." Later, he warned, via an editorial in the Times: "The Greatest single contribution the United States could make to world currency stability after the war is to announce its determination to stabilize its own currency."

Another memorable one of Hazlitt's editorials of the Times, from February 1945, is called "Supply Creates Demand." It warned against the fallacy that we could be "saved from disaster after the war only by a continuation of huge Government spending and deficit financing." The fallacy was based on the notion that "purchasing power" must be kept above "production." Hazlitt warned that would lead to the "crude inflationary theory that we can keep gong after the war only by the process of constantly increasing money payments regardless of production." Does this sound familiar?

The Hazlitt compendium also includes a celebrated editorial called "Gold vs. Nationalism," which was issued in the Times on March 17, 1945. It sketched one of the famous paradoxes, which is that agreements like Bretton Woods, which seem, on the face of it, to be archetypes of multi-nationalism are in fact the opposite. The real trans-national idea of a single standard to which all countries could, or could not, repair is gold. The opposite, the recipe for strife, was a "system under which each nation individually would be free to allow whatever unsound policies it wished, while the nations collectively would have to bail it out of the difficulties into which it fell as a consequence." Greece couldn't have put it better.

\* \* \*

Years later, Hazlitt himself was asked, in an interview by the Austrian Economics Newsletter, why he thought the editorials didn't have more effect. Quoth he: "As you will remember the guiding spirit at that conference was John Maynard Keynes. The delegates were making inflationary decisions every day. I was tirelessly pointing out that these decisions were inflationary. Nobody else seemed to be pointing this out and nobody paid any attention to what I was saying. In fact, I think an awful lot of people were astonished that the New York Times was taking this strange eccentric position. When the 43 nations represented all signed the agreement adopting the Bretton Woods program, Arthur Sulzberger, then publisher of the Times, called me into his office and said, 'Look, Henry, I've been letting you write these things, although I had misgivings about them, but now that 43 nations have agreed to accept the agreement, I don't see how the Times can continue to oppose it.' I replied, 'Mr. Sulzberger, if you feel that way, I can't continue to write any more editorials in the New York Times on the agreement; I believe it is too harmful.'"

The Times has stuck with the Keynesian errors all the way up through Professor Krugman, and it has been by no means alone in its willingness to swing behind Bretton Woods. But it has left, in the oeuvre of Hazlitt's editorials, a record that will repay a visit by the politicians of today, when the dollar — which under Bretton Woods was worth a 35th of an ounce of gold — is worth less than a 1,400th of an ounce of gold and when the 20 leading countries of the world are in disarray and when a new generation of politicians is rising in a new Congress that will be looking for a way forward.

— November 13, 2010

# The Ron Paul Question

We have received a number of queries from readers who are mystified that a newspaper like ours, which backs Israel and a strong American foreign policy, is offering support for Congressman Ron Paul in his campaign for honest money. Over the weekend we received a wire from a friend asserting that Dr. Paul is an anti-Semite. Producing a "puff piece" on him "because he has said a true thing about gold," wrote our friend in respect of one of our recent references to Dr. Paul, "is like saying Ezra Pound was a great poet . . . even though he wanted us all dead." The ellipsis is in the original.

By our lights, the analogy between Ron Paul and Ezra Pound fails to hold up. Ezra Pound, in his lifetime, stood formally accused of treason. He had made broadcasts from Italy that, during the time of Mussolini, gave aid and comfort to an enemy. Whether it could have been proved in court that Pound had been either "levying war" against the United States or "adhering" to an enemy, which is required under the Constitution for a conviction of treason, is unclear, as he wasn't tried. But one can speculate that justice would have been better served had Pound gone not to a psychiatric ward but to the gallows. His animus to America was no doubt related to his hatred of Jews, which he expressed often and over a long time.

Ron Paul strikes us as nothing like Ezra Pound. Dr. Paul's dissent from American policy may, at times, be as bitter as Pound's was, but, in sharp contradistinction to Pound, Dr. Paul has never broadcast against America from enemy soil or done anything else even remotely comparable to treason. On the contrary, despite Dr. Paul's dissent on policy, he has adhered to America and repeatedly sworn the constitutional oath. He served as an officer of the United States Air Force in a time of war. Since then he has made his career as a physician and as a congressman.

Dr. Paul, moreover, has a quality that we quite like. He

"thinks constitutionally," to use the phrase the editor of the Sun used, in a television interview, to describe the congressman. He may not be unique in that way, but he is unusual. He is fairly obsessed with following the plain language of the Constitution. Precisely for this reason he is coming in for a new look by many at a time when our country is in what we like to call a constitutional moment.

We are aware of Dr. Paul's attacks on neo-conservatives, including several heroes for whom our friendship is abiding, and there is no doubt that his views on foreign policy are at odds with those of this newspaper. Yet we don't believe that his views stem from a hostility to Jews. He is a libertarian and believes that war is a friend of the state, meaning that war invariably empowers the state over the individual. We don't disagree about that, only about whether the costs of war are justified in the current conflict. Dr. Paul is opposed to foreign aid on constitutional grounds; we're not so sure he's wrong about that. His aversion to both war and foreign aid have put him at odds with those of us who support the expeditions in Iraq and Afghanistan and also robust American backing of the Jewish state.

No doubt Dr. Paul's views have won him hosannas from some who oppose Israel for base reasons, but it is well to mark that the congressman is no friend of Osama bin Laden and his ilk. He is the leading advocate of using against Mr. Bin Laden one of the bedrock war powers of the Constitution, the letter of marque and reprisal. That constitutional instrument — which authorizes private parties to commit acts of war — was used against the Barbary Pirates. Letters of marque have issued only rarely since, but were advanced for use against terrorists back in the 1990s by the Jewish Forward.

Dr. Paul unsheathed the constitutional sword within days of Al Qaeda's attacks on New York and Washington, introducing the September 11 Marque and Reprisal Act of 2001 to authorize private parties to go after Osama bin Laden. He has pressed continually since then for legislation authorizing the granting of such letters, delivering an eloquent exposition to anyone who will listen. Say what one will about that strategy, but after so many hundreds of billions of dollars of outlays on conventional war, letters of marque and reprisal seem less chimerical than when Dr. Paul first proposed them.

* * *

Finally, a word about prejudice. The longer we are in the newspaper line the more we are disinclined to judge our public officials by their private prejudices. Harry Truman, as we have noted in these columns before, voiced privately the most astonishingly bigoted views toward Chinese, African-Americans, and Jews. Yet public life brought wisdom, and he went on to stand down opposition recognition of the Jewish state, to integrate the Army, and to defeat the Japanese tyranny that menaced, among others, Free China. We have met Congressman Paul only in journalistic settings. But we have covered him on monetary matters for three decades. He sees the struggle for sound and honest money as not just a constitutional matter but as a moral question, and we agree with him. Let those who feel he doesn't deserve our support step forward themselves to compete for the leadership in the campaign for the kind of monetary system our country deserves and the Founders envisioned.

— November 22, 2010

# 'Cruel Hoax of Humphrey-Hawkins'

It's going to be fun to see how the New York Times comes out in respect of Humphrey-Hawkins. That is the law that gave the Federal Reserve an additional mandate beyond stable prices, namely the assignment to promote full employment. In the face of the contretemps over the Federal Reserve's campaign of quantitative easing, the Wall Street Journal issued an important editorial last week calling for the repeal of Humphrey-Hawkins. The Financial Times followed this week, with its own argument in favor of repeal.

What puts us in mind of the Times is the fact that, back in February 1978, when the Humphrey-Hawkins was first proposed — by Vice President Humphrey's widow, Muriel, who'd been elevated to replace him in the Senate — the Times came out with a withering deconstruction of the ill-thought-out legislation. It ran its editorial under the headline "The Cruel Hoax of Humphrey-Hawkins." The Times acknowledged that the law had what it called "wide appeal," partly in tribute to the late vice president and partly as a reassertion of a "faded commitment" to full employment.

The law, however, was "deeply flawed," the Gray Lady warned, and would "legislate wishful thinking, not a reduction in unemployment." It observed that an earlier version of the bill promised too much and that the final version promised too little. So the Times concluded: "It deserves a harder look from its boosters and rejection by Congress." The Times editorial goes on to offer a fascinating glimpse not only of the inanity of Humphrey-Hawkins but of just how far the Times — and our times — have fallen from the days of what might be called "hard-headed liberalism."

It noted that Humphrey Hawkins would proclaim a goal of "4 percent unemployment by 1983" (the rate at the time, the dark days of the Jimmy Carter presidency, was 6.3%) but "by itself, would not create one job; it would merely legislate a good intention." The Times noted that the administration was offering a battle plan that included its "new tax cut proposal, its job program, and its voluntary anti-inflation initiative." But it noted that the plan was encountering resistance from legislators who feared either inflation or wage and price controls.

Then the Times offered a paragraph pregnant with a sense of the malaise of the Carter era of which Humphrey-Hawkins is a monument: "The uncertain consequences of any policy decision also impede action. Numerous levers can be pulled. Taxes, interest rates, job subsidies, training programs, wages or price restraints — all can be put to work. But the riddle no one can answer is how to use these tools to drive unemployment down to the promised land of 4 percent without triggering worse inflation and, perhaps, an accompanying deep recession."

It turned out that there were those who knew how to chart a way forward, one that involved taking a recession in the short run. One of them was Paul Volcker, who acceded to the chairmanship of the Fed shortly after Humphrey-Hawkins was brought into law. He promptly declared that dealing with inflation had been "elevated to a position of high national priority" and that success would require policy to be "consistently and persistently oriented to that end." Quoth he: "Vacillation and procrastination, out of fears of recession or otherwise, would run grave risks."

The other titan was Ronald Wilson Reagan, who ushered in the supply-side revolution. It combined Mr. Volcker's anti-inflation regime with strategic tax reductions, particularly at the top margins, and a commitment to deregulation and free trade. The result, after at 14-month recession in 1981 and 1982, was the Great Reagan Boom that rolled forward and helped bring, among other bounties, victory in the Cold War.

Now we are in an era of in which the malaise and befuddlement of the Carter years is being echoed under President Obama. The nature of the stagnation is slightly different. Consumer price inflation hasn't hit — yet. But the sense of frustration and malaise and policy indecision has hit. The questions are whether Congress will revise its mandate to the Federal Reserve or whether a new chairman with the capacities of a Paul Volcker will have to be brought in. And then the question of who will be emerge to rise, Reagan-like, to the presidency. How ironical it is that the debate is once again coming into focus over the cruel hoax of a law that required the soundness of our money to be compromised for the cynical promise of full employment.

— November 22, 2010

# How to Depoliticize the Fed

The secretary of the treasury, Timothy Geithner, issued a warning the other day, telling Republicans to stop politicizing the Federal Reserve. The warning was reported on the Bloomberg wire. "It is very important to keep politics out of monetary policy," the secretary was quoted as saying in an interview taped for broadcast on the show "Political Capital." It's a terrific idea — the idea of keeping the dollar from being whipsawed by politics. But there's only one tried and true way to do it. It's called the gold standard.

The idea is that the value of the dollar is set as a matter of law at a specified quantity of gold. Under the Constitution, silver could be used instead — or as well. Once the dollar is defined as a set amount of gold or silver, the politicians have nothing to say about it. This is how such figures as George Washington, James Madison, and Alexander Hamilton thought it was going to work. In the Constitution, Congress was granted the power to coin money and regulate its value. No sooner was the Constitution ratified than the Founding Fathers sat down and wrote the Coinage Act, which was passed in 1792 and defined a dollar as 371 ¼ grains of pure silver or the free market equivalent in gold.

Their expectation was that the constitutional dollar would be the standard for America. The power to coin it was granted to the Congress in the same sentence of the Constitution that grants Congress the power to fix the standard of weights and measures. The Founders figured that once the standard was set the politicians would have to adjust or deal with the consequences. But that has long since gone by the boards, and today a Federal Reserve, whose governors are appointed by the president and confirmed by the Senate, sits around and decides what it thinks the dollar should be worth.

To see how that is the recipe for politicization, feature what has happened in the past few weeks. The mandarins of the Fed got it into their heads that the dollar was too strong.

So they announced a plan to try to generate a little bit of inflation and bring down the value of the dollar. They would inject dollars into the economy buying more than half a trillion dollars of American government paper. This alarmed not only our trading partners overseas, from Britain to Germany to China, but also one of the most powerful institutions in America — Sarah Palin.

The former governor of Alaska, sensing a policy blunder ahead of the other politicians, used a speech in Phoenix to upbraid the Fed's chairman, Ben Bernanke. Before you could say John Maynard Keynes, every politician from President Obama to Speaker-to-be John Boehner jumped into the act. The Europeans went into a currency-war footing in respect of exchange rates. Even the Chinese communists doubled down. At the Group of 20 summit meeting in Seoul, President Obama's hectoring was spurned by the other leaders and he returned home humiliated.

Then a few days ago Sewell Chan of the New York Times reported that the Fed is getting into the Washington political game — "haltingly adopting the tactics of Washington, like strategically placed interviews, behind-the-scenes assuaging of opponents and reaching out to potential allies of Capitol Hill." The next thing you know, the Fed's chairman, Ben Bernanke, will be starting a political action committee. How about BenPac?

Backers of the Fed like to talk about the importance of the central bank's "independence." Translated into plain English what they mean is the freedom for the Fed to do whatever it wants, no matter what its political impact. The truth is that the idea of independence of the Fed went out the window formally in 1978, when Congress passed a law requiring it to adjust its monetary policy not only to protect the value of the dollar but also to protect jobs. The bill was put forward by the widow of Vice President Hubert Humphrey and named in his honor.

There is really only one way to take the Fed out of politics, and that is to return to a gold or silver standard. The idea is that there is a physical measurement of value that sits out there for everyone to refer to — the government, the banks, the housewife, the foreign potentates. They would all know what to expect. The politicians can then quarrel about their policies without getting involved in what the value of the dollar should be.

Is it possible to go back to such a system? There are lots of theories out there as to how it could be done. One way to start would be for Congress to remove the obligation of the Fed to worry about the unemployment rate and concentrate on steadying the value of the dollar. This is already being proposed by Congressman Michael Pence and as Senator Corker and endorsed by the Wall Street Journal and others. That would make it easier for the Fed to pay primary attention to the value of the dollar and, hopefully, stabilize it.

In the longer run, though, the betting is the Fed itself won't be able to solve the problem. It will have to involve action by Congress or the states. Or both. There are those — most pointedly the constitutional sage Edwin Vieira Jr. — who believe the states should begin exercising the power reserved to them in the Constitution to make gold or silver coins legal tender and set up a kind of competing money to which Americans could repair as the dollar collapses. There's also the hope that the national legislature won't want to get scooped by the states and will start working on a monetary system more in line with what the Founders of American envisioned.

— November 26, 2010

# Hi Yo, Silver...

The surge in the price of silver to near record levels puts us in mind of President Lyndon Johnson's now-much-ridiculed appearance in the Rose Garden, when, in July 1965, he signed the first new coinage act since the original that George Washington had signed in 1792. It was the 1792 act that defined the dollar in terms of silver; it was silver to which the Founders were referring when they used the word dollars in the Constitution. The law that Johnson signed gave us a quarter that lacks silver — call it a fiat two-bits — which is what prompted him to utter his now a now ridiculous seeming warning.

"If anybody has any idea of hoarding our silver coins, let me say this," drawled the Texan "Treasury has a lot of silver on hand, and it can be, and it will be used to keep the price of silver in line with its value in our present silver coin." At the time, the price of silver was $1.29 an ounce, meaning that the value of a dollar, at 0.775193798 of an ounce of silver, was down, but relatively slightly, from the 0.848571429 ounces of silver that the dollar was defined as consisting of in the first Coinage Act.

In short order, Johnson's promise proved to be hollow. The value of what was still being called a dollar began dropping. Within 15 years, the price of silver had soared to $49 an ounce. That was due in part, although only in part, to the attempt of Nelson Bunker Hunt and his brother William Howard Hunt to corner the silver market. Even after the attempted corner collapsed, the silver value of the dollar lurked well below that which had obtained between the Founding Era and Johnson's signing of the Coinage Act of 1965. Today the value of what passes for a dollar as collapsed to less than a 27th of an ounce of silver. CNBC is reporting that silver prices have soared 60% in 2010 — meaning that the silver value of the dollar has plunged sharply this year, and it attributes this partly to strong buying of exchange-traded funds, known as

ETFs, backed, as CNBC puts it, "by the physical metal." It reports that sales of silver coins are up 22% over year earlier levels and 30% since 2007.

What catches our attention about all this is simply the drama of the collapse of the dollar against silver in the two generations since the president who signed the Coinage Act taking silver out of most of our coinage vowed there wouldn't be such a collapse. It's just something to bear in mind amid the latest vows from various government officials about how they have an exit strategy available from the balance sheet distortions that are being created by the quantitative easing and other programs. History teaches that in respect of money it pays to be wary of the prognostications of politicians.

— December 1, 2010

# A Dodge on Judges' Pay

The dead-of-the-night deal that was struck in respect of the pay of New York State's judges is being hailed by the governor, the bar association, and, it seems, the judges. And why not? It establishes a system that takes the governor off the hook — and, for that matter, the legislature. Under the new system, the hard-put-upon taxpayers of New York State can be forced to give a raise to the judges of the state court system without the taxpayers' elected representatives having to give it so much as a hearing, let alone actually to vote on it.

Instead the deed will be done by a commission that includes only two persons appointed by the legislature and an equal number of persons who are appointed — wait for it — by the judges themselves. The judges will get to appoint two-sevenths of the commission that will decide their pay. This stunt was pulled the same week that unemployment benefits were ended for the rest of Americans because the taxman is already taking too much money from those few who are left working. There will come a day when this will be seen as a strategic error.

If it will be said that this newspaper is unsympathetic to judges, we will plead innocent. The fact is that judges are generally the most learned and most thoughtful of our public officials. And we recognize the special nature of judges' pay. The pay of judges was one of reasons America seceded from the tyranny of Britain. The grievance was enumerated in the Declaration of Independence itself, which noted that the British king, George III, had made judges "dependent on his will alone, for the tenure of their offices, and the amount and payment of their salaries."

So the Constitution of the United States — and, incidentally, of New York State — establishes that a judge's pay may never be diminished during the judge's tenure in office. To lower a judge's pay is unconstitutional. The principle is American bedrock. But it is also American bedrock that money mayn't be drawn from the treasury except through an appropriation by the legislature. And the record is clear in American law that a legislature can't delegate its powers to someone else. Why, after all, bother with a legislature in the first place?

In the case of the pay of New York State judges, the legislature has sought to evade this principle by reserving for itself the power to block the decision of the commission it is setting up to deal with judges' pay. That strikes us as a dodge. It would be like the legendary bank robber Willie "The Actor" Sutton — who put his hands in his pockets and poked a finger at the bank tellers — pleading innocent because he wasn't carrying a real gun when he demanded the money. By our lights, if a legislator is going to give someone a raise, he ought every time to look the taxpayers in the eye. It's their money he's spending.

The right way to address the question of judges' pay is to repair the dollar. For it is true that the pay of our judges has been reduced during their tenure in office. But what has been putting our judges in such extremis is not that anyone reduced the number of dollars they've been paid. It's that the value of the dollar has collapsed. If, for example, the chief judge of the state of New York was paid a decade ago with a dollar that was worth a $270^{th}$ of an ounce of gold and is today paid with a dollar that is worth barely a $1,400^{th}$ of an ounce of gold, his or her pay has been reduced. Unconstitutionally so, in our view.

The right way to rectify this is to pay our judges in constitutional money, meaning a set number of grains of silver or gold. That is what a dollar was understood as being by the same Founders who established in the constitutions of America and New York that a judge's pay may never be reduced. This, incidentally, would give most of our judges much bigger raises than they are going to get from the cornball commission the legislature has just set up. And it would throw into sharp relief the predicament of the rest of America. Judges, after all, aren't the only ones who have been robbed over the decades by the Great Thief of inflation.

— December 2, 2010

# Wikileaks and the Fed

"What we really need," Congressman Ron Paul said in respect of the Fed when we spoke with him on the phone this morning, "is a Wikileaks episode." He wasn't in any way suggesting that literally — or recommending any other kind of illegal raid on the Fed's books; all his points favor acting only in lawful ways. What he was underlining is that the big document disclosure from the Fed is just the tip of the iceberg of what the public needs, and deserves, to know about what our nation's central bank is doing.

The documents that have been released were disclosed by the Fed in the face of an array of pressures — from Bloomberg News, among others, and from the Congress, spurred by the socialist senator from Vermont, Bernard Sanders, against the backdrop of Congressman Paul's years long quest for some sunlight on the Fed. The disclosures show a vast rescue by the Fed of all sorts of institutions. "Santa Clause: Fed Aid Went All Over; Companies, Banks, Offshore" is the headline the Drudge Report put on the story.

It's quite a spectacle. The Fed disclosed 21,000 transactions in its multi-trillion emergency lending program. It turns out that the then-triple-A-rated General Electric was getting bailed out without any disclosure being made by its broadcasting arms, even while they're covering the Fed and the debate over the bailout. So vast was the borrowing by foreign banks that Senator Sanders was quoted by the Financial Times as asking: "Has the Federal Reserve of the United States become the central bank of the world?"

One analyst, Karen Shaw Petrou of Federal Financial Advisers, was quoted by the Washington Post as saying the "disclosure shows 'how really profound the financial crisis was in the fall of 2008 and the firepower the Fed mustered in response.'" But a former aide of the Atlanta Fed, Robert Eisenbeis, now chief monetary economist at Cumberland Advisors, told Bloomberg Television that "it's not clear that you get a real picture about the severity of the financial crisis from these data."

He elaborated on the point this way: "When you drop money out of a helicopter on Wall Street, rational people pick it up, and you know there's a question about how much was needed." One point Mr. Eisenbeis cited was the disclosure by the Fed that among the companies it bailed out was the motorcycle maker Harley Davidson. "It's hard to argue," he noted, "that that's a systemically important firm — may be to the motor cycle crowd, but certainly not from the broad base of the United States economy."

Mr. Eisenbeis said there should be a "strong forensic team" — an outside group — to go in and look a the vast Fed bailouts and do an analysis the way it was done after, say, the failure of Lehman Brothers. His comments were but an example of the logic of a proper, public, outside audit of the Fed, which has long been sought by Congressman Paul. His quest for a full audit may have gotten lost in the compromise of the Dodd-Frank legislation, but it is asserting itself. It is something that the poor suffering taxpayers, who are looking at all this with a sense of horror, will look to the 111th Congress to require.

* * *

The logic is for such an audit to go way beyond the workings of the alphabet soup of various rescue lines opened up by the Fed. The real issue is the much larger question — how is the Federal Reserve conducting monetary policy and was our system of fiat money, in and of itself, a cause of the Great Recession? Or, to put a more forward spin on it, the question that is really asserting itself is whether monetary reform is the route to getting us out of the current morass and returning us to a path of stable growth. It's an encouraging thing that Dr. Paul is in line to chair the subcommittee in Congress that has primary oversight of the Fed. If he gets the post he's in line to get we'd like to think the American people will start to get some answers.

— December 2, 2010

# Has America Already Defaulted?

"Insanity" is the word an aide of President Obama, Austan Goolsbee, is using to characterize a move in Congress to block the heretofore routine raising of the ceiling on the national debt. Members of the Tea Party, among others, are urging the Congress to refuse to authorize an increase in federal borrowing and instead to concentrate on keeping outlays within what we can cover with tax revenues.

The debt ceiling, after all, is already north of $14 trillion dollars. "If we hit the debt ceiling," Mr. Goolsbee, who is chairman of the Council of Economic Advisers, warned on ABC television, "that's essentially defaulting on our obligations, which is totally unprecedented in American history."

Totally?

Certainly it is possible to see America as a "sovereign default virgin," in the language of two economists, Kenneth Rogoff and Carmen Reinhart, who wrote a famous paper on the history of defaults. The paper was cited, on the eve of President Obama's accession, by Greg Ip in a dispatch in the Washington Post warning of the danger of America's growing debt.

If one wants to be particular about it, though, the picture is more ambiguous. Professors Reinhart and Rogoff make a point of noting that America counts as a sovereign default virgin only because they are excluding "events such as the lowering of the gold content of the currency in 1933, or the suspension of convertibility in the nineteenth-century Civil War."*

In other words, a default by the federal government on its obligations isn't entirely unprecedented. It starts to depend on one's definitions. Did we default on our obligations when President Nixon closed the gold window, ending Bretton Woods? After all, the Constitution establishes that treaties — and Bretton Woods was one —

are the supreme law of the land. Yet Nixon acted without consulting our treaty partners, which is why the default became known as the "Nixon shock." Has America defaulted on its obligations by permitting the dollar to plunge in value, albeit in a free market and over time, to less than a 1,400[th] of an ounce of gold?

Our own view is that the answer to that question is yes. Allowing the dollar to collapse to but a 1,400[th] of an ounce of gold is a default. A rising gold price may not fit the economists' definition of inflation, which they tend to measure in terms of the Consumer Price Index. And one may try to argue that inflation itself is not a default. One can still get scrip for a treasury bond. But our own world view reckons that the American people are not stupid. They know that what the law of legal tender requires them to accept in payment of a debt is not what they hoped or expected it to be — or what it used to be.

This is what we are starting to hear in the Congress. The Tea Party might not be able to halt a new raising of the debt ceiling. The Republicans' own leadership was plumping for a debt ceiling increase within hours after the election, with the speaker-to-be, John Boehner, famously remarking, "We're going to have to deal with it as adults."

Explained Mr. Boehner: "Whether we like it or not, the federal government has obligations and we have obligations on our part." Yet clearly the ground has shifted, and people are starting to see that there is also an obligation in respect of the dollar.

So it would not be surprising to see the rumblings in the Congress, by the Tea Party or others, grow harder to ignore. For honoring the obligation to pay one's debts by dishonoring the obligation to maintain a sound currency is a default by any other name. Eventually the default that Messrs. Obama and Goolsbee insist would be an "insanity" is going to look less insane than what is happening to the rest of Americans at the cash registers of grocery stories and at gasoline pumps. They are plenty capable of looking into their wallets and comprehending that the default that the government insists would be "unprecedented" has already happened.

— January 3, 2011

---

\* The phrase "American default " was current in the City of London after the gold devaluation of 1933, we are informed by a wire from a reader.

# Palin's Gold

So it turns out that the last segment of "Sarah Palin's Alaska," airing tonight, finds the former governor and her family out panning for gold. Mrs. Palin issued a brief advance about the segment on her Facebook page, where she noted that the gold price, at the time of the posting, was $1,368.90 an ounce — or, as we like to put it, the value of a dollar is at a near record low of less than a 1,368[th] of an ounce of gold. Panning for gold, it develops, is an annual expedition for the Palin family, and it occurs to us that this tactile sensitivity to gold and its price is part of Mrs. Palin's canniness about the economy.

No wonder she was the first politician to express alarm over the collapsing value of the dollar in terms of gold. No wonder that she was the first politician to spring into print in respect of the second round of the Federal Reserve's quantitative easing, with the journalists and intelligentsia scrambling behind her. She makes a point of connecting every year with the scarcity of gold, the difficulty of bringing it out of the ground in amounts that could rock the world's money supply, its rare feature as an inert element, and the way it is bound up in the history of her state and country as a store of value.

In some ways it reminds us of one of our favorite stories about President Reagan, which we've told in these columns before and relates to a politician who was underestimated in respect of his comprehension of the real economy. It was told to us by one of his ambassadors to France, Van Gailbraith, who at one point drew the assignment to go in to see Reagan and brief him on the big issue that was going to be on the table when Reagan would meet with his French counterpart, Francois Mitterrand. The issue was corn gluten, which played a huge role in the economy of France and in trade tensions between the two countries.

Ambassador Galbraith went into the Oval Office to brief

the president, and began by saying something to this effect: "Mr. President, to prepare you for your meeting with President Mitterrand I'm going to have to explain to you about corn gluten . . ." Before he could get any further, Reagan laughed and told the ambassador that he didn't need an education on corn gluten or its importance. He was from Illinois. Then he leaned forward, opened the bottom drawer of his desk, and said, "I keep a jar of corn gluten right here in my desk — I use it to feed the squirrels."

We wouldn't want to make too much of that story, but we wouldn't want to make too little of it either. Reagan had a far more tactile feel of the real economy than his critics gave him credit for. And one gets that impression about Mrs. Palin, with her involvement in oil, with her "Sarah Palin's Alaska" episode on fishing ("it smell's like fish money," she tells to her daughter as halibut are unloaded at a cannery), and now with her episode on panning for gold. We are in a period in which the connection between the dollar and something real seems ever more tenuous. It's nice to see a politician who understands the connection and the meaning of gold.

— January 9, 2011

# Loughner's Money

'Will Jared Loughner discredit the gold standard?" That is the question being asked, apparently in all seriousness, by the Reuters news wire in the wake of the reports that one of the killer's obsessions turns out to have been our fiat money. "Loughner's YouTube videos," Reuters reports, "are consumed with the idea of creating a 'new currency,' one that is nothing like our current, Federal Reserve-controlled greenback." The way the New York Times put it, in a profile of Mr. Loughner, is that the killer was obsessed with "certain grandiose tenets of a number of extremist right-wing groups — including the need for a new money system . . ."

Which "extremist right-wing groups" the Times was referring to the paper didn't deign to say. But, hey, the United Nations has been carrying on about the need for a new world currency. And as the Gray Lady was moving its profile of Mr. Loughner, the Wall Street Journal was moving an interview with the Communist Chinese strongman, Hu Jintao, who, on the eve of his visit to America, is questioning the dollar. He is, as the Journal put it, "calling the present U.S. dollar-dominated currency system a 'product of the past,'" and highlighting what the Journal called "moves to turn the yuan into a global currency." Get set for a column from Paul Krugman saying that if Sarah Palin wasn't responsible for Mr. Loughner's rampage then Ben Bernanke was.

Wisecracks aside, America is hurtling toward a serious moment in respect of its dollar, and we predict that the gold standard will look less and less crazy with every passing week. In his answers to questions posed by the Wall Street Journal, the Chinese communist party boss offered no ground on exchange rates, making it clear that China has its own internal pressures and rebuffing the condescending lecture he got last week from Secretary Geithner about how a stronger yuan is in China's own best interests. Hard to credit, no doubt, from a treasury secretary with a checkered record here at home. The fact is that in a world where the big powers are arguing over whether the yuan is too strong or the dollar too weak, only the gold standard offers a modern and scientific way to discern the difference. For only gold can tell us what is actually happening, whether the yuan is gaining in value and the dollar losing, or both are losing, or both gaining, just one faster than the other. And it will take more than the ravings of a Jared Loughner to discredit that enduring principle.

— January 16, 2011

# The Pence Possibility

An independent campaign to draw Congressman Michael Pence into the 2012 presidential race is under way, the Associated Press is reporting this morning, and it is clearly one to watch. An email alerting us to the story was sent by Ralph Benko, a former Reagan aide who is working to draft the Hoosier. It's too early for any endorsement, but there are a lot of things we like about the Mr. Pence, including a strong foreign policy position honed, among other places, during his years on the Middle East subcommittee of the House Foreign Affairs Committee. He is a Jack Kemp, Ronald Reagan supply-side Republican. But the feature of his emerging platform that most attracts us is the fact that when Mr. Pence talks about what needs to be done to pull us out of our economic predicament the number one item on his list is sound money.

He laid this out in a speech last year at the Detroit Economic Club, where he declared, "Sound monetary policy is the foundation of our prosperity. A strong dollar means a strong America." He quoted Lawrence Kudlow as saying, "The Fed can print money, but it can't print jobs." He opposed the Federal Reserve's campaign of quantitative easing. He said he wasn't laying blame "solely at the feet of the Federal Reserve." The problem for the Fed, he said, began in 1977 with Humphrey-Hawkins, which imposed the dual mandate that requires the Fed to look not only at stabilizing prices but at maximizing employment.

The congressman didn't come right out and declare for a gold standard, though he acknowledged that such is what Jack Kemp, were he alive today, would have urged him to do. But he did swing behind the call by the president of the World Bank, Robert Zoelick, to "re-think the international currency system, including the role of gold" — and, Mr. Pence added, "I agree." The time has come, he said, "to have a debate over gold and the proper role it should play in our nation's monetary affairs."

That puts Mr. Pence in a group of political leaders who are forming an avant-garde for what we believe will be the most important issue in 2012. These figures range from Ron Paul, who is the grand old man of the movement for sound money, to Congressman Paul Ryan of Wisconsin, who asked the famous question that got Chairman Bernanke to confess he didn't know what to make of the collapse in the gold value of the dollar, to Sarah Palin, who first addressed the collapse of the dollar — it's now down to little more than a 1,400th of an ounce of gold — in a speech in Hong Kong and has, more recently, made the highest profile challenge to Chairman Bernanke on the Fed's campaign of quantitative easing.

Our view is that the right place for the debate Mr. Pence speaks of is in the presidential campaign of 2012. President Obama, who will meet the Chinese communist party boss, Hu Jintao, this week at Washington, is positioning his administration to stand for a weaker dollar and a stronger Chinese communist scrip. But the uncertainty, the faulty price signals, and the difficulties in borrowing that bedevil Americans are not a matter simply of the relative price of the dollar against foreign paper. They can be traced to the fact that our currency has been cut loose from anything of real, permanent value. What an opportunity for the Republicans, and the movement to draft Mike Pence offers yet one more chance that there will be a politician prepared to seize it.

— January 17, 2011

# Virginia's Golden Opportunity

For a glimpse of the avant-garde in the coming battle for monetary reform, one place on which to keep an eye is Virginia, where the general assembly — the oldest legislature in the hemisphere — is considering whether the Old Dominion might establish its own currency as a hedge against the collapse of the fiat dollar now being issued by the American government. A measure called Joint Resolution 557 has been introduced that would establish a committee "to study whether the Commonwealth should adopt a currency to serve as an alternative to the currency distributed by the Federal Reserve System in the event of a major breakdown of the Federal Reserve System."

The new governor of the state, Robert McDonnell, has announced that he "can't support," as his position was characterized by the Associated Press, the legislation because the proposal violates the constitution. The Associated Press reports that Mr. McDonnell said that proposals like the one just made in Richmond stem from "fear about frightening levels of debt the federal government has taken on," as the governor is paraphrased by the Associated Press. The newswire reports that the governor reckons that currency, as the AP put it, "is the responsibility of the federal government, not the states."

The fact is that the Constitution does not make currency the exclusive responsibility of the federal government. It does give the federal government the power to "coin money" and regulate its value and the value of foreign coin and to fix the value of weights and measures, like the hour and the ounce. That's in Article 1, Section 8. The Constitution does prohibit Virginia and the other states from making anything other than gold or silver coin legal tender. But it specifically leaves to the states the right to make gold or silver coin legal tender.

So out of sync with the Constitution was Mr. McDonnell's statement that one can surmise that he misspoke.

He has, after all, shown great regard in the past to the constitutional principles he is sworn to uphold; he was also attorney general before he was governor. In any event, one would have expected the governor — any governor — to defend, rather than cede in casual fashion to the federal government, the powers and privileges that are, under the Constitution, so pointedly reserved to Virginia and the other states.

The resolution that has been introduced in the state's general assembly, moreover, would not establish a state currency. It would merely study the matter. The resolution — part of a nationwide turn to constitutional principles — couldn't be more timely and appropriate. The value of the dollar has plummeted so fast and far in the past year that it is now worth only a bit more than a $1,400^{th}$ of an ounce of gold. It may have strengthened a bit in recent days, but there some who are predicting it could collapse to a $3,000^{th}$ of an ounce, which would be less than a tenth of what it was worth at the start of the century.

Myriad schemes are being advanced for setting up currencies to compete with the collapsing dollar. The Chinese communist party is talking about it; the president of China, Hu Jintao, is visiting America right now, with the dollar one of his big agenda items. The Europeans are talking about a parallel or replacement reserve currency even while their own scrip is in jeopardy of going out of existence altogether. Even the United Nations is trying to horn in on the idea of new currency.

What is significant about the proposal in Virginia is that it involves the idea that a parallel or competing monetary system should be set up not internationally but within the United States and by the states themselves. This idea is, by our lights, one of the most powerful ideas in the coming debate. It has been nursed for years by Edwin Vieira Jr., who has written extensively on it and on his plan for an electronic gold currency to be established precisely by the states.

It happens that Mr. Vieira lives in Virginia, at the north end of the Shenandoah. It would be a smart thing for Mr.

McDonnell to visit Mr. Vieira and take the time to sit in his study and listen to the sage explicate the history of the dollar, the concept of the constitutional dollar, the centrality of the constitutional principles to the repairing our economy, and the distribution of the monetary powers and disabilities of the Constitution. We've made the trip to Front Royal, and it is hard not to think the governor would find it illuminating.

\* \* \*

America is at a remarkable moment in respect of the dollar. Suddenly a wide range of thinkers are waking up to the catastrophe that would be represented by the loss of the dollar. A former chairman of the Federal Reserve, Alan Greenspan, presented himself at the Council on Foreign Relations to warn that fiat money always goes to gold. The president of the World Bank, Robert Zoellick wrote an important op-ed piece in the Financial Times, of all places, to suggest that there may be a role for gold after all. The New York Times brought in no less a figure than James Grant to argue that the time has come to bring back the classical gold standard. The Wall Street Journal editorial page has been running a stream of important pieces on monetary reform. This week a committee has been set up to draft for the 2012 presidential campaign a candidate, in the person of Congressman Michael Pence, who might stand on a gold plank. The Congress of the United States has just put Ron Paul at the head of the subcommittee that oversees the Federal Reserve. What a golden opportunity for Virginia, which gave us so many fathers of the Constitution, to take the lead in studying what role the states themselves might have in a return to sound money.

— January 19, 2011

# The Moment for Gold

The speed with which money is flowing out of gold — and American government bonds — and into stocks reflects the improving economic outlook, according to a telegram sent out this afternoon by the economist David Malpass. He notes that gold has fallen $115 dollars since its $1,431 intra-day peak on December 7, while the 10-year Treasury yield has risen to 3.4% from a low of 2.4% on October 7. He reported on a recent conference at which investors passed around "large gold nuggets" and at which Paul Volcker pointed out that a rising gold price is, as Mr. Malpass put it, a "negative assessment of a central bank." But he thinks the trend in the past month reflects the economic outlook.

Not a bad moment to sketch this newspaper's interest in gold. We look at it not with the investor's eye or the speculator's motives, though we respect both investors and speculators. Our interest in this beat has to do with the long struggle for monetary reform. It's our view that the difficulties our economy have been going through have their roots in the un-soundness — the fiat nature — of what currently passes for American money. We comprehend that the dollar can gain in value even without a repair of the monetary system, as fiscal, political, and related matters and even the business cycle can change the outlook for growth.

If, however, we are to reduce the danger of future busts, the most important reform would be to restore sound money. By that we mean the kind of gold- or silver-based money contemplated by the Founders of America. It happens that during a period in which the value of the dollar is collapsing — such as the past decade when it fell from more than a 300th of an ounce of gold to, at one point, less than a 1,400th of an ounce of gold — the logic of monetary reform seems to be plain on its face. When the dollar is gaining in value, as it has been in recent weeks and as it began to do in the Reagan years, the logic of sound money isn't as pressing.

This is what happened in the early 1980s, which we'd thought was a marvelous moment for monetary reform. After the great inflation unleashed by the failure of the Johnson and Nixon administrations to make hard fiscal choices during the Vietnam War — Johnson insisted on both guns and butter — the dollar collapsed to less than an 800th of an ounce of gold from the 35th of an ounce that it had been at, by law, during the years of Bretton Woods. So in 1981 Congress set up the United States Gold Commission, also known as the Reagan Commission, to look into what role gold might play in a monetary reform in America.

Eventually the commission rejected the idea of a return to gold, though it issued a famous minority report by two of its members, Lewis Lehrman and Ron Paul. But the dollar was rescued, at least for a while, by the rise of Paul Volcker to the chairmanship of the Federal Reserve. His was a long reign of tight money that conquered inflation and started moving the value of the dollar back up. Mr. Volcker was able to do this because his tight money regime was operated in tandem with the tax cuts and other supply-side measures being put through by President Reagan.

The combination of policies touched off the Reagan boom, which ran through what the editor of the Wall Street Journal called "seven fat years," and eventually it was extended into the 1990s and, after some retreats, into the 21st Century under George Bush. It is astonishing, at least to us, to think that at the start of George W. Bush's administration, in January 2001, a dollar was worth a 265th of an ounce of gold.

What nags at us is the question of whether the momentum for monetary reform which gathered as the catastrophe of the collapse of the dollar has come into focus could be lost in the economic growth we are experiencing today. The position of the Sun is that there are three circumstances when it makes sense to move to a system of sound money. One is when a currency is collapsing. Two is when it is steady. And three is when it is appreciating. What one really wants, at any point, is the confidence that the dollar will remain exchangeable for gold over a long period and that people will have confidence in that.

David Malpass's conclusion is that the risks of severe inflation and deflation are abating at the moment. But he closed his wire to clients and others with a warning that information on debt problems is still coming out. He noted that the Congressional Budget Office had just put out what he called a "daunting" report on America's fiscal deficit, that Standard and Poore's has just downgraded Japanese debt, and that the Fed seems intent, following the meeting Tuesday of the board of the Open Market Committee, to plow ahead with its plan for a second quantitative easing. All the more reason for the leadership in Congress to heed Representative Paul Ryan's pointed reference to the need for sound money in the policy mixture currently being crafted by the Republicans and, one would like to at least hope, the Democrats.

— January 27, 2011

# The Eclipse of Ben Bernanke

It's a sign of the times that the chairman of the Federal Reserve Board, Ben Bernanke, testified before the House Financial Services Committee yesterday and the part of the hearing that everyone wanted to know about is what was said by Congressman Ron Paul. He is the chairman of the monetary policy subcommittee that directly oversees the Fed, and he is the one, who, in a poll some months back, was ranked as being neck and neck with President Obama. The reason people are more interested in what he has to say is that it is Dr. Paul who has the deeper understanding of our national predicament.

This was illuminated in in an exchange yesterday in which Dr. Paul asked the chairman of the Fed, which issues the currency notes Americans are required to accept in payment of debts, what was his definition of a dollar. Forgive us, but we've been waiting for years to hear that question asked of a Fed chairman the way Dr. Paul put it. And Mr. Bernanke walked right into it. "My definition of the dollar is what it can buy. Consumers don't want to buy gold. They want to buy food and gasoline and clothes and all the other things that are in the consumer basket."

If the Founders of America had been on the Committee, why, they might well have had the chairman brought up for contempt. They were fairly obsessed with the dangers of paper money, and they had a clear idea of the meaning of money. When, in the Constitution, they delegated to the Congress the power to coin money, they did so in the same sentence in which they also delegated to Congress the power to fix the standard of weights and measures. When, in the Second Congress, they exercised the coinage power, they defined a dollar in plain language — 371 ¼ grains of silver, or the equivalent in gold.

Now it would be unjust to heap upon Mr. Bernanke's head blame for all that has happened since the greenback was brought in by Lincoln (to pay for, as we have previously noted, a cause — namely, the Union — for which it was worth risking everything). But for Mr. Bernanke to appear before Congress in a week in which the value of the dollar plunged to the lowest point in its history, meaning a week in which the price of an ounce of gold has risen to its highest nominal price in history, and assert that consumers don't want to buy gold, well, it's just breath-taking. Marie Antoinette, *telephonez votre bureau.*

Mr. Bernanke had barely finished his dodge than Lawrence Kudlow, who knows a story when he sees one, got Dr. Paul on the air, broadcast the question about the dollar, and asked the congressman, "Did you hear a Bernanke plan, or is it just going to be 'destroy the dollar'?" Mr. Bernanke, Dr. Paul told Mr. Kudlow, "believes, like a liberal does, that you have to spend more money, you have to increase demand. That's all he talks about, not work and savings and investment, increased demand. So they pay us the money whether it's the Fed or the Congress. So he's not being exactly honest with us on that, I don't believe."

It happens that we've been on this beat for a generation and a half, and one thing we can say with confidence is that it's just not every day that one gets the chairman of the subcommittee that oversees the Federal Reserve stating in public that the Fed chairman has been less than honest. Mr. Kudlow went on to ask the congressman whether oil would be $102 a barrel today "if we had a sound dollar." Replied the Congressman: "Absolutely not." He then asked Dr. Paul about Mr. Bernanke's suggestion that the threat of inflation is temporary."

"I think he's dreaming," Dr. Paul replied. ". . . if I were there and I had to tell the truth, I would be telling what I'm telling now . . . it took years and years for that Bretton Woods agreement to break down. But eventually the market ruled and said, 'Look, you're abusing it. Gold is not at $35 an ounce.'" Mr. Kudlow then noted that he didn't recall Mr. Bernanke mentioning that the consumer price index in the past two months was running at a 5.1% annual rate . . . and that's before the gasoline price increases hit." Dr. Paul agreed, saying, "if you calculated with the old CPI, it's actually over 9% . . . You can fool the markets for a while, but even as much complaining as I do about the power of the Federal Reserve and the power of these spendthrifts in Congress, markets are more powerful."

\* \* \*

No doubt Mr. Bernanke knows that all he has to do is lift the interest rate a bit and value will start returning to the notes he's issuing. But whose point does that make? And no doubt value could be restored to the dollar if pro-growth, supply-side fiscal and regulatory measures were enacted, a point that was suggested brilliantly in a column in this morning's Wall Street Journal by Karl Rove. But by our lights it is no small thing that the congressman who has watched this issue the most closely in the past 30 years and who is now chairman of the subcommittee that oversees the Fed is prepared to walk out of a hearing at which the chairman of the Fed has been testifying and go on television to question, in essence, whether the chairman who has just testified has been giving the Congress the straight story.

— March 3, 2011

# A 'Unique' Form of 'Terrorism'

Here is a thought experiment concerning two men who have issued money. One issued gold and silver coins that will today bring more in dollars than he charged for them. The other issued paper notes that are today worth but a fraction the gold or silver they were worth at the time they were issued. One man is facing the possibility of years in prison after a federal jury found his issuing of money to have been a crime. The other man is walking around free and being treated by the authorities with great deference.

Which is which?

It turns out that the man walking free is Ben Bernanke, the chairman of the Federal Reserve. A one-dollar note that his bank issued used to be worth — as recently as, say, the start of President Bush's first term — a 265th of an ounce of gold; today it's value has plunged to less than a 1,400th of an ounce of gold. The man who issued the coins that will fetch more dollars today than when he issued them is Bernard von NotHaus, 67. He called his coins "Liberty Dollars," minted them with some similarities to government money, and even though they more than held their value it turns out they're against the law.

Von NotHaus promised a "spectacular trial" when, in 2007, he was interviewed by our Joseph Goldstein.* At the time von NotHaus was expecting to be indicted, as he eventually was, in connection with his minting of coins. His boast to our Mr. Goldstein was that he would "put this country's monetary system on trial." In the event, the trial of von NotHaus, which took place at Statesville, North Carolina, was over in but eight days. The jury deliberated only two hours before bringing in its verdict of guilty. It will stand for many as a lesson in the difficulties of illuminating the illogic of our monetary system.

We do not suggest that von NotHaus was wrongly tried or convicted. The United States code imposes a fine or imprisonment for anyone who, "except as authorized by law, makes or utters or passes, or attempts to utter or pass, any coins of gold or silver or other metal, or alloys of metals, intended for use as current money, whether in the resemblance of coins of the United States or of foreign countries, or of original design . . ." The Justice Department, in a press release about the verdict, asserts that von NotHaus was placing just such coins into circulation with the purpose of mixing them "into the current money of the United States."

Nor do we suggest that Mr. Bernanke and his colleagues at the Federal Reserve have been violating the United States criminal code by issuing their currency by fiat. Nor do we suggest that the officers and directors of the Fed are anything other than honest and honorable individuals. The Federal Reserve has, over the years, won most of its battles in the federal courts, though possible angles for constitutional challenges have yet to be exhausted.

What we do suggest is that the contrast between the Fed and von NotHaus is an example of how the scandal is not in what's illegal but in what's legal. When Mr. Goldstein interviewed von NotHaus in 2007, he had recently been selling a one-ounce silver coin for $20, which at the time was, Mr. Goldstein noted, several dollars above the spot price of silver. It was also at the start of a rapid collapse in the value of Federal Reserve Notes, which has plunged to the point where today a dollar is worth less than a 30th of an ounce of silver. So who is the injured party — the individual who acquired a one-ounce Liberty silver coin for $20 or the individual who kept his wad of twenty one-dollar Federal Reserve Notes?

"A unique form of domestic terrorism" is the way the U.S. Attorney for the Western District of North Carolina, Anne M. Tompkins, is describing attempts "to undermine the legitimate currency of this country." The Justice Department press release quotes her as saying: "While these forms of anti-government activities do not involve violence, they are every bit as insidious and represent a clear and present danger to the economic stability of this country." Such language strikes us as hyperbolic. It may be that the monetary authorities in America fear that their own currency will be exposed as unsound. The monetary terror for the rest of Americans is the danger that there will be a further collapse in the value of their dollars or, conversely, a deflation that will make it even harder, or impossible, to pay back their debts.

The Founders of America understood all this. No doubt they wanted a national coinage. The Constitution they wrote forbids the states from making legal tender out of anything but gold or silver coins, and it is to the Congress that the Constitution gives the power to coin money and regulate its value. But they promptly defined a dollar as 371 ¼ grains of silver, which was the same as in a coin called a Spanish Milled Dollar, or the then free market equivalent in gold. The record left by the Founders is replete with expressions of horror at paper money. They required our government officials to enforce the laws Congress has passed until a court tells them otherwise. But they would have understood the instinct of a man like von NotHaus to seek protection from a debasement that the Founders feared was, in respect of paper money, inevitable.

— March 20, 2011

———

* Now with the New York Times.

# The Verbal Dollar

The scariest moment of the next quarter will be April 27, when the chairman of the Federal Reserve, Ben Bernanke, will give the first of the four-times-a-year press conferences that the Fed, in a break with tradition, is vowing to hold. That is the report from Fast Money's John Melloy, who quotes a founder of TradeMonster.com, Jon Najarian, as saying that he would anticipate "a giant ramp up in volatility" ahead of Mr. Bernanke's press conference. "Traders react to one word removed from a paragraph in the policy statement and now he's going to hold a press conference?"

That may be why there had been a tradition of silence among central banks. It goes back at least to the Bank of England. Once, in 1929, its deputy governor was asked to explain the silence. His interlocutor, Lord Keynes himself, was serving on a parliamentary committee looking into the looming depression. He asked the Bank of England's deputy governor, Sir Ernest Harvey, whether it was a practice of the bank never to explain what its policy was. Sir Ernest suggested that it was the bank's practice to "leave our actions to explain our policy." When Keynes plowed on, Sir Ernest famously explained: "To defend ourselves is somewhat akin to a lady starting to defend her virtue."

The editor of Grant's Interest Rate Observer, James Grant, who reminded us of that exchange, has a newspaperman's skepticism of Mr. Bernanke's plan to start defending the Fed's virtue. He speculates that perhaps Mr. Bernanke "is reacting to the smoldering populist rage over the inflation he refuses to acknowledge." He notes that the Bank of England, in "its glory days managing the pre-World War I gold standard," said "next to nothing" but did "conscientiously exchange bank notes for gold, and gold for bank notes, at the statutory rate. Compare and contrast our Federal Reserve, which prints acres of money, manipulates stock prices, suppresses interest rates — and can't seem to stop talking."

Call it the verbal dollar. It seems to be the opposite of the gold standard, and why not, since gold and silence are linked. The Web site phrases.org.uk has a whole essay on the etymology of the aphorism "silence is golden." It turns out, phrases.org reports, that the first use of the phrase in English was from the poet Thomas Carlyle, who in 1831 translated the phrase from the German in Sartor Resartus, in which a character expounds on the virtues of silence. He spoke of how "all the considerable men . . . forbore to babble of what they were creating and projecting." Speech is great, he wrote, "but not the greatest." And then he cites the Swiss inscription, "Sprecfien ist silbern, Schweigen ist golden [Speech is silver, Silence is golden]." No wonder the markets are scared.

— April 1, 2011

# $1,500 Gold

One of the questions hanging over our politics today is whether President Obama appreciates the impact on his own legacy of the collapsing dollar. The futures market yesterday was putting the value of the dollar below a 1,500th of an ounce of gold on what the Bloomberg News attributed to concerns about "escalating U.S. debt." There's a lot of blame to go around in respect of the debt, including to Congress, which has the constitutional authority to regulate the value of the dollar. But it is not the portraits of the leaders of Congress that are put on America's currency. The portraits that normally go on our currency are portraits of the presidents,* whose treasury secretary signs the American scrip.

Yet as president, Mr. Obama has never given us a major speech in which he talks about how he views money or what he thinks of what has become of the dollar during his presidency. The value of the greenback has, for the record, fallen more than 43% from the 853rd of an ounce of gold that it was worth at the end of the day on which Mr. Obama acceded to the presidency. That is less of a decline than the 68% slide in the value of the dollar under President George W. Bush. But Mr. Bush was in office eight years. The steepness of the plunge under Mr. Obama is breathtaking.

All the more so in light of the things the future president was saying back when he was a candidate. A glimpse of it can be seen in a video on YouTube of Mr. Obama meeting with the editors of the Sentinel newspaper, which is issued at Keene, New Hampshire. The editor, Jim Rousmaniere, put the question of the collapsing dollar in a straightforward way. He noted that the dollar has been in a decline and asked, "Is that good or bad?" Mr. Obama began his response by offering a long discredited theory, saying, "There are some benefits from the dollar's decline, obviously it is just making our exports cheaper and we needed to get some balance in our trade deficits."

Then Mr. Obama signaled that he comprehended that there's another side of the question. "You haven't seen huge spikes in inflation as a result of the dollar's decline," he said. "There's some stickiness there. But it's not going to last forever. So the downside is we're going to see inflationary pressures as a consequence of this." The candidate went on to say that he was "less concerned" about the day to day gyrations of the dollar than "by the underlying economic fundamentals that are causing the dollar to decline," which he characterized as "that we're spending more than we produce, and you know we are losing our competitive edge."

The federal budget, he asserted, was "entirely out of whack." He said "we've been benefiting from this huge credit splurge, and we're not preparing ourselves for the long term competition that we're going to be engaging in with China and India and other countries." He went on to tell the editors of the Sentinel that he'd be "worried if there was such a big decline that at some point you started seeing a huge spike in interest rates and you know that had a depressing effect on the U.S. economy ... " Meantime, he would be more focused on the tax code, health care costs, education, and "getting our handle on energy so that we're not sending 800 million to a billion dollars every day to Saudi Arabia and Kuwait."

President Obama would no doubt be the first person to note that a lot happened between 2007 and his swearing in at the start of 2009. But no matter how one discounts for that, the difference between what Mr. Obama said and the way his policies have unfolded couldn't be more stark. He has done nothing but increase spending, while making it ever harder for our energy producers who exploit our own onshore and offshore oil reserves. The collapsing dollar has done nothing for our trade deficit, and the costs for food and fuel are soaring. It took a revolt by the Tea Party movement to spur any kind of action on deficits.

And still no preparedness to share with American voters — or the rest of the world, for that matter — his thinking about the dollar. A while back something called the Dollar Redesign Project started a contest to redesign the greenback on the theory that the dollar was so weak it that what had to be done is "rebrand" it. The winner of the 2010 submissions featured a piece of one-dollar scrip with a huge picture of Mr. Obama. It became something of a joke on the satirical Web site drinkingwithbob.com. Yet sooner or later Mr. Obama's reluctance to share with Americans his view on the dollar is going to lay him open to a challenge from the Republican candidates. And what better time than with the value of the dollar down to a 1,500$^{th}$ of an ounce of gold and the political conventions but 15 months away.

— April 19, 2011

---

\* There are exceptions, such as Benjamin Franklin, whose portrait is on the c-note.

# The Silver Bullet

'Now," said President Obama in his most soothing voice, "whenever gas prices shoot up, like clockwork, you see politicians racing to the cameras, waving three-point plans for two dollar gas. You see people trying to grab headlines or score a few points. The truth is, there's no silver bullet that can bring down gas prices right away."

Funny the president should choose those words. As he was delivering his weekly radio address, we were just thinking about gasoline and wondering how its value has been faring in specie. One can't tell that from its price, though, because we are dealing with, in the dollars issued by the Federal Reserve, a fiat currency that no longer has any connection with something real. But what if, say, we were to price gasoline in silver?

It turns out that if we price gasoline in ounces of silver, we discover that it has been falling in value. That is, a gallon of gasoline on the day President Obama was sworn in was worth about a sixth of an ounce of silver. Today, the value of the same gallon of gasoline has fallen to less than a 10th of an ounce of silver.

This is something to remember next time you pull up to the pump and get ready to pay four one-dollar greenbacks for a gallon, if you can even find gas at the $4 price Mr. Obama quoted in his weekly radio address. It's not that the gasoline has been going up in value. It's that the dollars you're using to pay for the gas have collapsed in value.

This is not something the politicians like to discuss — at least not those in the administration, whose treasury secretary, Timothy Geithner, signs the currency, or those in Congress, which has the constitutional responsibility to coin money and regulate its value. But the collapse of our currency is the most important fact in the economy.

Silver, of course, is not the only form of specie. The better measure of value is no doubt gold. But silver was the one that was favored as money by the Founders of America. In

French the word for money and for silver are the same. And silver bullets are the ones the mythologists reckoned would slay a werewolf. So why not the monster known as inflation.

— April 23, 2011

# Sarah Palin for the Fed?

The big question as Chairman Bernanke gets set for his first quarterly press conference is how Sarah Palin was able to figure out sooner than everyone else that the Federal Reserve's campaign of quantitative easing wouldn't work. Disappointment in the Fed's policies is being reported this morning at the top of page one of the New York Times. It reports that "most Americans are not feeling the difference" from the Fed's "experimental effort to spur a recovery by purchasing vast quantities of federal debt." It reports that "a broad range of economists say that the disappointing results show the limits of the central bank's ability to lift the nation from its economic malaise."

It's a terrific story, and well-timed, given that on Wednesday Mr. Bernanke will break tradition and meet with the press. It is part of the Fed's effort to get ahead of what is emerging as a public relations catastrophe, as gasoline is nearing six dollars a gallon at some pumps, the cost of groceries is skyrocketing, and the value of the dollars that Mr. Bernanke's institution issues as Federal Reserve notes has collapsed to less than a $1,500^{th}$ of an ounce of gold. Unemployment is still high. Shakespeare couldn't come up with a better plot. But how in the world did Mrs. Palin, who is supposed to be so thick, manage to figure all this out so far ahead of the New York Times and all the economists it talked to?

She did this back in November in a speech at Phoenix, which the Wall Street Journal, in a laudatory editorial at the time, characterized as zeroing in on the connection between a weak dollar and rising prices for oil and food. "We don't want temporary, artificial economic growth brought at the expense of permanently higher inflation which will erode the value of our incomes and our savings," the Journal quoted Mrs. Palin as saying. "We want a stable dollar combined with real economic reform. It's the only way we can get our economy back on the right track." Now here is the New York Times quoting a raft of economists who have reached the conclusion that Mrs. Palin's warning was right down the line.

It happens that Mrs. Palin's demarche coincided with a piece in the Financial Times by the president of the World Bank, Robert Zoellick, suggesting that a new international monetary system centered on the major currencies "should also consider employing gold as an international reference point of market expectations about inflation, deflation and future currency values." The FT is such a Keynesian bastion that the Journal likened Mr. Zoellick's mentioning gold in its pages to mentioning Sarah Palin's name at the Princeton Faculty Club. The FT issued an editorial attacking its own op-ed piece, while Mr. Zoellick's scoop so startled the New York Times that it brought in no less a heavyweight than James Grant of the Interest Rate Observer to write a piece on the virtues of the gold standard.

Alone among general interest publications, the Drudge Report has been fronting the gold price almost daily. And now the Times itself is out with its a story about how the Fed's quantitative easing has been a disappointment. It may have, as the Times puts it, "pumped up the stock market, reduced the cost of American exports and allowed companies to borrow money at lower interest rates," but "those benefits have been surprisingly small." Will any of this bring some humility to the Fed and its chairman? It will be something to watch for in his first big press conference Wednesday. No doubt it will be one of the most crowded press conferences in recent memory, and there will be lots to ask about. But one of the questions will be how in tarnation Mrs. Palin figured it out so far ahead of everyone else.

— April 24, 2011

# Forbes' Foresight

What is one to make of the fact that within minutes of Human Events publishing the prediction by Steve Forbes that America would return to a gold standard within five years, the Drudge Report put it up as its lead, banner headline? Is it that the logic of the gold standard is becoming clearer, even in the general interest press? Is it that moderately small newspapers, such as Human Events, can make a big difference? Is it that Matt Drudge has a keener nose for news on the monetary story than his competing editors? Or is it the fact that the Republican field of potential candidates is still at sea on the most important issue facing the economy?

The answer, by our lights, is all of the above. It's not that Mr. Forbes has departed from his past views in respect of sound money (he hasn't). Or that what he said would, in ordinary circumstances, seem newsworthy. All he said was that a return to the gold standard seems likely, in Human Events' characterization of the story, "because that move would help the nation solve a variety of economic, fiscal, and monetary ills." The magazine quoted Mr. Forbes as saying: "What seems astonishing today could become conventional wisdom in a short period of time."

What is newsworthy is that Mr. Forbes is the only major Republican to mark this point in plain language and in a way that is informed by history. He predicts that a restoration of a gold standard would — again in the language of Human Events' paraphrasing — "help to stabilize the value of the dollar, restore confidence among foreign investors in U.S. government bonds, and discourage reckless federal spending." He pointed out in the interview that America "used gold as the basis for valuing the U.S. dollar successfully for roughly 180 years before President Richard Nixon embarked upon an experiment to end the practice in the 1970s that has contributed to a number of woes that the country is suffering from now."

Mr. Forbes put into sharp relief the fact that fiat money

is a digression from what has been the American system. Its advocates seek to give the impression that fiat money is the default position, standard operating procedure for America. On the contrary, fiat money is a bizarre experiment, like the Soviet communism, that deserves to be abandoned. It may have seemed logical to some when it was first toyed with during the Civil War, and we could make a case that war trumps all, particularly a war on which the very existence of our constitutional compact depended. But it is becoming clearer by the day that the 40-year experiment in fiat money on which we've been embarked since the presidency of Richard Nixon has been a failure.

The gold standard, in other words, is not a flakey idea. On the contrary, it is fiat money that is the flakey idea. A standard of sound money, defined in gold or silver, is the default monetary system for America, one that has served it in the vast majority of its years. It's a sign of the times that it is big news when a public figure learned in history, such as Mr. Forbes, points this out and points out the logic of a gold standard reasserting itself. One of the points illuminated by Mr. Forbes is that these days the people are way ahead of the politicians. "People know that something is wrong with the dollar," Forbes told Human Events. "You cannot trash your money without repercussions." Too bad he is not running for president himself.

— May 11, 2011

# For Whom Mundell Tolls

The link on the Drudge Report to the Financial Times' headline on the dollar losing global reserve status is as good a time as any to remark on what may be the most important development of the past several weeks in respect of money — namely the endorsement by the Nobel laureate Robert Mundell of gold convertibility for the Euro. This has been written about by, among others, Ralph Benko of the American Principles Project, and it's an important story, not only because Professor Mundell himself is such a titanic figure in the debate on political economy in our time but also because he is himself known as the Father of the Euro.

Your editor has often remarked that one of the most illuminating encounters of his career was a few days he spent with Professor Mundell and a number of others interested in monetary matters at the villa Mr. and Mrs. Mundell own at Tuscany. There, among the ancient hills, we remember looking across the table and asking the question, "What is a dollar, anyhow?" It ignited a tumult of conversation, some saying an "obligation," other's a "unit of account," others a "measurement of value," some a "commodity," while Mr. Mundell regarded the conversation with a merry twinkle.

In any event, the professor's statement on gold and the Euro is the most important of the recent warnings. No less an establishment figure than Robert Zoellick issued late last year an op-ed piece in the Financial Times calling for consideration in monetary reform of a role for gold, a call that was endorsed by the Sun but sneered at by the Financial Times, which issued an editorial attacking its own contributor. Mr. Zoellick's piece referencing gold followed the statement earlier that fall by the former chairman of the Federal Reserve, Alan Greenpan, warning that fiat money always goes to gold, a statement that echoed widely.

Mr. Mundell's statement is the most important of the three. Mr. Benko calls him "the world's most distinguished living economist" and "the primary source of the original supply-side manifesto, 'The Mundell-Laffer Hypothesis,' which led to the low-tax-rate, strong-dollar policy at the heart of Reaganomics." He has also, Mr. Benko noted, been advising the Communist Chinese during their 30-year surge. Mr. Benko has also argued that Mr. Mundell had much to do with the rise in global output to something like $60 trillion today from $11 trillion in 1980.

In any event, Mr. Mundell's statement was made on a Bloomberg News broadcast, in an exchange with Pimm Fox in which Mr. Mundell was asked whether he thought "we're going to see any kind of return to the gold standard." Replied The Great Mundell*: "[T]here could be a kind of Bretton Woods type of gold standard where the price of gold was fixed for central banks and they could use gold as an asset to trade central banks."

It's not our purpose here to dispute the details of monetary reform with TGM (we tend to favor the restoration of a definition of the dollar in law as a set number of grains of silver, as the Founders had it, or gold, which has been a superior measure of value; we tend to distrust governments to hew to schemes of convertibility, a point about which the New York Times warned, in the editorials written by Henry Hazlitt, at the time of Bretton Woods). It is our purpose merely to mark the moment that we now have three significant figures — Zoellick, Greenspan, and Mundell — referencing things in terms of gold.

The speed with which the Financial Times denounced Mr. Zoellick for even gingerly advancing the idea of a role for gold in world monetary affairs was astonishing. But what will be establishment thinking, if that's what it is, in the wake of the FT report about the survey of central bankers? The survey was done by UBS; its results, according to the FT's own report, "point to a growing role for bullion, with 6 per cent of reserve managers surveyed saying the biggest change in their reserves over the next decade would be the addition of more gold." Wouldn't it be something were a return to gold start the salvation of a continent that once sneered at its significance in the monetary affairs of a modern world?

— June 28, 2011

# The ' Error' of 1971

It is going to be illuminating to see how the candidates for president pick up, if any do, on the fact that this week is the 40th anniversary of President Nixon's closing of the gold window. That default, announced on August 15, 1971, signaled the end of the monetary system crafted by the soon-to-be victorious allies in World War II. The conference at which the system was originally agreed upon was held at the Mount Washington Hotel at Bretton Woods, New Hampshire. The centerpiece of the system was a gold exchange standard among governments that measured the dollar at a 35th of an ounce of gold.

Now, four decades after the collapse of Bretton Woods, recognition is spreading that the system of fiat money that emerged in the 1970s has not only been a failure but is at the root of our current travail and needs to be reformed. "Abandoning the gold standard was a  error we're now all paying for," is the headline over the latest dispatch to that effect. It appeared over the weekend in London's leading broadsheet, the Telegraph. The piece was by its former economics editor, Edmund Conway, who is now at the school of government at Harvard that is named after President Kennedy.

Kennedy is a reminder that both liberals and conservatives in the American political tradition understood the logic of the role of gold in our international monetary system. He himself had vowed to maintain a dollar that was good as gold. It was Nixon, supposedly the more conservative of the two, who announced, after a secret meeting at Camp David, his plans for a new monetary system that, although he didn't mention it at the time, would turn out to be fiat money with no constitutional basis and without backing of any kind.

In the short term, the closing of the gold window precipitated what Lewis Lehrman, writing in today's Wall Street Journal, describes as "a decade of one of the worst inflations of American history and the most stagnant economy since the Great Depression." The situation was righted by the combination of President Reagan's supply-side fiscal policies and the tight money regime of Paul Volcker at the Federal Reserve. Yet there was no permanent repair of the world monetary system, no restoration of the legal checks of government over-reach.

The absence of any legal connection between the dollar and gold permitted the combination of fiscal and monetary over-reach that has, today, delivered us a dollar with a value of barely more than a 1,800th of an ounce of gold, less than a percent of the value of the constitutional dollar. It is noteworthy that the top contenders for the Republican nomination for president, Michele Bachmann, has said she's prepared to look at a gold standard and that the close runner up, Ron Paul, has made sound money his central issue throughout his entire long career in the Congress.

Governor Pawlenty had also declared for sound money. So that the three top finishers in Iowa were either in or open to a campaign on sound money. Governor Pawlenty has since dropped out, prematurely in our view. Governor Perry is unclear to us on this head. Governor Romney has indicated he won't challenge the Federal Reserve's chairman, Ben Bernanke — a strategic error. It would be silly to make too much of an anniversary. But there's no reason to let it slide entirely. The record these past 40 years is more than enough time to make it clear that fiat, electronic paper ticket money is a recipe for ruin, and with the value of a dollar having collapsed to historic lows, the moment strikes us as ideal to take the issue to the voters.

— August 15, 2011

# Waiting for De Gaulle

Governor Perry's remarks on Chairman Bernanke's debasement of the dollar were greeted with widespread complaints owing to the governor's raucous tone. So how could he have better made his case? For an example, we commend none other than Charles De Gaulle. We comprehend that the general-turned-president of Free France is renowned for his haughtiness and, for that matter, his mixed view, to put it mildly, of America. Let's lay that aside for the moment and feature the prophetic remarks he made in February 1965, warning of the incipient monetary crisis that would, absent a return to gold-backed money, engulf the world. When these columns speak of our hope that some leader of our time will address this issue, this is the kind of talk for which we are hankering.

De Gaulle didn't fool around when he wanted to make a statement. He gathered 1,000 journalists in the salle de fetes of the Elysee Palace, where, according to the dispatch by Richard Mooney of the New York Times, he seated them in gilded chairs. The president of the Fifth Republic sat himself at a cloth-covered table in front of them and spoke for 20 minutes in language that was slow, didactic, profound. He warned that the dollar had lost its transcendent value and called for a return to, in the gold standard, a system that was not particular to any one country but imposed the same measure of value and thus of discipline on all of them. "In truth," he declared, "one does not see how one could really have any standard criterion other than gold."

His remarks caused an immediate stir. "Perhaps never before," rumbled Time magazine, "had a chief of state launched such an open assault on the monetary power of a friendly nation." It called De Gaulle's remarks "a particularly nettling irritant" coming, as they did, "just as the U.S. was deeply involved in making some hard decisions about its monetary policy." President Johnson, pursuing his course of guns in Vietnam and butter at home, was facing a balance of payments crisis. But this did not prevent the more serious commentators from recognizing both the importance and the wisdom of De Gaulle's demarche. These included, most notably, the Wall Street Journal, which issued an editorial upbraiding the American Treasury for denouncing the French president.

The Journal's editorial, a classic, was called "A Gold Star for De Gaulle." It noted that De Gaulle was not recommending an immediate return to a true gold standard from the so-called gold exchange standard that had been set up at Bretton Woods in the closing months of World War II. It acknowledged all the difficult questions of what it called "mechanics." But it insisted that such issues did not mean that the French president was talking nonsense. It praised his adviser, the economist Jacques Rueff. And it said that it was "a splendid commentary on the quality of financial thinking when a man is bitterly resented for stripping off the mask of illusion and talking sense about money."

In addition, the Journal rolled out two columns by its famed editor at the time, Vermont Connecticut Royster, praising De Gaulle's demarche. The first one quoted Scartlett O'Hara's remark as Rhett Butler rode into the sunset, "I'll think about that tomorrow." In the second, Royster responded to President Johnson's petulant attack on De Gaulle, criticizing LBJ for buying into the notion that the gold standard had caused the Great Depression. The column ran under the headline "Muddling History." Royster didn't gainsay the monetary system's role in precipitating the Depression, but said the system was very like the one we had then under Bretton Woods. "General De Gaulle is better on history," he concluded.

\* \* \*

Who is going to be the De Gaulle of our time? Who can gather 1,000 journalists in a room, sit them in gilded chairs, park himself or herself before a baize-covered table and talk to them seriously about the monetary crisis? We are there now, with the value of the dollar having collapsed to less than an 1,800th of an ounce of gold. It is hard to imagine President Obama rising to this task. Or, for that matter, Prime Minister Cameron or President Sarkozy. The Chinese party boss has an over-hang on his economy (we speak of slave labor) worse than the monetary overhang that bedevils us. Chairman Bernanke doesn't believe in it; worse, he confides — if that is the word — to Congress he is mystified by the gold price. Angela Merkel? Stephen Harper? Our guess is that the leadership here is going to have to come from the individual who emerges as the Republican nominee. For our part, we don't have the slightest doubt that the American public is fully capable of digesting the warning that De Gaulle sounded and that our leaders brushed aside half a century ago. Since then there's been a lot of history from which to learn.

— August 19, 2011

# The Next De Gaulle?

Our editorial yesterday in respect of Charles De Gaulle raised the question of whether someone could be found today who could talk about the monetary crisis with the sense and gravitas the leader of Free France brought to the monetary crisis that came into view in the mid-1960s. De Gaulle himself is now gone, of course, having died in 1970. He had his faults and had become, in many ways, an irritant to America. But his late career call for a return to a system of sound money that would — by virtue of being based on gold — hold all countries to the same standard is now echoing across the decades. And it turns out there is an heir to the economist who emboldened the French president to make his famous declaration.

The economist was Jacques Rueff, who helped save the Fifth Republic by guiding De Gaulle to establish the convertibility of the French franc. His agitation for a return to the gold standard in the late 1950s and 1960s was based on his comprehension that holding dollars as a reserve currency was a recipe for global inflation. It was on his advice that De Gaulle put through the polices that made the franc convertible and balanced the budget and turned France, in the decade after 1959, into the fastest growing economy in the developed world. Rueff himself died in 1978 at the age of 82. The question is whether his formula could be used by America.

Well, the heir to Rueff turns out to be actively pursuing his ideas right here in America now, as a new crisis swells up around us. This is Lewis Lehrman, a New York businessman and student of monetary affairs who in 1982 came within a whisker of being elected governor of New York and is now working full time on a return to the gold standard. For a candidate wanting to achieve in America the kind of turnaround that De Gaulle achieved at France, Mr. Lehrman would be the man to call.

We first started covering Mr. Lehrman in 1981, when he was on the United States Gold Commission that had been convened by President Reagan at the urging of Senator Jesse Helms. Congressional input ensured that the commission was stacked against advocates of sound money. Its most notable achievement was a famous dissent, written by Congressman Ron Paul and Mr. Lehrman and later republished as a book called "The Case for Gold." Later Mr. Lehrman established a prize, the Prix Rueff, to reward those who best carried on in the spirit of Rueff.

An institute established by Mr. Lehrman is now issuing a Web site, thegoldstandardnow.org, to serve as a bulletin board for those who reckon a return to sound money will be a precondition to sustained growth in America's and the world's economy. In recent months he has written a number of important op-ed articles for the Wall Street Journal. It strikes us that for Mr. Perry, who has so pointedly marked the monetary issue, or any other candidate who wants, like De Gaulle, to craft a serious strategy around the monetary issue, Mr. Lehrman has the potential to be a game-changing figure. Our impression is that he is not wedded to any one candidate but rather to the principle of sound money and the convertibility of the dollar into gold.

His central point is that monetary policy is the most important issue today — more important than, say, the debt ceiling and more important, even, than the deficit, as he puts it in a recent video on thegoldstandardnow.org. He calls it more important than regulation, because it is the key to long-term savings and long-term investment, thus to long-term economic growth and full employment. He would ask candidates: "What is the monetary policy that will get us out of the age of inflation, which the paper-dollar standard has put us on now for as much as two generations?" He has emerged as the tribune for the idea that the right answer to that question is gold convertibility and for the practical programs for moving forward to the time-tested standard that could make America the fastest growing developed economy in the decades ahead.

— August 20, 2011

# Looking Forward to Gold

As President Obama was getting set to address the Congress in respect of jobs, our attention was on James Grant. We're adding the editor of Grant's Interest Rate Observer to our list of sages who can articulate the case for monetary reform in the spirit of Charles de Gaulle. Mr. Grant didn't summon 1,000 journalists to a press conference in the salle de fetes the way the president of the Fifth French Republic did in 1965. He went him one better, appearing this week on an edition of CNBC's Squawk Box devoted to the gold standard. The result is a memorable piece of journalism that is yet another instance of an important institution — CNBC — taking a new and suddenly more respectful look at what has in recent decades been set down as, to use Keynes' phrase, a barbarous relic.

The show starts off with a piece by the CNBC graphics department that traces the history of the gold standard. It is followed by the host, Steve Liesman, senior economics correspondent of CNBC. He tells the audience that he "came into this with the economic orthodoxy that a gold standard is a stupid thing." More recently, however, he is now "a little more in the middle on this." This reflects a newsworthy phenomenon. People are rapidly getting ahead of the government on this. We have this sense not only from our own interviews but from the astonishing poll rankings of, say, Congressman Ron Paul, whose entire career has been centered on a campaign for sound money.

This in and of itself is not surprising. The dollar, after all, is in a historic collapse, its value having plunged to well less than an 1,800th of an ounce of gold. What is surprising — or, if not that, gratifying — is the raptness of the attention now being paid to a journalist like Mr. Grant, who offers the gold standard not in absolute terms but as "the least imperfect monetary arrangement available."

Quoth Mr. Grant: "If one were interested in the

following properties for a monetary standard, one might look to a gold standard. For example, you'd want something that is synchronous, that is reciprocal, that links . . .All nations together," Mr. Liesman interjected. "Rather than what is happening now, which is that the G20 seems to be really fraying really at the center . . ."

"You'd want a monetary system that is objective, in which there were certain known rules. Now we have an improvisational one, with the mandarins at our Federal Reserve making stuff up as they go along ... perfumed clouds of algebra and differential calculus ... what are they talking about?"

Here Mr. Liesman interjects again: "Right now, when you read the Fed minutes, when you listen to all the Fed talkers, it is something again that recommends the gold standard. Because what is the monetary policy? It is the policy that is the compromise of the Fed officials and all their disparate views."

"It is a compromise," Mr. Grant responded, "among people who really seem to have no first or fixed principles. If you read Bernanke's speech at Jackson Hole, he begins to tell us what the Treasury ought to do about the deficit, he begins to tell us what Congress might do to improve the process of budgeting, he tells us that we are deficient in K through 12 educational standards. What does the secretary of education think about QE3? I want to know."

Mr. Liesman greets this point with an appreciative guffaw, then a cackle, which strikes us as what has to be a sobering moment for Messrs. Bernanke and Co. We are at a point where a major speech by a Fed chairman is seen as being met by one of our most serious journalists with merriment and laughter, which Mr. Grant returned with this straightforward point: "So what we want it seems to me is a monetary system that is objective, that we can understand, that has something at its bottom, as its root something that we can recognize as money. Gold is recognized as money most places on the planet."

\* \* \*

We wouldn't want to get so far up on our high horse that we fail to acknowledge that Mr. Bernanke has some things he could do to cause value to flow back into the Federal Reserve notes he has been issuing. Chairman Volcker showed us that in the 1980s. But it's going to be hard for Mr. Bernanke absent a president to work with of the vision of the Reagan that stood in the White House for much of the period that Mr. Volcker ran the Fed. The irony is that President Obama will shortly be giving a speech on jobs. We are in a cru in which, as Ralph Benko, among others, has been pointing out, sound money is the most important plank of a real jobs program. This has so far eluded the Obama administration, and the chorus grows for the kind of profound, era changing reform that is being called for by Mr. Grant and those who are prepared to move forward to a gold standard.

— September 1, 2011

# A Hole in the GOP Jobs Plan

It's encouraging to see the Republicans put forth a jobs bill, but — confound it — the measure as outlined by Senators Portman, DeMint, Paul, Jordan, and McCain is missing an essential element. This is sound money, the lack of which is emerging as a central cause of America's current travail. The failure of the GOP jobs bill to address this point is all the more troubling, because leaders like Messr. DeMint and Dr. Paul understand so clearly the monetary issue, as they made clear when, earlier this year, they introduced a bill known as the Sound Money Promotion Act, which this newspaper was the first to endorse.

The new GOP jobs bill gives excellent legislative shape to the fiscal facet of job creation. It abjures the Keynesian approach of borrowing and spending our way to prosperity. If such a strategy ever made any sense (we don't see it, but some do), it certainly doesn't make sense in an economy with near zero interest rates, a collapsing dollar, and budget deficits and government debt already at astounding levels. Instead, the new bill offers restraint on spending, reduction of tax rates, an end to prohibitions on drilling for oil, the promotion of free trade, the repeal of growth-inhibiting regulations, and liberation from Obamacare.

Absent a simultaneous demarche in respect of the dollar, however, the fiscal approach just offered can be defeated by a Federal Reserve that appears happy to facilitate congressional spending by purchasing government debt until the cows come home, even if milk goes to $100 a gallon.* There is a growing recognition of this problem among the Republican leadership, which was made clear during the debate on the economy Tuesday at New Hampshire. Speaker Gingrich in the most recent debate called for "hard money," which surely is an allusion to the gold standard as well. It was a good moment for the speaker.

Herman Cain, a former chairman of the Federal Reserve

Bank in Kansas, has spoken well of the gold standard and made commitments to keep the dollar stable and, at New Hampshire, spoke critically of the current leadership of the Federal Reserve. Congressman Ron Paul gave a classic performance on this question at New Hampshire, cementing his role within the candidates in contention as being best able to articulate the monetary issue. Our own view of Dr. Paul is that his failure to gain traction in the polls is due to other planks of his platform than the monetary one.

In any event, there is no time to lose for the Republican leaders working on growth and jobs. Our own recommendation would be for Messrs. DeMint, Paul, Portman, Jordan, and McCain to summon for a private meeting Lewis Lehrman, who has been advancing a practical, step-by-step plan for returning America to a true gold standard of the kind that would ignite a new generation of growth and thus jobs. Mr. Lehrman has a new book out and gave earlier this month at Washington an important speech laying out the case that a return to sound money is eminently do-able. It has, after all, been done before in our history. Bringing the fiscal and regulatory planks of a growth plan together with a monetary plank will be essential for the best platform for the coming election.

— October, 14 2011

---

* For the record, between January and the end of August, milk prices rose in dollars to $3.70 a gallon from $3.30 a gallon but fell in value to a 491th of an ounce of gold from a 428th of an ounce of gold.

# Bernanke's Forgotten Footnote

As the markets settle down after the big move by the central banks to stabilize the situation in respect of Europe, we find ourselves thinking of the speech the Federal Reserve's Ben Bernanke gave at the National Press Club on November 21, 2002,* when he was but a governor and not yet chairman. The speech, entitled, "Deflation: Making Sure 'It' Doesn't Happen Here," offered an explanation of how the Fed would operate, hypothetically, once it had already brought its main monetary policy tool, the Fed Funds rate, to zero.

It was this speech that contained the reference to the Fed's ability to print dollars that earned Mr. Bernanke the sobriquet "Helicopter Ben," after Milton Friedman's explanation that the Fed could figuratively drop money from helicopters if it had to. Now that the Fed has held the Fed Funds rate near zero for several years and has committed to keep it there at least through mid-2013, the speech has turned into a kind of playbook or checklist of all that Mr. Bernanke has done since and may yet do.

The famous footnote came in where the chairman, in the course of explaining the ways in which the Fed could inject money into the economy, asserted that that the Fed "has the authority to buy foreign government debt, as well as domestic government debt. Potentially, this class of assets offers huge scope for Fed operations, as the quantity of foreign assets eligible for purchase by the Fed is several times the stock of U.S. government debt."

There the Fed's own publication of the speech offers footnote 16. "The Fed," it says, "has committed to the Congress that it will not use this power to 'bail out' foreign governments; hence in practice it would purchase only highly rated foreign government debt." We wonder if anyone in Congress other than Ron Paul will remember this commitment. "Highly rated government debt" seems such a quaint concept today, nine years later, especially since the

United States itself has been downgraded. And the commitment to not "bail out" foreign governments seems practically naïve given what has transpired during the crisis.

No doubt the Fed will insist that on various technical grounds joining in the coordinated move to use swap lines more aggressively does not amount to a 'bail out' of foreign governments. Fair enough. One could spend the rest of one's days parsing the paltering among issuers of fiat money. But given the relationship between European governments and European banks and, for that matter, the Euro itself, it strikes us that the Fed is skating close to the line it promised Congress it wouldn't cross. The fact is that it is becoming ever clearer by the day that the Federal Reserve is now the central bank to the world.

At some point one would think Congress would want to get in on this question. It established the Federal Reserve, after all. It established the dollar as the American unit of account, for that matter. One would think it would have its own interests in respect of whether the Fed is supposed to be the central bank of the world. Is it supposed to look out for both price stability and employment on the continent, like it is here? And against what sort of standard is it formulating policy in respect of the Euro? Few in the Congress are focusing on this issue, and only Congressman Ron Paul is working the issue on the stump. Eventually, though, the election will be over and there will accede a new Congress, the 113th, in which this will be one of the most urgent questions.

— December 2, 2011

---

* The value of the dollar on that day, incidentally, was a 317.65th of an ounce of gold, according to the Kitco historical gold chart; the greenback's value has since plunged to below a 1,740th of an ounce of gold.

# Gingrich Goes for Gold

The call by Newt Gingrich for the creation of a commission on gold to examine how America can return to a system of hard money is a step forward for him and the Republican Party as we go into the most formative months of the campaign. The former speaker issued his call at Columbia, South Carolina, at a policy forum on American global leadership. He used the phrase "hard money" to speak of a gold standard of the kind the Founders of America had in mind. It would mean, he said, "you can't just hide from your problems. You've got to solve them."

Mr. Gingrich's call is the most clarion yet among a Republican field that has been dancing around this issue since the start of the campaign. We're delighted — thrilled — to see it, because we have been stressing the centrality of the monetary issue since before this campaign began. Let us say, though, that our country is way past the point where we need another commission. A commission, as President Reagan learned in 1981, is a recipe for burying an idea, not putting it into law. It will be important for Mr. Gingrich to get past the commission idea in a hurry.

The fact is that we know how to get back to a gold standard. This has just been outlined by Lewis Lehrman in a new book, issued in October, on exactly this point. It is called "The True Gold Standard: A Monetary Reform Plan Without Official Reserve Currencies — How We Get From Here To There." Mr. Lehrman, a businessman turned scholar, is not just any gadfly. He was a member of the United States Gold Commission set up under President Reagan in 1981. The commission, in a historic blunder, recommended sticking with the old system of fiat paper money.

It's most noteworthy achievement, still widely discussed today, was the minority report, which was written by two of the commission members — Mr. Lehrman and a relatively new member of Congress named Ron Paul. Their minority report, later issued as a book called "The Case for Gold," recommended a return to hard money. But it was swept aside in the tumult of the early Reagan years. That was a time when the supply-side measures of Mr. Reagan were combining with the tight-money policies of a Federal Reserve headed by Paul Volcker to bring us back from the precipice. We had been teetering on the brink because of the inflation unleashed by Lyndon Johnson's campaign of guns and butter and President Nixon's abandonment of Bretton Woods.

So we don't need another confounded commission. We need a political campaign that knows where it's going. It sounds to us like Mr. Gingrich understands these principles; he's well acquainted with Mr. Lehrman's work, as he made clear in an interview with Lawrence Kudlow in December, where he also praised Steve Forbes, another honest money advocate. Congressman Paul knows the issue cold. Governor Perry has also indicated that he comprehends the issue. Our own estimate is that Governor Romney, who blundered at the beginning by telling Mr. Kudlow that he would not challenge Chairman Bernanke's quantitative easing, is educable; he's already indicated he wouldn't reappoint the chairman. We'd prefer the Republican Party Platform Committee to another government commission.

The thing that needs to be done is go get the best of the Republican candidates and the platform writers together with Mr. Lehrman and his brain trust, which includes a number of figures who understand this issue down to the ground. Among them are James Grant of the Interest Rate Observer and policy experts already grouped under the umbrella of The Gold Standard Now. The ideal outcome, in the view of this newspaper, would be a platform plank that could be carried into the general election by whoever wins the Republican nomination. If that candidate wins the election, the platform plank becomes a genuine mandate for restoring America to the era of sound money under the president and Congress that will be in office for the 100'th anniversary of the founding of the Fed.

— January 18, 2012

# Gingrich's Gold Group

The announcement by Newt Gingrich that he intends to appoint Lewis Lehrman and James Grant to co-chair a new Commission on Gold will serve as a signal that he has determined, if given the chance, to undertake monetary reform in a serious way. The former speaker made his announcement only days after declaring for a return to the gold standard so that it would be radically more difficult for America to dodge its fiscal problems. After he made his announcement, these columns expressed the concern that we don't need another commission, for in American politics commissions are normally a way to bury an idea.

The choice of Messrs. Lehrman and Grant signals that Mr. Gingrich is already past the question of whether to go for sound money and is focusing on getting it done. Of Messrs. Lehrman and Grant, the former speaker said: "They are both distinguished students of monetary policy and long-time advocates of a return to hard money — a dollar as good as gold." Mr. Lehrman was a member of the United State Gold Commission that was set up under President Reagan, and Mr. Grant, editor of the Interest Rate Observer, has emerged as one of the most distinguished journalistic voices in support of gold-backed, honest money.

The moment Mr. Gingrich announced for gold, Messrs. Lehrman and Grant had sent him a congratulatory letter that is a classic of concision and point. They noted that between 1792, when the Congress first defined a dollar, and 1971, when President Nixon abrogated the Bretton Woods Treaty, "Congress defined the dollar by statute as a specific weight unit of gold." They noted that between 1971 and 2011 — that is, the period of fiat money that is being used today — the dollar has shed 85% of its value. They stressed the importance of establishing convertibility of the dollar to gold a value that will hold for "many generations."

Mr. Gingrich, in his statement today, signaled that he

would be unlikely to prejudge the details of how to end the era of fiat money. "While I am not presently committed to any one version of reform," he said, "if elected I will be eager to work with Lew Lehrman and Jim Grant in achieving a dollar that once again can hold its purchasing power for many decades to come." Mr. Gingrich also gave an important salute to Congressman Ron Paul, who has done so much to keep the issue of the collapse of the dollar at the center of the current campaign.

"I have had, and will continue to have, many strong disagreements with Congressman Paul during the campaign," Mr. Gingrich said today. "But I believe he has made an important contribution in the field of monetary reform." His salute to Dr. Paul came the same day on which the Wall Street Journal issued what will be a closely read column by one of its stars, Kimberly Strassel, warning that the "real aim" of the libertarian from Texas is hold the GOP hostage to his issues, including his isolationist foreign policy.

Mr. Gingrich's demarche can be seen, at least in part, as a counter maneuver, an effort to seize Dr. Paul's most important issue for what might be called the his own wing of the party. By our lights the backers of honest money can take heart either way. From the beginning of this campaign, these columns have argued that the question of money — of monetary reform — is the issue of the hour, one that deserves to be taken to the hustings. The Republicans could still let it slip from their grasp. But thanks to Mr. Gingrich, this week has certainly been an encouraging one.

— January 20, 2012

# The Missing Gold

"The U.S. government did two dramatic things after World War II. They created a GI Bill which enabled literally millions of returning veterans to go to college for the very first time. My father, when — who was in the Second World War, went to college on a GI Bill. So there was an enormous expansion of opportunity that enabled them to integrate into a new, emerging society. The second thing they did is, they dramatically cut taxes, and the economy took off and grew dramatically, and it absorbed the workforce."

\* \* \*

Newt Gingrich may have had a great debate last night, but by our lights he missed several opportunities to mark what we believe is the most important issue facing the country today — the need for monetary reform. The speaker listed, as quoted above at Charleston, two of the dramatic things the U.S. government did after World War II to set the stage for the generation of growth that followed. But we'd have thought his list would have included the signing, at Bretton Woods, of the treaty that established the post-war gold exchange standard. That set up a gold-linked monetary system that served as the superstructure for the post-war success.

The speaker's failure to mention gold was a disappointment. Just the day before the debate Mr. Gingrich had declared for a return to sound money backed by gold. He went so far as to call for the establishment of a new Gold Commission to chart the way. It is an important demarche, particularly in a state, South Carolina, that itself is so concerned about the collapse of the Obama Dollar it is exploring making gold and silver coins legal tender in the state. One of its senators, James DeMint, is already playing a leading role in pushing the monetary issue in the Congress.

Mr. Gingrich had another chance to bring up the crisis of the dollar when he was being ridiculed by Senator Santorum for his penchant for grandiosity. Mr. Gingrich acknowledged the jibe, pointing out his role in daring to imagine — and in winning — a Republican majority in the House. And also in passing the largest tax cut in American history. We kept waiting for him to park out there the next major reform waiting to be enacted, which is a restoration to the dollar of a legal definition as a specified number of grains of gold.

If Mr. Gingrich is going to lead this fight, as he suggested this week he is prepared to do, he's not going to be able to miss the kinds of opportunities the debate last night presented him. The Federal News Service transcript of the debate doesn't even once contain the word gold. Mr. Gingrich, or whoever wants to lead on this issue, is going to have to talk about it at every turn, the way Congressman Ron Paul has done so obsessively, consistently, knowledgeably, and heroically. Dr. Paul, however, has lashed himself to a critique of his party's foreign policy that makes it difficult, at least so far, for more than a quarter of Republican primary voters to swing behind him.

This is not a problem that Mr. Gingrich has. He is with the party on foreign policy. He understands that the costs of our fight against terror are more than manageable in a growing economy and, in any event, are dwarfed by the mandates, regulations, and entitlements that are such a drag on our growth. Nor is Mr. Gingrich a stranger to the gold question, as was pointed in these columns on the eve of the debate by Andresen Blom of the American Principles Project. He was, as far back as 1984, a sponsor of Jack Kemp's Gold Standard Act.

Mr. Gingrich is magnificent when he gets his dander up, as he did when John King brought up at the start of the debate the question of his long-ago marital problems. The way to put the politics of personal destruction behind this campaign is for someone to lift it up to the larger issues, like monetary reform. It is a perfect plank on which to stand against President Obama, under whom the value of the dollar has collapsed to less than a 1,600th of an ounce of gold. If Mr. Gingrich doesn't want to talk about his former wife, that is how he can seize the lead on the issue that he signaled this week he understands so well.

— January 20, 2012

# Romney Resisting Reform

Governor Romney's exchange with Lawrence Kudlow, with whom the governor resisted talk of a gold standard, is an important moment in this campaign. It was aired on CNBC yesterday. It reminds us of an exchange we had some years ago with Milton Friedman.

At a lunch in Hong Kong, we asked Friedman for his view on the gold standard. "The problem with the gold standard," Friedman replied, "is that you can go off it." So we asked him: "Isn't there the same deficiency in the law against murder? It can be broken. How can that be a reason not to have such a law in the first place?"

It was a cheerful and friendly exchange and ended there. But it's the same question we'd put to Mr. Romney today, after Mr. Kudlow asked him pointedly about the Gold Commission that Mr. Gingrich has declared he would establish to chart a way forward to the gold standard. Mr. Kudlow shrewdly gave Mr. Romney an opening, noting that Mr. Gingrich "hasn't really endorsed" a gold standard. Then he asked Mr. Romney: "You looking at gold? You looking at a dollar link?"

"You know," Mr. Romney replied, according to the transcript of the CNBC interview posted at Real Clear Politics. "I'm happy to look at a whole range of ideas on how to have greater stability in our currency and in our monetary policies. I know that in the past when we had a gold standard, the idea that somehow it was detached from or free from any interference by Congress was simply wrong because even with the gold standard someone has to decide what is the conversion rate between the gold and the dollar."

"Hmmm," Mr. Kudlow commented.

"And Congress," Mr. Romney continued, "can inflate the dollar simply by changing the exchange rate, as was done in the past. So I don't think there's any, if you will, magic bullet substitute for economic restraint, for not spending more money than you take in, for having the nation that's the most productive in the entire world. That's how you get wealth for the middle class is making America a more productive nation with high savings rates and a government that only spends what it takes in."

It happens that the gold standard has among its virtues precisely that it serves as an alarm system against over-spending of the kind Mr. Romney describes. To avoid getting caught up in Milton Friedman's dodge, which Mr. Romney is but the latest politician to use, these columns have strived to keep the focus not on economics but on the Constitution. The crisis in which our country finds itself stems from a failure to adhere to the enumerated monetary powers and disabilities of the United States Constitution.

We would not want to suggest that the proposals Mr. Gingrich has made are not important. The controversy he generates generally does not take away from the significance of his plan for a commission on gold and honest money. He has sent a confidence-building signal in saying the chairmen he would name to the commission are Lewis Lehrman and James Grant — they couldn't be better. We would suggest that Mr. Gingrich is still going to need more than the promise of a commission.

Particularly because Congressman Ron Paul is so far ahead of the Republican pack. Whatever doubts one has about him, he has stood on principle on money. While Mr. Romney resists and Mr. Gingrich plans his commission, Dr. Paul is moving way beyond a Gold Commission. He already has before the Congress one of the most visionary pieces of legislation of our time, the Free Competition in Currency Act. The measure, called H.R. 1098, is drawn from the seminal work of Friedrich Hayek, another Nobel laureate.

Hayek concluded toward the end of his career that the best course was to denationalize currency. Dr. Paul's bill would end the legal tender laws and legalize the private issuance of money.

The congressman is not the only legislator who gets the issue. Senator Mike Lee of Utah and James DeMint of South Carolina get it, as does Senator Rand Paul, to name but three. The danger for Messrs. Romney and Gingrich is that if either one of them becomes president they are going to find that themselves playing a catch-up game among the savviest Republicans on Capitol Hill.

— January 26, 2012

# Sarah Palin for the World Bank?

In respect of the candidacy of Hillary Clinton to be president of the World Bank, let us just say that it's a terrible idea. This is not a quarrel with Mrs. Clinton per se; had we been endorsing in the Democratic primary for president in 2008, we'd have put in a word for her, even if by our lights Barack Obama has a more presidential personality. It happens, though, that we've followed the World Bank for decades, and the key feature of the whole World Bank system is the conditionality it imposes on its lending. Its presidency is a pulpit in which a tribune of free markets, sound money, limited taxation, and growth could help the banks' shareholders and borrowers. Whatever it is that Mrs. Clinton is for, these are not the causes that come to mind.

Sarah Palin would make a more credible president of the World Bank than Mrs. Clinton. Laugh not. We understand that no one (leastwise, President Obama) is going to nominate her and she wouldn't take the job, anyhow. But she's a radical, pro-growth politician. She understands natural resources policy, she is a leader on energy policy, she knows fishing down to the ground (so to speak), and she came up through a fight against corruption. She is prepared to lead on sound money, as her demarche against the quantitative easing of the Federal Reserve — made before the other politicians woke up to the issue — shows. And feature the rock-star receptions she got in such places as Hong Kong and India. Sarah Palin is exactly the kind of spark-plug one would need at the World Bank — if one needed the World Bank at all.

But do American taxpayers really need to set up on the scale of the World Bank a government-capitalized pulpit for free market, pro-growth policies? We wouldn't put another nickel into it. What really needs to be done about the World Bank is to examine the question of whether there's any logic at all to any of the institutions conceived at Bretton Woods. The longer we've covered this beat, the more plain it becomes that the clear-eyed vision of the treaties that emerged in the closing hours of World War II was that of Henry Hazlitt, whose editorials for the New York Times warning of an inflation trap will be read for generations. As he predicted, the gold-exchange standard that the Bretton Woods system set up among governments collapsed.

So what is the logic of any of the institutions left standing? This is the question left hanging by the outgoing president of the Bank, Robert Zoellick. What we will remember his tenure at the World Bank for is that he used it to call for a restoration of a role for gold in the international monetary system. He did this in November, 2010, in an op-ed article in the London Financial Times on the eve of the failed G20 summit at Seoul. He called for a cooperative monetary system that would employ gold as an international reference point. "Although textbooks may view gold as the old money," he wrote, "markets are using gold as an alternative monetary asset today." For this, he was roundly mocked the next day in the very newspaper that published his proposal.

Mr. Zoellick himself is lucky to be leaving the World Bank, and it can be hoped that whoever emerges from the Republican pack will bring him into the coming campaign. Particularly if it turns to the question of monetary policy. Mr. Zoellick isn't an advocate of returning to Bretton Woods. Nor is he a gold standard man per se. He was asked about it point blank by Newsweek a year ago. He did respond by pointing out that gold is "already being viewed as an alternative monetary asset because holders of money perceive uncertain prospects in all countries and currencies other than China, and the renminbi is not free for exchange and investment. The antidote is for major economies to pursue sustainable, pro-growth policies based on structural reforms, open trade, and sound money." If we're going to have a World Bank, its ideal next president would be someone committed to that direction.

— February 18, 2012

# Bernanke 101

Chairman Bernanke's decision to use the first of his four lectures at George Washington University to attack the gold standard certainly puts the hay down where us mules can get to it. "Ben Bernanke's first lesson on economics: Forget about the gold standard," is how Politico led its story. The Fed chairman used a series of slides to guide his remarks to a bright looking group of students. The "strength of a gold standard is its greatest weakness too," one slide said. "Because the money supply is determined by the supply of gold, it cannot be adjusted in response to changing economic conditions." Mr. Bernanke insisted he understands "the impulse" behind the gold standard, "but I think if you look at actual history the gold standard didn't work well."

The way Mr. Bernanke sketches his lesson one gets the feeling that the whole scheme of the institution he heads is as an alternative to the barbarous relic. So we reached into the stack of books beside our typewriter to see what might be there. The first one we found was "An Adventure in Constructive Finance," the memoir of Carter Glass, the congressman who led in the creation of the Fed. It turns out that as the Federal Reserve Act of 1913 was moving through the House, it was hit with what Glass calls a "feverish outbreak about an imaginary 'assault on the gold standard'." It seems a group of Republicans was concerned that it would rescind the Gold Standard Act of 1900, which had settled the great battle over bimetallism that erupted in the late 19th century.

It turns out that Congress reacted to the assault by adopting an amendment put forth by an Ohio Republican, Simon Fess. It declared, as Glass put it, that nothing in the bill should be construed as a repeal of the law "providing a gold parity for all forms of money." It was only against that assurance in law that the Federal Reserve Act actually made it through the House. Why Mr. Bernanke leaves this history out of his lecture one can but surmise. He also leaves out the fact that under the Federal Reserve System the dollar has lost more than 95% of its value. Nor does he mention the sheer drama of the collapse of the dollar on his watch. A bit of value has flowed back into it in recent weeks, but it is still below a 1,600th of an ounce of gold.

None of this back-story is in Mr. Bernanke's lecture. Nor does he dwell on the failures of the Fed itself. The whole reason he is appearing in these classes, in the first place, is that there is a rising tide of distrust of the Fed within the Congress that created it. The bill to audit the Fed started out as one of Ron Paul's chimeras. Eventually it was passed, albeit in a watered down form, overwhelmingly in the House, and the Fed has been fighting a so-far losing battle against it in court. This has led Mr. Bernanke to begin his quarterly press conferences, and now his college lectures. It seems he is happy to appear in any place save where his testimony can be compelled.

The question is why, if the Federal Reserve and the system of fiat money are so superior to sound money, has our country been in such a pickle these past few years. The Fed has tried every trick in the book and some that aren't in the book. Yet so far the economy seems impervious to its monetary ministrations. It has met neither of its dual mandates of stable prices and employment. The Fed chairman did acknowledge that his institution failed at crucial moments, most notably in his view in the Great Depression, when it "did not use monetary policy to prevent deflation," as he put it yesterday. But what about its failures in the current time, when it has run the value of the dollar down to a level that was once unthinkable and millions are still out of work?

It's always possible that Mr. Bernanke will confront these questions in the remaining three lectures he is scheduled to give at George Washington, but given the preview yesterday, it looks unlikely. The full accounting of the Fed is going to have to come from the body that created it in the first place. We are less than two years away from the centenary of the institution, and there will be plenty of legislation around which this accounting could take place. One bill, H.R. 1098, would establish a free competition in currency and end the system centered on making legal tender out of the kind of scrip that Mr. Bernanke circulates. No doubt it will be a long battle, and it wouldn't be surprising to us were some of the bright-looking students to whom Mr. Bernanke spoke yesterday to end up in the lists.

— March 21, 2012

# Ron Paul's Man at the Fed

The man Congressman Ron Paul would install as chairman of the Federal Reserve was, in a little noticed but remarkable moment, invited the other day to address the Federal Reserve Bank of New York. It seems the bank wants to hear from its distinguished critics. It picked, in Mr. Grant, not only the man that Dr. Paul wants to run the Fed but the man that Newt Gingrich wants to see installed, with Lewis Lehrman, as one of the chairmen of a reconstituted United States Gold Commission. We weren't lucky enough to be at the Fed when Mr. Grant delivered his remarks, but we read them in in the latest number of his newsletter, the Interest Rate Observer.

Now, it also happens that the Fed has a less secure system for storing the gold in the vaults in its basement than Grant's Interest Rate Observer has for guarding its intellectual property. So one doesn't just reprint remarks from Grant's; the full read is normally reserved for Mr. Grant's subscribers. In this case, Grant's has made the full text available to all on the Web under the headline "Piece of my mind," which starts with a lament on the replacement of the gold standard with what Mr. Grant calls the "PhD standard." He calls the changes he seeks "re-reforms" and notes that "my program is very much in accord with that of the founders" of the Federal Reserve

Mr. Grant then suggested that the congressman who led a century ago in founding the central bank, Carter Glass, would "skewer" today's Fed. "He had an abhorrence of paper money and government debt," Mr. Grant reminded his audience. "He didn't like Wall Street, either, and I'm going to guess that he wouldn't much care for the Fed raising up stock prices under the theory of the 'portfolio balance channel.'" This "enflamed" Glass during the congressional debate over the creation of the Fed system, Mr. Grant said. He noted that when Senator Root of New York maligned the anticipated Federal Reserve notes as "fiat" currency, Glass snorted angrily;

he had no reason to doubt that the country would remain on the gold standard.

We rather like this resurrection, if that is the word, of Carter Glass (we attempted the stunt ourselves the other day), even as we prefer his Republican skeptics at the time. The virtue of dredging up Glass's protestations lies in the reminder of how far the central bank has strayed from the plan — or promises — of its founders. Mr. Grant pressed this point in the context of the pending double jubilee of the Fed. The institution originally envisioned, Mr. Grant said, "would operate passively, through the discount window. It would not create credit but rather liquefy the existing stock of credit by turning good-quality commercial bills into cash — temporarily."

"This it would do," quoth Mr. Grant, "according to the demands of the seasons and the cycle. The Fed would respond to the community, not try to anticipate or lead it. It would not override the price mechanism — as today's Fed seems to do at every available opportunity — but yield to it." Mr. Grant reckons it would be easer to carry on that modest role were we once again on a classical gold standard. He said that were Ron Paul ever to become president, Mr. Grant would (from his new post at the Fed) invite in for lunch the Wall Street Journal's Jon Hilsenrath and explain to him that the Fed is "now well over its deflation phobia and has put aside its Atlas complex."

Then, Mr. Grant said, he would call the president of the New York Fed, William Dudley, and warn him that "we're not exactly leading from the front in the regulatory drive to reduce the ratio of assets to equity at the big American financial institutions." Then he would instruct the Fed's research division "enough with 'Bayesian Analysis of Stochastic Volatility Models with Levy Jumps'" and refer them instead to the work on a gold standard for the 21st century. Mr. Grant ended his remarks to the central bankers by quoting the editor of the Skibbereen, Ireland, Eagle,* who, in 1899, warned the Russ tsar: "The Skibbereen Eagle has its eye on you."

\* \* \*

Whether any of this sank in at the Fed, one can but speculate. We cover the remarks at length because if such truth-telling fails to prosper at the Fed, it will be all the more important that it trickle up through the public discussion to the Congress. Mr. Grant himself is, despite Ron Paul's vow to install him at the Fed, entirely his own man and but one particularly eloquent and knowledgeable figure among scores who are now working this problem. They are not, incidentally, all on the right. Congressional pressure for Ron Paul's plan to audit the Fed has become bipartisan. And Carter Glass, in addition to the points above, is a reminder that there was a gold tradition among the Democrats, both before and after the road show known as William Jennings Bryan. Not a bad thing to remember as the value of the dollar edges back down toward a 1,700th of an ounce of gold and unemployment is stuck above 8%.

— April 3, 2012

\* One of its shareholders, Wikipedia reports, was Michael Collins himself.

# Krugman's 'Lust'

'The position of the Sun is that there are three circumstances when it makes sense to move to a system of sound money. One is when a currency is collapsing. Two is when it is steady. And three is when it is appreciating. What one really wants, at any point, is the confidence that the dollar will remain exchangeable for gold over a long period and that people will have confidence in that."

\* \* \*

Those words were part of an editorial issued in the Sun in January, 2011, one of the all-too-rare moments when value was flowing back into the dollar, as it has been in recent weeks. We thought of them when we read Professor Krugman's column in this morning's number of the New York Times. It ran under the headline "Lust for Gold."

What the Nobel laureate does in the column is mock what he calls "goldbuggism." With what bug he himself has come down is unclear. On the one hand, he asserts that "gold is like a very long-term bond that's protected from inflation." On the other hand, he asserts that the "the modern world's closest equivalent to the classical gold standard is the euro."

The jibe about the euro has got to be one of the most fantastic claims ever issued by the New York Times, a feat, to be sure. The columnist's idea seems to be that the euro puts the European countries "back under more or less the same constraints they faced when gold ruled." He neglects to mention that if you, say, tried to ski down a chart of the Euro's value against gold, it would be like plunging over the Headwall at Tuckerman's Ravine.

It is hard to imagine that Mr. Krugman is going to be the last of the advocates of fiat money who are going to try to make a megillah out of the fact that the value of the dollar has been appreciating — to, in a sharp move in recent hours, above a 1,500th of an ounce of gold. This is a moment to mark one of the key point in this whole great debate. It is not the desire, or even the prediction, of advocates of sound money that the price of gold will rise, meaning that the value of the dollar will fall.

If that is what Mr. Krugman means by "goldbuggism," count this newspaper out (and we have written a whole book's worth of editorials calling for the gold standard). What we mean when we write of sound money and the gold standard is a return to a system of money like that envisioned by the Founders of America. They twice used the word dollars in the Constitution of the United States, and the record is crystal clear in respect of what they meant by a dollar. They meant 371 ¼ grains of pure silver or a 15th as many grains of gold.

The Constitution they crafted delegates to Congress the power to coin money and regulate its value, but we find it hard to imagine the Founders intended anything like what Congress has permitted to happen to the dollar they entrusted to it. They comprehended, from their own experience in the Revolution, what damage could be done by inattention to the soundness of the national unit of account. They gave the Congress enormous powers to prevent the kind of catastrophe our country has experienced this past decade.

\* \* \*

This is the context in which the Joint Economic Committee of the Congress will convene this week to begin what will no doubt be a series of hearings in connection with the 100th anniversary of the Federal Reserve. The chairman of the JEC, Kevin Brady of Texas, has two measures before Congress. One is the Sound Dollar Act, which would remove the dual mandate on the Fed so that it can concentrate on stable prices without having to worry about the unemployment rate. The other is a bill to establish a serious, bipartisan monetary commission to look at the Federal Reserve as it begins its second century. What role has monetary policy played in the Great Recession? These are among the most important bills before the Congress, and it's nice to see that someone will start addressing the monetary question in a more open-minded way than has been done by Mr. Krugman and the other partisans of fiat money.

— April 12, 2012

# 'Don't Ask, Don't Tell' at the Fed

The big message from the meeting Friday of the Shadow Open Market Committee is that Congress is wising up to the Federal Reserve. This is implicit in the legislation that was the centerpiece of discussion at the meeting of Fed watchers. The measure, the Sound Dollar Act, was introduced in March by a Republican congressman from Texas, Kevin Brady, and a companion bill in the Senate was introduced by one of the leading advocates for honest money, Senator Lee of Utah. The measure would bring to an end the era of "Humphrey-Hawkins," which is the law, named for Vice President Humphrey* and a California Democrat in the House, Augustus Hawkins, that requires the Fed work toward not only stable prices but also full employment. The measure has caused nothing but mischief since it was signed by President Carter. If the Sound Dollar Act is passed, the Fed can swing back to its original assignment, which is price stability.

The act itself isn't as good a strategy as a return to what we like to call constitutional money, meaning a dollar defined in terms of silver or — to use the better specie for modern times — gold. The Sound Dollar Act doesn't seek to restore a proper gold standard the way, say, the program being advanced by Lewis Lehrman would do. Nor does it address the problem of legal tender. It wouldn't pass what one might call a Ron Paul purity test. Dr. Paul's own measure, H.R. 1098, is called the Free Competition in Currencies Act and would do what really needs to be done in the long run, which is end legal tender for the fiat money being issued by the federal government and open the way to the use of privately issued money, an idea advanced by the Nobel laureate Friedrich Hayek.

The Sound Dollar Act, however, is calculated to have a better chance of actually passing the House and Senate, a point that was made at the Shadow Open Market Committee by Mr. Brady. So in this sense it could be called an important interim measure. Ending Humphrey-Hawkins, in and of itself, would be a boon for the economy, since price stability and full employment are sometimes — even often — contradictory goals. It would be like trying to travel east and west at the same time. Mr. Brady pointed out yesterday that the first time ever that the Fed invoked the employment half of its dual mandate was to justify the tripling of the size of its balance sheet in the course of its vast program of quantitative easing. Yet Mr. Brady reckons that "protecting the purchasing power of the dollar over time provides the strongest foundation for lasting economic growth and job creation."

Ending the dual mandate is but one of several steps the Sound Dollar Act would take to rein in the Fed. It would improve the way the Fed watches prices. It currently concentrates on consumer prices. The Sound Dollar Act would require the Open Market Committee to monitor and report to Congress on what Mr. Brady characterized as "broad classes of assets including equities, corporate bonds, state and local government bonds and agricultural, commercial, industrial, and residential real estate." It would also require the foreign exchange value of the dollar to be thrown into the mix. And, most significantly, it would require the Fed to watch the price of gold, which, alone, would have, had the Fed been paying attention to it, have signaled the current crisis.

The Sound Dollar Act would also give a permanent vote on the Federal Open Market Committee to the presidents of each of the regional Federal Reserve banks. The measure would challenge the power of the Federal Reserve chairman, who has recently met dissent from some of the regional presidents. Mr. Brady told the Shadow Open Market Committee meeting that there might be other ways to achieve the diversity he wants in decision making, "but I'm seeking change that will provide Main Street with a greater voice in determining monetary policy." The reforms would break up a system that has been in place for something like 70 years, but that doesn't bother Mr. Brady. On the contrary, he reminds that it was the Congress that created the Fed in the first place and that surely Congress can reform it.

And his bill has a number of other reforms in it. It would curb the ability of the Fed to serve as an allocator of credit among various sectors of the economy, a role that Mr. Brady charged yesterday "exposes the Federal Reserve to political interference." Noted he: "In Washington D.C., subsidies die hard." His Sound Dollar Act would limit the kinds of securities in which the Federal Open Market Committee could deal. It would also require the Fed to publish its lender-of-last-resort policy. "In nearly a century of existence," Mr. Brady said Friday, "the Federal Reserve has never articulated this critical policy." He quoted Allan Meltzer as warning that the absence of clarity invites political solutions and risk taking by banks looking for a rescue, all adding up to "the well-known moral hazard problem."

The Sound Dollar Act would also start to curb abuses of the Exchange Stabilization Fund, which Mr. Brady called a "slush fund that has been abused by Secretaries of the Treasury in both Democratic and Republican Administrations." Over the years the fund received the profits from FDR's nationalization of privately owned gold and the devaluation of the dollar that followed. Mr. Brady's bill would steer the fund toward reducing federal debt. Finally, the Sound Dollar Act would nip in the bud one of the most outrageous abuses building at the Fed, funding for Elizabeth Warren's Consumer Financial Protection Bureau. The measure would end the diversion of the Fed's profits to the CFPB and force the agency to seek an annual appropriation from Congress, like any other agency.

* * *

The Sound Dollar Act is one of those measures whose importance is greater than the sum of its parts. One participant at Friday's meeting, Marvin Goodfriend of Carnegie Mellon University, likened the measure to ending "Don't Ask, Don't Tell." It is a signal that, as the Federal Reserve gets ready to mark its 100th anniversary, the legislature that created the central bank is not satisfied with its performance. The Fed was originally launched to end panics only to see a raft of them during its tenure, including a Great Depression in the 1930s and the Great Recession we are experiencing today. We don't question the loyalty or integrity of the Fed's chairman or governors. They were handed, particularly after the collapse of Bretton Woods, an impossible task of maintaining their credibility while dealing in fiat money. Guarded optimism about passage of the Sound Dollar Act was voiced to our J.V. Bennett at the Shadow Open Market Committee meeting. If the measure fails to prosper in the next congress, it would be logical to expect more radical measures to be pressed.

— April 21, 2012

---

* Vice President Humphrey's membership in the Senate when the dual mandate was introduced was by virtue his election as a regular senator from Minnesota rather than as vice president of America.

# Hat-Tip for Hollande

To mark the election of Francois Hollande as the second socialist president of France, we went to our closet and retrieved the Motsch Fils. It's the finest hat we've ever owned, a supple brown fedora that is "garanti pur castor," which is French palaver for guaranteed pure beaver. It is in the nature of beaver that it is so durable that, well, we're still using the hat more than 25 years after we purchased it. The reason we retrieved it from the Sun's hat rack today is that we could never have afforded it were it not for the election of Francois Mitterrand as the first socialist president of France.

The elevation of Mitterrand to the Elysee Palace precipitated a collapse in the value of the franc to the nadir at which we, a young foreign correspondent in Europe in the mid-1980s, were finally able to afford the finest of hats. We'd spotted it at the Motsch shop at 42 Avenue Georges V at Paris. The hat was priced at the once towering sum of 1,100 francs. But when we proffered a Reagan-era portrait of Benjamin Franklin, the man at Motsch responded, "Mais, oui," and we walked out with our hat at what may yet stand as a record exchange rate.

Of course, those were the days when there was a franc. Measuring the collapse of France that is likely to be precipitated by the accession of Mr. Hollande is going to be more difficult now that there is no franc. The French government stopped redeeming the scrip once and for all earlier this year, and commerce is conducted in a marker called the euro. So it will be more difficult to separate out the failures of France from the rest of Europe. That will take place only over time. It will also be more difficult to separate out the successes of the other European countries, if there are successes.

There are no doubt those who will suggest that this socializing effect is the whole idea of the euro. But it has been able to survive as a construct mainly because we are in the era of fiat currencies and the dollar itself has no legal definition, either. It is hard to make a whole lot out of the collapse of the euro if the dollar has also collapsed. Nor can one say a whole lot about the future of the Communist Chinese yuan. It is going to be hard to get a true picture of national strategies of political economy until there is a restoration, at least somewhere, of sound money.

DeGaulle understood this, a point we marked in an editorial last year recalling how the founder of the Fifth Republic once gathered 1,000 newspapermen into a press conference at the Elysee palace and called for a restoration of the international gold standard. Our own hope for President Sarkozy was that he might have hearkened to the Gaullist call for the gold standard as providing not only a way for France to lead but a standard that would allow smaller countries to find the same footing as larger ones.

Alas, in the end Monsieur Sarkozy proved not up to the task, and the possibility that he might pull off an upset victory — sketched by our erstwhile man in Paris, Michel Gurfinkiel — proved unattainable. So let us offer a tip of the Motsch Fils to the *president-elect de la republique*. It is a moment to remember that if the dollar and the euro are at the end of their days, one of the earliest and most durable currencies was the pelt of the beaver itself. If Mr. Hollande has any interest, we can point him to a suitable shop.

— May 6, 2012

# The Munger Games

One would think that a man as wealthy, as smart, and as old as Charles Munger would have known better than to suggest that persons who buy gold are uncivilized. "Gold is a great thing to sew into your garments if you're a Jewish family in Vienna in 1939," Mr. Munger told Rebecca Quick of CNBC, "but I think civilized people don't buy gold, they invest in productive businesses." The fact is that people who bought gold a decade ago were far better positioned than those who put their money in Mr. Munger's company, Berkshire Hathaway. For the value of a share of Berkshire Hathaway has collapsed over the past decade to barely more than 74 ounces of gold from the 238 ounces it was worth a decade ago.

Ms. Quick had beckoned Mr. Munger into this morass by telling him he was one of the greatest investors of all time and asking him whether there is anything happening that seems "like déjà vu." Mr. Munger replied that the panic that "came as a predecessor of the Great Recession had common themes that are always the same — the crazy greed, the crazy leverage, the crazy delusions, and I think we were very lucky that the outcome wasn't worse. . . . Of course, we knew it was coming, and we always used to say, well, what do you think about the crazy consumer credit or the crazy this or the crazy that, well, what's going to happen. I would always say, it's going to have a very bad result, but I can't tell you when."

Where the uncivilized boors who adjusted early to this crazy period gained the judgment to buy gold is a mystery Mr. Munger didn't pursue, though they better protected their investors than Mr. Munger and his partner, Warren Buffett, did. Mr. Munger dodged Ms. Quick's query about the current campaign among central bankers in respect of easy money. "They went to the whip," Mr. Munger mused. "They don't have an unlimited number of weapons. We'd be in way worse shape if both political parties hadn't backed huge central bank intervention. The big mistake was made by allowing the boom to go so crazy, so much evil and folly to run so rampant."

Mr. Munger credits Alan Greenspan for having recognized that he was wrong. "He's the only one that's done that," Mr. Munger said. "Everyone else has managed to look at this enormous [word unclear] and leave the previous ideas intact. . . ." He then began talking about economic virtue and sin. "What happens is that in an economy with a certain among of basic virtue, like a bunch of Germans or Japanese or something, can resort to a lot of extreme Keynesian intervention and help things. But if your whole cultural system disintegrates — say the way it did in Greece where everyone was living with no work and a lot of make believe and fraud and what have you — then the Keynesian stuff won't work."

Ms. Quick said she took it that Mr. Munger was "not in Paul Krugman's camp." Mr. Munger allowed that Professor Krugman "is one of the smartest and most articulate people we have, and he is very often right." But not before remarking that Mr. Krugman "doesn't sufficiently understand the kind of sin that the Democrats like. You know, the crooked plaintiffs lawyers. That stuff affects the body politic, and affects how well the economic principles work." Then he moved on to talking about how Chairman Greenspan was "blind not to step on the boom." The problem, he said, was that Mr. Greenspan "really overdosed on Ayn Rand."

Hmmm. Was it Ayn Rand on which Mr. Greenspan overdosed? In 1966, the future Fed chairman wrote for her newsletter an essay called "Gold and Economic Freedom." It begins with the sentence "An almost hysterical antagonism toward the gold standard is one issue which unites statists of all persuasions. They seem to sense — perhaps more clearly and subtly than many consistent defenders of laissez-faire — that gold and economic freedom are inseparable. . ." The essay ends with the assertion that "[i]n the absence of the gold standard, there is no way to protect savings from confiscation through inflation" and that "[t]he financial policy of the welfare state requires that there be no way for the owners of wealth to protect themselves."

"This is the shabby secret of the welfare statists' tirades

against gold," Mr. Greenspan warned. "Deficit spending is simply a scheme for the confiscation of wealth. Gold stands in the way of this insidious process. It stands as a protector of property rights. If one grasps this, one has no difficulty in understanding the statists' antagonism toward the gold standard." So maybe it was something else on which Mr. Greenspan was over-dosing when he arrived at the Fed. And maybe the reason that Berkshire Hathaway shares have collapsed in value is that neither he nor Mr. Munger were paying attention to the civilizing effect of gold and economic freedom.

— May 6, 2012

# The Last Call

The fact is that we were sitting in our study the other evening thinking how the Republican Party needs a clear plank on monetary reform, when the doorbell rang and we discovered on our stoop the lanky frame of the editor of the Interest Rate Observer, James Grant. Our neighbor had told us he would be stopping by with something he wanted us to see.

It turned out to be a beautifully bound volume of the issues of Barron's, the national business and financial weekly, from the second half of 1952. There marked with a yellow Post-It note was the page-one editorial of July 14, which ran under the headline "Golden Plank: It's a Test of Republican Promises." It was about the call of the Republicans, in the 1952 presidential platform, for a "dollar on a fully convertible gold basis."

One could be forgiven for thinking that, by 1952, we were already in a period of hard money. The country was, after all, a few years into the Bretton Woods Treaty, which bound America to redeem the dollar at $35 an ounce. But that was only when it was asked to do so by corresponding governments. The hapless American citizens had been divested of their gold by President Franklin Roosevelt, who spent the Depression setting the gold price out of thin air as he sat in bed in the morning. And there were already signs that Bretton Woods would be just what Henry Hazlitt had warned of — an inflation trap.

The plank on which Barron's fixed was therefore a serious marker, designed to put the Democrats in a corner. It was passed at the Republican convention that nominated General Eisenhower. It was a plank that, Barron's noted in its first paragraph, the general "is now committed to support." The measure, Barron's said, "reflects a deep and legitimate yearning on the part of the American people for a return to hard money."

"Yet if this yearning and this hope are to come to anything," Barron's warned, "it is the part of honesty to point out that much more is required than payment of lip service to a golden phrase." The fact is, Barron's wrote, "that before gold convertibility, or a return to the gold standard, can be contemplated, certain great conditions must be met. And whether the Republican Party works to fulfill these preconditions will in turn show how seriously it is dedicated to conservative economic principles both at home and abroad. Gold, in short, is the test of larger intentions."

The preconditions Barron's was citing were set down in the Republican platform as being a balancing of the budget and establishing independence of the Fed, which was being pestered something awful by President Truman's treasury department. It also dilated on what would have to happen after the institution of a gold standard, namely the establishment of international arrangements. The old gold standard, it noted, "was not a game of solitaire."

It turns out, though, that all these preconditions didn't sit too well across the hall at the offices of Barron's sister publication, the Wall Street Journal, which issued its editorial the day after Barron's cover. "What the Republican platform says about monetary policy is pretty good — but only pretty good," the Journal declared. It was irked by all the shilly-shallying.

The Republican platform wanted the Federal Reserve to be able to function in the money and credit system "without pressure for political purposes from the Treasury or the White House." The Journal didn't like the qualifying phrase about political purposes. "If the word 'political' in that sentence was not intended to leave a door open to pressure which might plausibly be defended as non-political it has no significance," the Journal growled. "It should have been deleted."

More substantively, the Journal was worried that the way the platform was nailed together it was asserting that "this country's return to a gold convertible currency must await the restoration of both a sound domestic economy and a stable world economy." Quoth the Journal: "When, if ever, will all the world have a stable economy?"

Rather than using our influence to bring into existence a stable world economy, the Journal suggested that there is "ample reason to believe that the return of the United States to a gold-convertible currency would exert a more powerful influence on the side of stable world economy than anything else we could do."

If that's not a schematic of the current debate, we don't know what it is. It's a reminder of the timeless nature of the principles that are being fought over today. It validates our own sense that all this to and fro about fiscal and trade imbalances relates to a problem that, while important, is subsidiary. The real issue facing our country is monetary reform and the need to bring to an end the failed experiment in fiat money.

\*\*\*

The Republican platform of 1952 turned out to be the party's last call for full convertibility of the dollar into money, which is what this newspaper likes to call gold. Once Eisenhower got to the White House, he rejected, along just the lines the Wall Street Journal feared, a return to convertibility. "[W]e should first begin to work for a healthy trade as the basis for programs affecting money, both their convertibility and their relationship to gold," he wrote to an adviser, George Whitney. One can almost hear the advisers to Governor Romney today using the echoes of that debate to tune up their arguments for the next nominee. All the more important the effort to prepare for Tampa a platform of monetary reform on which to stand against a president, in Barack Obama, on whose watch the dollar has collapsed to below a 1,500th of an ounce of gold.

— May 31, 2012

# Jawbone of an Ass

So it turns out that the great scandal of the London Interbank Offered Rate has spilled over to the Federal Reserve. It seems, according to a dispatch of Reuters, that the Federal Reserve Bank of New York "may have known as early as August 2007 that the setting of global benchmark interest rates was flawed." It was consulted when the problems first arose at Britain, and it sent some suggestions for reform. But these are now looking inadequate. "As one of the world's most powerful regulators, the New York Fed has the power to 'jawbone' banks to force them to make tough decisions," Reuters reported, attributing the point to a former associate general counsel at the Federal Reserve in Washington, Oliver Ireland.

This is something to consider. If Samson could use the jawbone of an ass to slay a thousand men, how come the Federal Reserve can't jawbone a few banks into fixing their interest rate the right way? After all, the Fed has a lot of experience in the jawboning line. That's what it does for a living. Its governors set their own rate for federal funds by talking about it without so much as a howdy-do to gold or anything else of value. In theory, they're supposed to keep prices stable, but the value of the dollar has plunged in recent years to less than a 1,500th of an ounce of gold. It has lost nearly half its entire value during President Obama's first three years in office and something on the order of four fifths of its value since President George W. Bush was sworn in.

They're also supposed to set their rates with an eye to maintaining full employment. But they've been lathering trillions of dollars over to the federal government and to banks. Yet it seems the more they do it, the more contented the unemployment rate seems to be resting above 8%. That doesn't even count hidden unemployment and underemployment and persons dropping out of the search for work. It's gotten so bad that members of Congress are starting to think about whether they want to end the employment mandate. A key committee unanimously called for a tough, unprecedented audit of the Fed, and the chairman of the Fed, Ben Bernanke, is so concerned that he's broken precedent and started holding quarterly press conferences.

So, while we don't want our biblical references to be construed as rude in tone, it's time to ask the question: Who is the jawbone here, and who is the ass? Or to put it another way, what is the difference between, on the one hand, the kind of rate setting done by Barclays and the others involved in the London Interbank Offer Rate, and, on the other hand, the kind of rate setting that is done by the Federal Reserve? In the one case, the chairman of Barclays, Robert Diamond, is given the heave-ho as unceremoniously as Samson dealt with the Philistines, and the thing is being written up as a scandal. In the other, the chairman of the Fed, Ben Bernanke, is given deference as a genius of rate-setting and the thing is being written up as a proper monetary system.

Our own prediction is that out of this debacle will come greater impetus to monetary reform and the introduction into the conduct of monetary policy of a reference to gold. This may be done through the kind of legislation being advanced by Congressman Ron Paul in the Free Competition in Currencies Act, which would end legal tender laws altogether in the United States and open the monetary sphere to the introduction of privately coined and printed money. It might involve the establishment of the kind of classical gold standard being advanced by, among others, the American Principles Project and Lewis Lerhman. Or it may come from, say, another country or an international organization. But it's hard to look at the LIBOR scandal and not conclude that jawboning has its limits, as poor Samson found out the hard way.

— July 10, 2012

# Ron Paul's Triumph

Congratulations are in order for Congressman Ron Paul, whose long campaign for a full audit of the Federal Reserve has finally passed the House in what the Washington Times, in a dispatch linked on the Drudge Report, calls "a move that serves as a capstone" to the Texan's career. The measure didn't just pass the House. It was approved by a bipartisan vote of 327 to 98, sending the bill to the Senate in which the majority leader, Harry Reid, supports an audit, at least in theory. Yet the Wall Street Journal reports that there are no plans, at least at the moment, to bring up the measure in the Senate.

The lesson of this saga is to redouble the drive for an audit. No one could imagine, when Dr. Paul began his quest for a decade ago, that the measure would pass the House with the kind of bi-partisan support it garnered today. A while back a kind of faux audit was passed, but it was so watered down that Dr. Paul was against it. The measure that passed today is a much tougher audit, one of the kind Dr. Paul has been seeking. The more the Democrats resist, more the need for an audit will come into focus, particularly at a time when more and more people are starting to come to grips with the possibility that errors of monetary policy are at the at the root of the Great Recession.

Chairman Bernanke has been digging himself in more and more against an audit. Were he the chief executive of a publicly held company, his shareholders would stand aghast at his recalcitrance and start asking why. Yet as recently as this week Mr. Bernanke told the Congress that an audit of the kind Congress is looking for — it could get into, among other things, the closed-door meetings at which Fed policy is made — risks a "nightmare scenario" that opens the Fed to meddling in monetary policy. "That will politicize the making of such policy, and I think it's a bad way to go," Reuters quoted the number two Democrat in the House, Steny Hoyer, as warning.

In fact, the politicization of the Fed has long since happened, and it was not the drive for transparency that did it. The politicization came with the era of fiat money, an era in which Congress stopped defining the dollar in terms of gold or any other specie. Congress threw up its hands and left matters to the Fed, interrupting only to require the Fed to work not only for stable prices but also for maximum employment. No less a figure than Secretary Geithner has been warning against politicizing the Fed, but, as these columns pointed out nearly two years ago in "How To Depoliticize the Fed," the only proven way to take politics out of monetary policy is to restore a classical gold standard.

So we welcome the showdown that's ahead. What is shaping up is a historic opportunity for the Congress to open up the question of the Fed, the whole question of the dollar, on the eve of the centenary of a central bank on whose watch the value of a dollar has collapsed to less than a 1,600th of an ounce of gold or less than a 77th of what it was when the Fed was created. The audit isn't the only process through which Congress is starting to assert its monetary powers in the Constitution. Congressman Kevin Brady has a bill, the Sound Dollar Act, that would, among other things, repeal the misguided Humphrey Hawkins Act, which requires the Fed to conduct monetary policy with an eye to employment and return it to a goal of price stability. Congressman Paul himself is pressing the Free Competition in Currencies Act, which would end legal tender and permit the introduction of privately issued money. Auditing the Fed, though, is the right place to start, so the Congress and the voters can get a true picture of where we stand at the end of a century in which the Fed had its way.

— July 25, 2012

# The Gold Platform

News that the Republican platform is going to call for the establishment of a new Gold Commission, to explore the route to monetary reform, is the most encouraging thing we've heard out of the convention about to gather at Florida. Drafts of the GOP platform to be voted on next week, according to the report in the Financial Times, will "call for an audit of Federal Reserve monetary policy and a commission to look at restoring the link between the dollar and gold." Good for the GOP, good for Governor Romney, Congressman Paul Ryan, and Congressman Ron Paul, good for the American Principles Project, and good for the legions who have moved the question of monetary reform toward the center of the national debate.

Long experience on this beat, though, has taught us to be only guardedly optimistic. Your editor covered the United States Gold Commission that was established in 1981 to look at the possibility of a return to a gold-backed dollar. The commission was established at the behest of no less a pair than President Reagan and Senator Helms at a time when the value of the dollar had collapsed to well less than a 10th, if that, of the 35th of an ounce of gold it was valued at under the Bretton Woods Treaty. In the event, the overwhelming majority of the commission turned out to be content with the system of fiat money that had emerged from Congress after President Nixon closed the United States gold window.

The commission drew a dissent in which two of its members, Congressman Ron Paul and Lewis Lehrman, declined to endorse its final report. Their dissent was eventually published as a book called "The Case for Gold." During this year's GOP primary campaign, the former Speaker, Newt Gingrich, vowed that if nominated he would convene a new Gold Commission and name as its chairmen not only Mr. Lehrman but also the publisher of the Interest Rate Observer, James Grant. "Our country," we said at the time, "is way past the point where we need another commission. A commission, as President Reagan learned in 1981, is a recipe for burying an idea, not putting it into law."

Having said that, we rather like the lede the FT put on its news dispatch this afternoon. "The gold standard has returned to mainstream US politics for the first time in 30 years . . ." it began. That's a nice turnaround from two years ago, when the newspaper, in an editorial, ridiculed its own op-ed contributor, Robert Zoellick, then president of the World Bank, for daring to suggest that it would be wise do consider a role for gold in the monetary system. The FT reckoned then that it was "instructive to ask what useful role gold can play in today's world economy." The answer, it said, "is probably none at all."

Back then, the FT reckoned that there was "no sign that confidence in central banks is about to collapse," brushing off the flight to gold that had reduced the value of the dollar to, at the time, to less than a 1,380th of an ounce of gold. Since then, the value of the Bernanke-managed greenback has plummeted even further. So Congress is starting to look to its own reputation, with the House of Representatives passing — in an astonishingly strong, bipartisan vote — a bill that would require a prompt audit of the Fed.

That the GOP's draft platform endorses the Fed audit is, combined with Governor Romney's confirmation yesterday that he would like to see a new chairman at the central bank, a sign that things are moving fast. All the more reason to remember that the last time a Republican platform called for a gold standard was 1952. General Eisenhower stood on the plank for the campaign but abandoned it once in office. So one of the tasks in the campaign ahead will hold the candidate to the plank of monetary reform platform being erected at Tampa. It has the potential to be a transformative moment, as the

Federal Reserve approaches its centenary and the Congress considers whether it wants to buy in for another generation of an irredeemable dollar.

— August 24, 2012

# The Missing Element

The one missing element in the news stories just put up in respect of the quantitative easing by the Federal Reserve is the comment issued by the one of the individuals who sits directly above Chairman Bernanke in the constitutional pecking order. This is the chairman of the House subcommittee on domestic monetary policy, Ron Paul. He's none too pleased with the direction in which the Fed is going. "The Fed's only solution for every problem is to print more money and provide more liquidity," Dr. Paul said in a statement today. "Mr. Bernanke and Fed governors appear not to understand that our current economic malaise resulted directly because of the excessive credit the Fed already pumped into the system." Added he:

"For all of its vaunted policy tools, the Fed now finds itself repeating the same basic action over and over in an attempt to prime the economy with more debt and credit. But this latest decision to provide more quantitative easing will only prolong our economic stagnation, corrupt market signals, and encourage even more misallocation and mal-investment of resources. Rather than stimulating a real recovery by focusing on a strong dollar and market interest rates, the Fed's announcement today shows a disastrous detachment from reality on the part of our central bank. Any further quantitative easing from the Fed, in whatever form, will only make our next economic crash that much more serious."

Dr. Paul's remarks were underscored by the market for constitutional money — i.e., gold and silver. The Kitco chart for gold is dramatic. In the space of an hour or so, it shows the value of the dollar collapsing to less than a 1,770th of an ounce of gold from more than a 1,720th of an ounce. The way Kitco's chart works, it's a green line suddenly shooting straight up against a side rail representing the gold price. What an astonishing vote of no confidence in what the Federal Reserve is doing. No doubt Mr. Bernanke will mark, as the Fed did in its formal statement, the fact that the mandate it has from the

Congress is to keep an eye on both prices and employment.

Of course, we've been easing quantitatively for years now, and unemployment is still above 8%, even as an astonishing number of would-be workers drop out of the labor force altogether. Not only is quantitative easing failing to solve the problem it was ostensibly undertaken to solve, but, according to one of our favorite economists, David Malpass, it is actually making things worse. "In our view, Fed bond purchases are weakening the economy's output by misallocating capital — channeling capital into [mortgage backed securities], government bonds, gold and commodities rather than allowing a market-based allocation of capital to job-creating businesses. The stronger the Fed's forward guidance, the more self-fulfilling the economic weakness."

What one can take from today's commitment by the Fed to a long period of further quantitative easing is that the impetus for monetary reform will be with us well after the election in November. So win, lose, or draw at the polls, the Republican Party has put itself in a strong position by including in its platform a call for a new gold commission to look at a metallic basis for money in a new monetary reform. Congressman Paul himself will not be in the Congress to nurse this question from the chairmanship of the subcommittee on monetary policy. We look forward to the possibility that a gold commission is constituted and he becomes a part of it.

— September 13, 2012

# Germany Eyes Gold Standard

It would be too much to say that the government of Free Germany, as we are still wont to call it, is taking steps toward the gold standard. After all, no committee beckons in the Bundestag. The government is entangled with Spain and Greece in the scrip known as the Euro. The newspapers are mum. It would not be too much, though, to say that the latest report from the Deutsche Bank, the country's leading private bank, is a newsworthy document, even if it will slide past the *bien pensant* salons of Europe.

Deutsche Bank's report is "Gold: Adjusting for Zero." It reckons we're in a situation that is "Zero for growth, yield, velocity and confidence." It says: "We believe there are nearly zero real options available to global policy-makers. The world needs growth and is willing to go to extraordinary lengths to get it." It forecasts bluntly that the value of the dollar will plummet in the first half of 2013 to less than a 2,000th of an ounce of gold. It reckons "the growth in supply of fiat currencies such as the USD will remain an important driver."

That's just for openers. The report then goes on to assert that gold is misunderstood and doesn't really belong in the basket of "commodities" used by so many economists. Gold is money, according to the Deutsche Bank. Says it: "We would go further however, and argue that gold could be characterized as 'good' money as opposed to 'bad' money which would be represented by many of today's fiat currencies." It refers to Gresham's Law and suggests "the undervalued money (good) will leave the country or disappear from circulation into hoards, while the overvalued money (bad) will flood into circulation."

There follows a discussion that would make Ron Paul blush, though it doesn't mention the congressman who, with the businessman scholar Lewis Lehrman, has been pushing this issue all these years. Deutsche Bank notes that discussion of the gold standard has become a common theme, a development that "says much about the change in attitudes by investors, many who would have ridiculed the mere mention of such a thing as little as five years ago." It suggests the talk "perhaps gives a hint as to the desperation of investors."

In any event, the Deutsche Bank concluded that "[w]hile a gold standard could work," it remains skeptical that it will be considered. This is owing to what it calls the power of culture. "The world economy has, over the past century, morphed into a highly integrated, government dominated system guided by conventional wisdom (group think)," says the Deutsche Bank. "The self-reliant, individualism of the free market has been left behind in favor of a 'new age' of coddled consumerism. Culturally this represents a very powerful force in our view, one which minimizes creative options/solutions to economic impasses."

\* \* \*

What startles us is that this is being issued by the one of the world's major banks. It was brought to our attention by James Grant of the Interest Rate Observer, who says when he read it, he could have been knocked over with a feather. For his part, your editor remembers the way gold was dismissed by the then president of the Bundesbank, Karl Otto Poehl, when your editor met with him in Frankfurt. That was a generation ago. When pressed, Herr Poehl suddenly exclaimed that Germany was the second biggest gold holder in the world. It still is, according to one of the many nifty charts in the Deutsche Bank's "Gold: Adjusting for Zero." This gives rise to the thought that if America is not going to lead on monetary reform, Germany is in a position to do so. There has, after all, been a bit of talk lately about how it should be not Greece but Germany that leaves the Euro. If Berlin wanted to take that course, a campaign for "good" money, as the Deutsche Bank calls it, would certainly be the strategy.

— September 22, 2012

# Bernanke Warns His Creator

'Bernanke warns congress to butt out of interest-rate policy discussions . . ." is the headline up on the Drudge Report following the speech today by the Federal Reserve's chairman at Indiana. It sounds to us like the chairman is warning Congress against passing Congressman Ron Paul's audit-the-Fed legislation and Congressman Kevin Brady's Sound Dollar Act, both of which would open up Fed policies to inspection. The chairman's speech marks another step in the Fed and the Congress toward what might be called open, if polite, confrontation.

It's an important story. The fear the Fed chairman is trying to instill is that by conducting an audit of the Fed that includes its interest rate policy discussions, the Congress would open the Fed up to political interference. It strikes us as an illogical reach. The Fed, after all, is running one of the most radical interest rate programs in the history of the central bank. It's been many an election since we've seen the Fed so close to the center of the presidential campaign.

Indeed, the Republican nominee is running on, among other things, a promise to replace the Fed chairman — and also to establish a gold commission to take a more fundamental look at monetary policy. The chairman himself has entered the fray, declaring at George Washington University that he is against advancing to a gold standard. He has also broken with tradition and started holding regular press conferences to get his own voice into the fray. Now he has the brass to suggest that the Congress butt out?

Our own view is that everyone — the Congress, the Federal Reserve, and the American people — would be better served were this issue opened up on every front. This is a moment for our leadership to acknowledge, nay, to declare that the topic of monetary reform needs to be put on the table and debated. Value was seeping out of the dollar even as Mr. Bernanke spoke. At the end of the day today, it was down to less than a 1,775th of an ounce of gold.

The value of the dollar, in other words, has collapsed to less than half of the number ounces of gold it was worth when President Obama acceded to the presidency and to less than a sixth of what its value on the day, say, George W. Bush acceded. Is there a candidate in either party — or for any seat in the Congress — who thinks this collapse, breath-taking in its rapidity and depth, is unrelated to our national economic travail?

What needs to be said is that it is way past time for the Congress to open up the Fed's operations for a proper inspection. The audit-the-Fed bill, more formally known as HR 459 or the Federal Reserve Transparency Act, passed the House by vote of 327 to 98. Does one think the House could be trying to tell the chairman something? Where does the Federal Reserve chairman come off entering the political fray to campaign against the passage of such a measure by the Congress that created the Fed?

Congressman Brady's Sound Dollar Act is even broader. It would just end the era of Humphrey-Hawkins, the law under which job creation was brought into the Fed's mandate. It would bring gold into a role, if only a modest one, in respect of monetary policy. And it would radically increase the ability of Congress and the public to get a handle on what the Federal Reserve was trying to do. Mr. Brady gave a brilliant presentation on his bill in April at the meeting of the Shadow Open Market Committee in New York.

This week, as the debates are about to begin, is a perfect moment for the political leadership — and we would include most pointedly Governor Romney and Congressman Paul — to tell the American people that they are not going to stand for the Federal Reserve's compulsive secrecy. Transparency is not the same as political interference, and every time Mr. Bernanke goes out on the hustings to argue otherwise, let the alarms go off. What is it that the Fed doesn't want the Congress and the American people to know?

— October 1, 2012

# Is Legal Tender Next?

It's going to be illuminating to see whether the government appeals the big ruling on judges' pay that was handed down last week at Washington. The case is called *Beer v. United States*. The Sun has written about it in "Kagan's First Case" and the editor of the Sun in "Beer on Tap." The plaintiffs are Judge Peter Beer and a rainbow coalition of some of the most distinguished judges on the federal bench. They have just won a ruling that prohibits Congress from suspending a system of automatic pay increases designed to protect their honors from inflation.

The United States Court of Appeals for the Federal Circuit, sitting en banc, handed down the ruling on Friday. The ruling hasn't received much coverage in the press, though — at least in our view — it's one of the most important cases of our time. The reason is that it has to do not only with the question of need for Congress to keep its promises and the need to attract a first class judiciary but also the question of constitutional money.

The judges turn out to be a special case because it is unconstitutional ever to diminish their pay. This is American bedrock that was laid down by the Founders because of the British tyrant George III. The king made judges dependent "on his Will alone, for the tenure of their offices, and the amount and payment of their salaries," as America's revolutionaries put it in the Declaration of Independence. So it was written into the United States Constitution that the compensation of judges "shall not be diminished during their Continuance in Office."

In Beer, the judges sued under that clause after Congress suspended automatic pay increases it had established to protect their honors from inflation. What the appeals court just ruled is that Congress, in suspending the automatic pay increases, diminished the judges' pay, particularly because when Congress legislated the automatic pay increases, it also established limits on the outside income judges are permitted to earn.

More broadly, at least by our lights, the ruling says, in effect, that the legal tender laws don't apply to judges' salaries. That is, the court is suggesting that, at least in the case of judges, 100,000 dollar bills will not suffice in 2012 for a contract to pay $100,000 that was entered into in, say, 2000. The Appeals Court packed its opinion with some prime language from the founding era.

"[N]othing can contribute more to the independence of the judges than a fixed provision for their support," the Court quoted Alexander Hamilton as writing in 79 Federalist. It noted that at the constitutional convention at Philadelphia, where the Founders sat that summer in 1787, James Madison urged that variations in the value of money could be "guarded agst. by taking for a standard wheat or some other thing of permanent value."

Madison's wheat gambit was rejected, the court noted, and Founders did not tie judges pay to "any commodity." Quoth the United States Court of Appeals for the Federal Circuit: "The framers instead acknowledged that 'fluctuations in the value of money, and in the state of society, rendered a fixed rate of compensation [for judges] in the Constitution inadmissible.'" It was quoting 79 Federalist again. It noted that the constitutional convention voiced concerns "to protect judicial compensation against economic fluctuation."

It turns out, though, that the historical record is clear what the Founders thought dollars were. They used the word "dollars" twice in the Constitution. By a dollar they meant 371 ¼ grains of pure silver or a 15th as many grains of gold. That's the way Congress defined a dollar in law under the Articles of Confederation and the way Congress defined it in law in the first Coinage Act of the constitutional era.

The idea that a dollar could be worth a different number of grains of silver or gold at the end of a contract than it meant at the beginning of a contract would have horrified George Washington and nearly all of the other Founders (Benjamin Franklin, a printer, had a vested interest in paper money). So would the idea that the dollar would be permitted to decline over a decade to but a sixth of the number of grains of gold at which it was valued at the start of a decade. That is what has just happened in America.

The court deciding *Beer* didn't get into legal tender per se. But the legal tender question is the elephant in the courtroom, so to speak. If a dollar can't be diminished for judges — that is, if the legal tender laws are not good enough for judges — why should they be good enough for the rest of us? If they are not good enough for the contract between the government and judges, why should they be good enough for contracts between private parties?

Or, to put it another way, the rest of us Americans might as well be amici as the courts start to grapple with constitutional money. The diminishment of their salaries has driven the federal judges nearly to distraction, and understandably so, precisely because they are honest men and women. The chief justices — most recently Chief Justices Roberts and Rehnquist — have been warning about it for decades. The Great Scalia issued an impassioned warning about the problem here in New York just the other day.

We don't know whether the Supreme Court will be asked to hear an appeal of *Beer*. If it is asked, it may decline. But if the Nine are asked to take a final look at the case, the question for them to start thinking about is less the promises of Congress — although breaking such a promise is enough of a diminishment for us — and more about the meaning of money. The fact is that Americans are just as upset about the harm being done to them by fiat money as the judges are.

— October 8, 2012

# Romney's Ace-in-the-Hole

It's starting to look like Governor Romney is going to attempt to go this whole race without playing what might be called his ace-in-the-hole. He had a chance to play it relatively early at the debate in Hempstead. It was put on the table by one of the questioners, Phillip Tricolla, who asked the president whether he agreed with his energy secretary that it's not the policy of his department to lower gasoline prices. President Obama rattled on with his usual gift for gab without substance, and then, when the question was put to Governor Romney, the Republican let it pass.

The fact is that the value of gasoline has been plunging. If one were to look at a chart of gasoline priced in terms of gold it would look like a downhill ski slope. The reality is that it's not the gasoline that has been going up. It's the value of the Obama dollar that has been going down. We've made this point repeatedly in these columns in recent years, but, as our friends at the Wall Street Journal like to say, it takes 75 editorials to pass a law. At the rate Mr. Romney is going, it'll take 750 editorials. All the more reason to keep marking the importance of the issue of honest money.

Mr. Romney had another chance to play this ace. It came when the candidates were talking about Communist China. The governor was particularly forceful, saying that America is "going to have to make sure that as we trade with other nations that they play by the rules." He asserted that China hasn't been playing by the rules and said that "one of the ways they don't play by the rules is artificially holding down the value of their currency." He argued that this means "their prices on their goods are low, and that makes them advantageous in the marketplace."

Fair enough, but what rules is he talking about? If the Chinese communists are running down their currency, what are Chairman Bernanke and President Obama doing in respect of our own currency? The fact is that the value of the

Obama dollar has plunged over the course of his presidency against the Communist Chinese scrip. And the Obama dollar has plunged faster than the Communist currency against the real measure of money, which is gold. So if Mr. Romney intends to name the Chinese communists as currency manipulators — and do so on "day one" of his administration, as he said again last night — what standard is he going to use?

The logical standard is gold. It's the only tried and true international, non-political standard. Mr. Romney is in a good position to use this ace, because it is his party that has laid claim to the monetary question. Mr. Romney is running on a platform that calls for the establishment of a new gold commission to take a look at putting America onto a modernized version of the gold standard. He has vowed to replace the chairman of the Federal Reserve, Ben Bernanke, who has come out publicly against the gold standard and in favor of retaining the fiat system.

If that's the plan, it strikes us that the time is past due for Mr. Romney to start talking about monetary principles. A key element of leadership, as Reagan taught so well, is educating and explaining. The issue of honest money works particularly well with the rest of Mr. Romney's tax-reduction, pro-growth, pro-jobs strategy. One of the things that the two candidates' strong performances* in the debate last night reminded us is that this election could be razor close. It's not a race up from which Mr. Romney will want to awake on November 7 to discover he might have won if he played the ace he had in his hand.

— October 16, 2012

---

* Three strong performances if one counts the moderator, Candy Crowley, though she tilted to Mr. Obama, particularly in correcting Mr. Romney on what the president said in the Rose Garden after the terrorist attack at Benghazi; it turns out that Mr. Romney was correct in how he characterized the president's remarks.

# After the Dollar

"What is your opinion on ending the dollar bill?" came the cable from one of the readers with whom we have had the liveliest debates about money and gold. He was referring to the news dispatches that Congress is considering doing away with the famous piece of scrip and replacing it with a metal slug, on the theory that the slugs don't wear out so quickly. Our answer is that the question we are focusing on in respect of this reform is not whether these new slugs are going to be better than the paper scrip but what color they are going to be.

This issue sprang into focus for us when we were writing our editorial on the scandal of the presidential coins. ABC news issued a expose on it in July 2011. It seems that the United States Mint has been cranking out 2 million of these slugs a day, but, because no one wants to use them, it's been putting them in plastic bags and piling them up in a warehouse, which eventually irked Congress to the point where it started asking questions. One ABC headline over the story was "$1 Billion in Coins Nobody Wants."

How we got from there to the latest plans to replace paper scrip with these new slugs, this is a mystery we'll leave, at least for the moment, to the psychoanalysts. The color of the coins, however, strikes us as of more than passing interest. The one-dollar presidential coins have no gold in them — not even a molecule — but are colored gold. "What does one figure the government was thinking?" these columns asked when we last wrote about the issue. "Why not color them green or purple or embed them with rhinestones?"

"Surely," we noted, "the government didn't mean to trick people into thinking the coins were gold." But then the question presented itself. "[W]hy," we wrote, "with all colors of the rainbow, make these coins look, at first blush, as if they might be gold." A "mystery" is how we summed it up at the time. It's a vexing one, too, because the chairman of the

Federal Reserve, Ben Bernanke, has recently given a lecture against the gold standard. He's also belittled the idea of a gold standard when he's testified before the monetary affairs subcommittee in the House.

All this would be undercut, however, by coloring the coins gold. It would subject the issuer of the coins to charges that they are trying to palm off as specie a slug that has no intrinsic value. There are those who reckon the coins should be colored red, to connote the deficit that plagues the federal government, or green, since they replace green-colored irredeemable paper money. There are others who think they should be made of transparent glass or plastic, so that holders of the coins can look through them and see that there's nothing of value there.

— December 1, 2012

# Getting Beyond the Fed

Let us be the first to endorse the Centennial Monetary Commission Act, which has just been introduced in the Congress. It is being advanced not by one of the so-called marginal figures but by the chairman of the Joint Economic Committee, Kevin Brady. The measure would establish a serious, bipartisan committee on monetary reform as we begin the second century under a Federal Reserve System that, in recent decades, has had an increasingly illogical dual mandate and is churning out money that is convertible by law into nothing but more fiat money.

Mr. Brady is emerging as an important figure in the monetary debate. He has not endorsed a gold standard, per se. Nor has he signed on to some of the more radical measures, such as Ron Paul's Free Competition in Currency Act, which would end the whole system of legal tender and open the way for privately issued money to compete with government scrip. Instead, Mr. Brady has been pressing a measure called the Sound Dollar Act, which he has just reintroduced. It would, among other things, end the Fed's dual mandate to both stabilize prices and boost employment.

Mr. Brady's Centennial Monetary Commission Act, which is also known as H.R. 1176, is a parallel measure that would establish a commission "to examine the United States monetary policy, evaluate alternative monetary regimes and recommend a course for monetary policy going forward." It is not a repeat of the United States Gold Commission, which was established at the start of President Reagan's first term. That was an important body, to be sure, but it was stacked with advocates of fiat money and is today remembered primarily for its dissent, written by Congressman Ron Paul and another commission member, Lewis Lehrman, calling for a restoration of gold-based money.

Mr. Brady's bill would establish a much more balanced and bipartisan commission, without a predisposition for or against a gold — or any other — standard. It offers a chance not only to light the way to the repair a broken monetary system but also to illuminate the danger that our reliance on fiat money is itself the cause of our long economic travail. This alone is important. Congress is consuming itself with the fiscal debate at a time when a growing number of our best economists and political leaders are coming to the view that the real problem is the fiat nature of the dollar.

* * *

Regular readers of these columns will note that the Sun has been impatient with the idea of commissions. They are all too often a place to bury a movement for reform. What we like about Mr. Brady's commission is, among other things, that it is tied to the centennial of the Federal Reserve. Once in a century is not too often to take a look at questions this serious. Our politicians seem to have forgotten that the enumerated power to coin money and regulate its value was delegated in the Constitution not to a central bank or the president but to the Congress, which is also the body to which the parchment granted the related power to borrow money on the credit of the United States. The one thing the recent record shows above all else is that the impetus to reform will not come from the Federal Reserve itself. It is the Congress that will have to step up, and it looks like Mr. Brady has given it the chance.

— March 21, 2013

# Speaking of Money

L et us pause, amid all the monetary turmoil, to reason out the way we talk about gold — particularly all these confounded references to its "value." This struck us while reading a dispatch of Reuters saying that "every time the price of gold falls by $100 an ounce, as it did on Friday and it has done again today, the value of the world's gold falls by more than $500 billion." Reuters is hardly the only offender. ABC news notes that "for years the value of gold soared to fresh highs as its boosters fretted over the risk of hyper-inflation." Beneath the streets of Manhattan in a vault of the Federal Reserve, the New York Times reports, "the world's largest trove of gold — half a million bars — has lost about $75 billion of its value."

To the ears of a copy editor of the Sun, this is like the screech of chalk pushed the wrong way on a blackboard. We don't mean to suggest that Reuters, ABC, and the Times are alone. A Google search turns up thousands of references to "value of gold," including in all the best newspapers, and each of them is entitled to its own stylebook. But the "Reporters Handbook and Manual of Style of The New York Sun" includes a pointed warning against referring to the "value of gold," terming the phrase a "tautology." The logic of the Sun stylebook is that the value of gold is, in practical terms, constant. We prefer to talk about the value of the dollar. That's what does all the changing.

This is why one reads relatively few references in the Sun to the price of gold. We're not against referring to prices. We prefer, though, not to say that the price of gold fell to below $1,400 an ounce. Our preferred style is that the value of the dollar soared to above a 1,400th of an ounce of gold. It is gold, not the dollar, that is the measure of value. The Sun stylebook also urges reporters to avoid using the verb "to sell" if the object is gold. One doesn't "sell" gold; one "spends" it. There is an ideology stalking our policy precincts that reckons gold is a "commodity" or an "asset." This fits fine in an era of fiat money. But in the view of the Sun, it is gold that is the money.

Now we are not so solipsistic as to suggest that the Sun stylebook is the last word on this subject. It is merely our standard of style. We are not shy, however, about suggesting that the language in which we speak about the dollar has implications. The value of the dollar barely rose above a 1,400th of an ounce of gold yesterday and already the American Broadcasting Company was talking about how the development "may have damaged the case for any eventual return to the gold standard." Could be. But it will be less likely if the Congress of the United States, which is preparing to hold potentially historic hearings on the Centennial Monetary Commission Act, pays attention to the language in which we speak of the money the Constitution grants to Congress the power to coin.

— April 16, 2013

# The Tett Offensive

'How the Fed lost its cred" is the headline this morning over Gillian Tett's column in the London Financial Times. The rising FT scribe is praising a new book by President Reagan's former budget director, David Stockman. The book argues that at the heart of "The Great Deformation," which is the title of the tome, is, in the Fed, a "rogue central bank that has abandoned every vestige of sound money." Ms. Tett, who has been traveling a good bit around America, reports that Mr. Stockman's view "is creeping more and more into mainstream debate."

Ms. Tett insists that "most ordinary Americans," as she calls us, "do not really understand how quantitative easing does — or does not — work, nor are they articulating Stockman's fury that America left the gold standard." She writes, nonetheless, that on her travels she "was struck by how many people — be they economists, businessmen or cab drivers — volunteered a sense of unease about the central bank." Our own view is different. We think that Americans do understand how quantitative easing does not work and that this is precisely why Mr. Stockman's view is creeping more into mainstream debate.

What arrests us about Ms. Tett's coverage is the refreshment it offers from the editorial line of the Financial Times. The FT announced its opposition to any talk of the gold standard back in 2010, when its editors picked up their own paper to discover — to their horror — that on its own op-ed page no less of an establishment figure than Robert Zoellick, then president of the World Bank, had suggested it might be time to return gold to a role in the international monetary system. The FT turned around and issued an editorial denouncing the very op-ed piece it had just run.

We wrote about it at the time in "Zoellick Tossed Under the Bus." Ms. Tett emerged as a dissenter from the FT's stodginess a few months ago, when she came out with a devastating column on the "rising uncertainty over the Fed's effectiveness." She warned against a third round of quantitative easing. Her piece followed a column by the FT's editorial page warhorse Martin Wolf about how Chairman Bernanke "deserves praise for bold and ethical move." Her latest column followed by a week an FT editorial denouncing moves in Congress to repeal Humphrey Hawkins.

That is the law that assigned the Fed the task not only of stabilizing the value of the dollar but of also keeping the unemployment rate down. The reform effort is being led on the Capitol Hill by the chairman of the Joint Economic Committee, Kevin Brady of Texas, who wants a Centennial Monetary Commission to be established on the double-jubilee of the Federal Reserve Act. In addition to the prudence of such a commission — can once a century be too often for the Fed's creator to look at its handiwork? — it will be quite a spectacle to watch those Europeans who don't read Ms. Tett try to keep up.

— May 11, 2013

# Verbosity of Money

The debacle ignited by the Federal Reserve this week invites this question: What would have happened had Chairman Bernanke refrained from saying anything? He held on Wednesday one of his press conferences, announcing that, as the Associated Press put it, the Fed would likely slow its $85 billion-a-month program later this year and end it next year if the economy continued to strengthen. The stock market collapsed, and the value of the dollar soared — to more than a 1,300th of an ounce of gold at last check — and alarm is spreading.

Well, let it not be said that The New York Sun failed to warn of this kind of chaos. We did this a bit more than two years ago, in an editorial called "The Verbal Dollar." It quoted a founder of TradeMonster.com, Jon Najarian, as warning Mr. Bernanke's press conferences would ignite a "giant ramp up in volatility." He reasoned that traders "react to one word removed from a paragraph in a policy statement" and remarked, "now he's going to hold a press conference?" It reminded us that there had long been a tradition of silence among central banks, going back at least to the Bank of England.

Our editorial related the story of the question that Lord Keynes put in 1929 to the deputy governor of the Bank of England, Sir Ernest Harvey. He asked the governor whether it was a practice of the bank never to explain what its policy was. Sir Ernest suggested that it was the bank's practice to "leave our actions to explain our policy." When Keynes plowed on, Sir Ernest famously explained: "To defend ourselves is somewhat akin to a lady starting to defend her virtue." We quoted James Grant, editor of the Interest Rate Observer, as remarking that the Bank of England in its glory days said "next to nothing" but conscientiously exchanged bank notes for gold.

Now it does the opposite — and, as Mr. Grant said, "can't seem to stop talking." What in Sam Hill is the point of it? What would have been the harm in holding the meeting the Fed just held and having Mr. Bernanke refrain from trans-fogging the airwaves with a lot of ambiguous blather about what the Fed might or might not do and, instead, simply go to a baseball game or something? It's not as if Mr. Bernanke knows what he will do later this year. He only knows what he might do, and he might not even know that. Economists have a phrase called the "velocity of money," which is the rate at which a unit of money is involved in a transaction. How about the "verbosity of money," which would be the rate at which the Fed chairman talks about what he *might* do?

There was a time when we knew what the central bank or the other issuing authorities would do. Those were years when the law defined a dollar in terms of a given amount of gold. There was a period in our history where the law also specified the dollar in respect of silver. But the bimetallism debate was brought to an end with the Gold Standard Act of 1900 and, the Congress thought, with the Federal Reserve Act of 1913, which was passed on the condition that it not be taken to authorize an end to the convertibility of the dollar into gold at the value the Congress legislated using its constitutional authority to coin money and regulate its value and to fix the standard of weights and measures. Those years of dollar convertibility were, on a net basis, years of great prosperity and growth.

It turns out that the Congress is taking another look at things as we are coming up on the 100th anniversary of the Federal Reserve. The chairman of the Joint Economic Committee, Kevin Brady, is pushing the Sound Dollar Act, to relieve the Federal Reserve of the duty to pay attention to jobs and instead return its focus to the value of money. He is also pushing a bill to set up — on what he calls a "brutally bipartisan basis" — a Centennial Monetary Commission, that would use the double-jubilee of the Fed to look at the strategic question of monetary reform. It could include a law saying that if we do have a Fed, its directors adhere to the central banker's code and let their actions speak, knowing that silence is golden.

— June 21, 2013

# 'A Strange Glow'

So what does one figure is the explanation for the fact that when Chairman Bernanke testified before Congress today the value of the dollar began rising? The way the New York Times retailed the news is that the chairman "sharpened his insistence" that "the Fed remains committed to its economic stimulus campaign" and had not intended to signal in recent weeks that it was "lowering its sights." Yet the dollar finished the day with a higher value — more than a 1,277th of an ounce of gold — than when it started.

Our own theory is that it was the story on the Associated Press about how "a strange glow in space has provided fresh evidence that all the gold on Earth was forged from ancient collisions of dead stars." We're not making it up. That's the story that was being circulated as Mr. Bernanke was speaking. The AP was citing a report Wednesday by researchers. It seems high-powered telescopes have detected a collision of neutron stars that European supercomputers predict could produce gold, platinum, and other heavy metals.

"The observation," Alicia Chang of the AP reports, "bolsters the notion that gold in our jewelry was made in such rare and violent collisions long before the birth of the solar system about 4½ billion years ago." It quotes one Edo Berger of the Harvard-Smithsonian Center for Astrophysics as saying that people "walk around with a little tiny piece of the universe." The AP paraphrased researchers as saying that an infrared light in the glow it detected in intergalactic space "could be evidence that heavy elements like gold had spewed out of the cosmic crash."

If that seems fantastic, feature the exchange that occurred today between Mr. Bernanke and Congressman Keith Rothfus of Pennsylvania. The Quaker State Republican posed what he called a "simple question" about an individual who is "looking to make an investment" and goes to his bank or broker and purchases a Treasury bill. "Where does the Fed get its money to buy its Treasury bills?" the congressman asked.

"When we buy securities from a private citizen," the chairman transponded, "we create a deposit in their bank, and it shows up as reserves. So if you look up our balance sheet, our balance sheet balances. We have Treasury securities on the asset side. On the liability side we have either cash or reserves at banks, and on the margin that's what has been building up as excess reserves at banks."

"You create the reserves?" Mr. Rothfus rumbled.

"Yes," the chairman replied.

"Is that printing money?"

"Not literally," Mr. Bernanke answered in what we predict will be one of the most-remembered of all the remarks he's made before Congress.

It went over wonderfully with the Committee on Financial Services, we gather. "The shabby condition of the economy has become the constant background for Mr. Bernanke's public appearances," the New York Times reported today. It noted that unemployment "remains stubbornly common" and growth is "tepid." But it quotes Congresswoman Carolyn Maloney as telling Mr. Bernanke, who may have made his last appearance before the committee as Fed chairman, "You have never been boring." And it quotes the chairman of the committee, Jeb Hensarling, a Republican of Texas, as telling Mr. Bernanke, "You acted boldly and decisively and creatively — very creatively."

A strange glow, indeed.

— July 17, 2013

# The Female Dollar

James Thurber once drew some cartoons of a woman playing poker. In one, she is seated at a table clutching her cards to her breast, eying the capacious pot, and inquiring, "What do four ones beat?" In another she is glaring across the table, demanding to know, "Why do you keep raising me when you *know* I'm bluffing?" Whether Brother Remnick of the New Yorker could get away with publishing such japes nowadays, we don't know. But we were put in mind of the cartoons by the alarm at the New York Times over the possibility that President Obama might pass over Governor Janet Yellen as the next chairman of the Federal Reserve.

What is the world to make of the fact that as America approaches the 100th anniversary of the Fed the big question is whether the next chairman will be a woman? The Times headline is, "In Tug of War Over New Fed Leader, Some Gender Undertones." It characterizes the battle to succeed Ben Bernanke, who is widely expected to depart after his current term, as being between Mrs. Yellen, a former president of the San Francisco Federal Reserve Bank, and Lawrence Summers, an acolyte of Treasury Secretary Rubin. Or, as the Times puts it, "between the California girls and the Rubin boys."

Are we entering the era of the gender-backed dollar? We don't discount the issue of discrimination against women in America or the importance of cracking the glass ceilings. Your editor has spent a career cheering on high octane women. But what good is a gender-backed dollar going to do in an era of fiat money? The debate about the next Fed chairman has been conducted absent any attention to the question of whether America, or the world, is being well-served by a system in which the nation's money is convertible into nothing other than other pieces of fiat money.

We know how we are going to measure Mr. Bernanke's performance — by the value of the dollar entrusted to his care by the Congress. He may reclaim things between now and the end of his tenure in office, but as things now stand his tenure has been a disaster. The value of the dollar, at but a 1,333rd of an ounce of gold, is substantially less than half of the 568th of an ounce of gold it was valued at on the day Mr. Bernanke acceded to the chairmanship of the Fed. Would this record have been any better were he a woman? Where does that leave Governor Yellen?

The Times characterizes her as "one of three female friends, all former or current professors at the University of California, Berkeley, who have broken into the male-dominated business of advising presidents on economic policy." The other members of the triumvirate are Christina Romer, who headed President Obama's first Council of Economic Advisers, and Laura D'Andrea Tyson, who had the same post under President Clinton. None of them, in so far as we're aware, has made it her business to plump for an end to the system of fiat money.

On the contrary, the choice facing Mr. Obama in respect of the Fed is described by the Times as "roiling Washington because it is reviving longstanding and sensitive questions about the insularity of the Obama White House and the dearth of women in its top economic policy positions." Writes the Times: "Even as three different women have served as secretary of state under various presidents and growing numbers have taken other high-ranking government jobs, there has been little diversity among Mr. Obama's top economic advisers." It quotes Professor Romer as saying: "Are we moving forward? It's hard to see it."

Indeed. As the 100th anniversary of the Fed approaches the Joint Economic Committee of the Congress has been nursing a bill to establish a Centennial Monetary Commission. The idea would be to make a formal assessment of the Fed as it commences its second century. It struck us as a terrific idea, but the prognosis it is given from the Web site govtrack.us is a 14% chance of getting out of committee and a 2% chance of being enacted. Maybe the Joint Economic Committee could expand its bill to take in the question of whether the collapse of the dollar follows from the fact that it has been managed for the past century by men. It could be that Thurber was onto something.

— July 27, 2013

# ‘Freud and the Fed

‘I've been saying for a long time that we aren't having a rational argument over economic policy, that the inflationista position is driven by politics and psychology rather than anything the other side would recognize as analysis. But this really proves it beyond a shadow of a doubt; if you really want to understand what's going on here, the Austrian you need to read isn't Friedrich Hayek or Ludwig von Mises, it's Sigmund Freud.”

\* \* \*

So writes the Nobel laureate Paul Krugman in his Web log at the Times. He is reacting to our editorial, “The Female Dollar,” and to the Wall Street Journal's more substantive debunking of the way gender has eclipsed monetary policy in the debate on the next chairman of the Federal Reserve. And, by George, if it doesn't appear that Professor Krugman has stumbled onto something.

For Freud grasped the psychological propensity of people to fix on gold, which is at the heart of the monetary debate. Some of Freud's references are a bit scatological; at one point he traces the obsession with gold back to the trauma of toilet training. But elsewhere he makes reference to the monetary problem, referring to “the case of one who gives a beggar a gold piece in place of a copper or a silver coin.”

Freud's reference is under the heading “Erroneously Carried-Out Actions.” He characterizes the solution of such “mishandling” of coins as “simple” — “an act of sacrifice designed to mollify fate, to avert evil, and so on.” If so, what is one to make of tendering paper or dross where gold is owed? No doubt Freud would discover a desire not to mollify but to tempt fate and not to avert evil but to court it.

So it's not going to be easy for Professor Krugman to palm off the libel that advocates of sound money are simply crazy. For Freud had his own feel for the verities of the marketplace and the psychological dimension to the mystery of money, glimpsed in a reference he attributes to a report by another Austrian psychoanalyst, Otto Rank.

It involves a fellow who, shortly before Christmas, goes to the Austro-Hungarian Bank to "obtain ten new silver crown-pieces destined for Christmas gifts." He sees many people going in and out of the bank and thinks to himself he should be quick. "I shall put down the paper notes to be exchanged, and say, 'Please give me gold.'"

His mistake — he intended to ask for silver — awakens him from his fantasies, only to notice the approach of an acquaintance named Gold, who could help him in his career. Hence he imagined himself asking "the cashier for gold instead of the inferior silver." The essay speculates that the fellow's mind was "attuned to the material" and "guided my steps from the very beginning to buildings where gold and paper money were exchanged."

Dang the subconscious. Dang those Austrians. And add the Swiss psychoanalyst, Carl Jung. It turns out that Jung wrote a whole treatise on alchemy. He was nigh obsessed with the legend of turning lead into gold. We wouldn't want to make too much of the point. But we wouldn't want to make too little of it either. It's not just members of the Tea — or Republican — parties who think in terms of specie.

What would the psychiatrists say about Krugman's denial? Or his characterization of Janet Yellen, in the headline of his blog post, as the "she-devil of Constitution Avenue"? No one else used — or suggested — that kind of language. Nor was it the Sun or the Wall Street Journal that brought gender into this debate in the first place. That was Mr. Krugman's own newspaper, the Times.

It did so Friday in a story on page A1, under the headline "In Tug of War Over New Fed Leader, Some Gender Undertones." Mr. Krugman would have his readers believe that the Sun and the Journal have objections to a woman chairman the Fed. That's because he dasn't open up the question of the value of the dollar in the terms the framers of our constitutional system intended.

The fact is that the founders of America would be appalled at the monetary system that obtains in America today. Every last one of them — including George Washington, James Madison, Thomas Jefferson, Alexander Hamilton. Chief Justice Marshall, who wrote, in McCullough v. Maryland, the Supreme Court's famous opinion vouchsafing a central bank, he, too, would be appalled.

So would the creators of the greenback and the founders of the Federal Reserve itself. One hundred years ago Congress established the Fed on the express condition that, as it was put by the Fed's leading congressional supporter, Carter Glass, nothing in the bill should be construed as a repeal of the law "providing a gold parity for all forms of money." We have our doubts about what Keynes himself would have made of a dollar valued at but a 1,300th of an ounce of gold.

So forgive us if we react with a wry smile to Professor Krugman's lament over the lack of "rational argument" in respect of economic policy. In our experience those who measure the value of dollar in the terms in which the Founders measured it are a rational and cheerful lot. What a contrast to Mr. Krugman. In all of newspaperdom there is no more strident, ad hominem, angry column than his. No wonder he's thinking in terms of Freud.

— July 30, 2013

# Bernanke's Moral Hazard

President Reagan used to say that the nine most terrifying words in the English language are "I'm from the government, and I'm here to help." For an example of what he was talking about one is likely to gain a glimpse via a deposition scheduled as soon as later this month, when the chairman of the Federal Reserve, Ben Bernanke, is scheduled to be forced to answer questions under oath.

Let us just say that this sort of thing doesn't happen every day. The suit is being brought against the United States by the Starr International Company, which was an owner of AIG. Starr is headed by AIG's former chairman, Maurice "Hank" Greenberg, who contends that when the government bailed out AIG, it wiped out the equity of the company's shareholders.

If that sounds like ingratitude, feature the Fifth Amendment. It is at the heart of the Bill of Rights. It says, among other things, that no person shall be deprived of property "without due process of law" and prohibits the government from taking private property for public use "without just compensation." That's American bedrock.
Greenberg, who built AIG and ran it for decades, is arguing that, in effect, the government nationalized AIG at a fraction of its value, costing Starr, a major shareholder, billions of dollars. He concedes that AIG needed a bailout, but he disputes that the government needed to seize AIGs shares and suggests the government singled out AIG for particularly onerous — punitive — terms.

When Starr International issued a notice that it would depose Mr. Bernanke, the Obama administration went into a panic, at least to judge by the intensity with which it sought to get Mr. Bernanke off the hook. It filed a motion in the case suggesting that because Mr. Bernanke "is essentially responsible for the orderly operation of the United States financial and banking systems," bothering him "for even a day" could have "untoward results."

The judge in the case, Thomas Wheeler of the United States Court of Federal Claims, is no dummy. He ruled in no uncertain terms that Mr. Bernanke would indeed have to testify. "The court cannot fathom having to decide this multibillion-dollar claim without the testimony of such a key government decision-maker," he wrote.

To top things off, the judge said he'd attend the deposition personally and be prepared to deal with objections and procedural matters on the spot. It may be that Mr. Bernanke can squirm out of this on appeal, but it may be that someone — for the first time — will get Mr. Bernanke into a position where he won't be able to dodge the hard questions.

Like his own moral hazard. That is a phrase that connotes a situation in which someone is tempted to take an undue risk because someone else is bearing the cost. Mr. Bernanke used the phrase in testimony about AIG he made to Congress. He said that to mitigate concerns that the bailout of AIG would "exacerbate moral hazard" and "encourage inappropriate risk taking," the Fed imposed significant costs and constraints on AIG's owners.

What does that mean in plain English? Starr International's complaint refers to what it calls a banker hired to represent the interests of the Federal Reserve Bank of New York. It quotes the banker as remarking that "the basic terms of these transactions amounted to an attempt to 'steal the business.'"

Nor was all this without controversy behind the scenes. The treasury secretary at the time, Henry Paulson, has written a book about the 2008 financial panic. In a meeting at the time with congressional leaders, including Senators Reid, Dodd, and Gregg, and Congressmen John Boehner and Barney Frank, Mr. Paulson reported that Mr. Dodd twice asked "how the Fed had the authority to lend to an insurance company and seize control of it."

Mr. Paulson related that Mr. Bernanke explained that the Federal Reserve Act "allowed the central bank to take such actions under 'unusual and exigent' circumstances.'" In his own book, "The AIG Story," Mr. Greenberg asserts that the statute, in fact, did not authorize the Fed to seize control of private property. He argues that the constitutionality of any such provision would be doubtful.

Mr. Paulson goes on to quote Senator Reid as telling Mr. Bernanke: "You've heard what people have to say. I want to be absolutely clear that Congress has not given you formal approval to take action. This is your responsibility and your decision." Later, when in 2009 Mr. Bernanke was being questioned by an angry Senate, he confessed, "If there's a single episode in this entire 18 months that has made me more angry, I can't think of one, than AIG,"

So it looks like Starr International and Mr. Greenberg have a lot to ask Mr. Bernanke when they have him under oath. We do not suggest that Mr. Bernanke has been less than straightforward when he's not under oath. But the deposition could offer a glimpse of whether Mr. Bernanke kept his head in a time of his own moral hazard, since he, too, was taking a risk with other people's money. It will be a moment to remember the wisdom of Ronald Reagan and his warning about the danger that lurks when someone from the government says he is here to help.

— August 6, 2013

# The Class Backed Dollar

After disclosing some "gender undertones" in the maneuvering over the next chairman of the Federal Reserve, the New York Times is out with a new scoop — this one over the issue of class. "The most obvious topic for a Democratic Fed leader to emphasize is the sharp growth in income inequality, which many scholars think has destabilized the economy," writes the paper's Washington correspondent, David Leonhardt. He goes on to quote one contender for the job, Lawrence Summers, as saying he thinks "the defining issue of our time is: Does the economic, social and political system work for the middle class?"

Mr. Summers, a former treasury secretary, is important in part because, according to the earlier dispatch in the Times, Mr. Summers is the individual who is being advanced for the job by the faction that favors a man. The reporters who broke that story, Binyamin Appelbaum and Anne Lowrey, disclosed that the individual favored by the faction that wants the next Fed chairman to be a woman is the vice chairman of the Fed, Janet Yellen. At a time when the monetary debate is in a state of flux, the idea that the dollar should be based not on gender but on class is a scoop.

Call it the third mandate. The first mandate would be your basic price stability, which mandate has obtained since the founding of the Fed a century ago. The second mandate would be your full employment, which was legislated by the Congress in 1978 in a law called Humphrey Hawkins, after two Democrats, Hubert Humphrey and Augustus Hawkins, both men. The measure was signed by another Democrat and man, President Carter. The combination of the price stability and the full employment is your dual mandate. The third mandate would be to manage the dollar in a way calculated to help the middle class.

Why it's the middle class that the dollar should be managed to help isn't dwelled on by the Times. But the thinking of the Times must be that your poor people don't have many dollars to worry about, so the question of whether their dollars hold their value doesn't affect them as much. The rich people have so many dollars that they, too, don't care whether the dollar holds its value. So one can start to see the outlines of how Messrs. Summers and Leonhardt are thinking. It prompted us to type into the New York Times's search engine the phrase "rise of the American middle class."

One of the first cables it turned up, if sorted by relevance, is a post by Paul Krugman, introducing his Web log in September 2007. In it the columnist offers a paean to the middle class, which the future Nobel laureate says he grew up in and was created by the New Deal. He offers a chart that traces the "share of the richest 10 percent of the American population in total income," which Mr. Krugman calls "an indicator that closely tracks many other measures of economic inequality." It illuminates four periods in our recent history. Mr. Krugman focuses on one, which he labels Middle Class America.

The span labeled middle class America were years when society was "without extremes of wealth or poverty, a society of broadly shared prosperity, partly because strong unions, a high minimum wage, and a progressive tax system helped limit inequality." But the odd thing about it — about Mr. Krugman's column — is that he fails to mention one other feature of the period. The dollar was defined as a matter of law through most of the period as being a 35th of an ounce of gold. Mr. Krugman's chart shows the American middle class period running from the 1930s right up until the early 1970s.

What brought that era to an end? Well stub our toe if it wasn't the beginning of the period of fiat money. This is the period in which Congress stopped defining the dollar in terms of gold and turned to the concept of fiat money, when the dollar was whatever the Federal Reserve said it was and was, in any event, convertible into but another piece of government issued scrip. Mr. Krugman calls the period "the great divergence." We call it the fiat years, when the value dollar has collapsed to, at last check, less than a 1,385th of an ounce of gold. So here's the real scoop: If the Times wants to recapture the era when the middle class soared, history suggests the thing to do is to define the dollar not in terms of employment or gender or class but in terms of gold.

— September 1, 2013

# Mercy for the Fed

It's not often that this newspaper calls for mercy for the Fed. But this morning the Nobel laureate Joseph Stiglitz is devoting his column on inequality to endorsing Governor Yellen, currently the vice chairman, as the next chairman of the Federal Reserve. It's one of a raft of pieces endorsing Mrs. Yellen that have appeared in the New York Times. But why, Mr. Stiglitz asks, "is this a matter for a column usually devoted to understanding the growing divide between rich and poor in the United States and around the world?" The answer, if he says so himself, is "simple." It's that "what the Fed does has as much to do with the growth of inequality as virtually anything else."

Isn't the Fed having enough problems with its *dual* mandates of price stability and full employment? Do we really want to stick the Fed with the task of bridging the divide between the rich and the poor? It would be unfair to blame this entirely on Professor Stiglitz. Only a few days earlier, the Times's Washington correspondent, David Leonhardt, issued a column suggesting that "[t]he most obvious topic for a Democratic Fed leader to emphasize is the sharp growth in income inequality, which many scholars think has destabilized the economy." We wrote about it in an editorial called "The Class-Backed Dollar," calling the idea a "third mandate" for the central bank.

Professor Stiglitz calls for the new mandate without so much as a howdy-do to an earlier generation of the Times. The fact is that when the employment mandate was laid on the Fed — via the Humphrey Hawkins Full Employment Act, which was signed by President Carter in 1978 — the Times was against the measure. That was back in the Carter years, the last time the country was in the grip of a left-wing, Democratic presidency. The Times warned of the consequences of uncertainty and called for a rejection of the law, labeling it a "cruel hoax on the hard-core unemployed, holding before them the hope — but not the reality — of a job."

Our own view is that it's long past time to declare Humphrey-Hawkins a failure and to relieve the Fed of the assignment to boost employment. This isn't the Fed's fault. Alfred Nobel himself couldn't have made Humphrey-Hawkins work. All the hectoring by the left-wing economists and pundits isn't going to change that. Yet another mandate is the last thing the Fed needs as it marks its double jubilee. The right move is for the Congress to take a hard look at the Sound Dollar Act, which would repeal Humphrey Hawkins and diversify the board of the Fed to include the regional presidents (a route through which Mrs. Yellen rose).

Here's the thing to remember. If the gap between the rich and the poor has been getting wider, it is a feature of the era of fiat money. This was commenced in the early 1970s, with the collapse of the gold-exchange standard that had obtained during the era of Bretton Woods. It has led to two generations of hedging and speculation that is, under the circumstances, natural and even admirable, but has only exacerbated the inequalities about which the Times complains so much. A sound currency would be the best way to regulate the banks and the government. The centennial of the Fed is as good a moment as any to start this reform, so that whoever is named chairman or chairwoman of the Fed will have a mandate that is clear.

— September 7, 2013

# Mr. Bernanke's Motto

A particularly trenchant editorial — "Mr. Bernanke Blinks" — is now on the rotary presses of tomorrow's Wall Street Journal. The whole editorial repays a read, but the part of it that we like best is the reminder that in all of history no Fed chairman "has put more stock in offering 'forward guidance' to financial markets" than has Mr. Bernanke. "For him now to shrink at the market reaction he must have anticipated to his tapering guidance suggests a large failure of nerve," the Journal said. "It also undermines the credibility of the Fed's future policy guidance."

This underlines what another sage, James Grant of the Interest Rate Observer, likes to call the "PhD standard." His phrase is a reference to the conceit that a few highly educated technocrats could be so able to out-think the market as to be the basis for monetary policy. It's a kind of "hubris-backed money," as the editor of the Sun has been heard to mutter into his Manischewitz. The sign that Mr. Bernanke has become unmoored from even that standard is his infernal penchant for talking. He shares the tendency with the President.

We first wrote about this in an editorial called "The Verbal Dollar." That was two-and-a-half years ago, when Mr. Bernanke was preparing to start the quarterly press conferences that have become a fount of the "forward guidance" that has just been upended. We had been steered by Mr. Grant to the famous exchange between the deputy governor of the Bank of England, Sir Ernest Harvey, and Lord Keynes. His lordship had asked Sir Ernest whether it was a practice of the bank *never* to explain what its policy was. Sir Ernest suggested that it was the bank's practice to "leave our actions to explain our policy."

When pressed, Sir Ernest explained: "To defend ourselves is somewhat akin to a lady starting to defend her virtue." We quoted Mr. Grant as speculating that Mr. Bernanke was "reacting to the smoldering populist rage over the inflation he refuses to acknowledge." Mr. Grant noted that the Bank of England, in "its glory days managing the pre-World War I gold standard," said "next to nothing" but did "conscientiously exchange bank notes for gold, and gold for bank notes, at the statutory rate." He invited a comparison with "our Federal Reserve, which prints acres of money, manipulates stock prices, suppresses interest rates — and can't seem to stop talking."

His point seems to have been proven truer by the month. It wouldn't surprise us were the verbal nature of the Bernanke dollar to be reckoned by historians as its defining trait. It seems, we said two years ago, to be the opposite of the gold standard, and, we added, "why not, since gold and silence are linked." In English, the first use of the phrase "silence is golden" turns out to have been in 1831 by the historian Thos. Carlyle, who translated the phrase from the German in Sartor Resartus, in which a character speaks of how "all the considerable men . . . forbore to babble of what they were creating and projecting." Speech is great, he wrote, "but not the greatest." He cited the Swiss aphorism, "Sprechen ist silbern, Schweigen ist golden*," which could be trans-configured as "speech is *money*, silence is golden" and adapted as the motto of the Bernanke era.

— September 18, 2013

---

* "Speech is silver, Silence is golden."

# Mr. Bernanke Gets the Jones

*C*hairman Bernanke: *"We could raise interest rates in 15 minutes if we have to. So there really is no problem with raising rates, tightening monetary policy, slowing the economy, reducing inflation at the appropriate time. Now that time is not now."*

*Scott Pelley, CBS 60 Minutes: "You have what degree of confidence in your ability to control this?"*

*Mr. Bernanke: "100%."*

\* \* \*

No doubt that exchange of 2010 will go down as the most famous of Mr. Bernanke's tenure as chairman of the Federal Reserve. It is the context in which to savor — if that is the word — the news of today's "surprise," as the headlines labeled the announcement of the Federal Open Market Committee's decision to keep on pumping. On the one hand the Fed has been signaling it's getting ready to start ending the regime of quantitative easing by which it has been trying to keep the sluggish economy from falling back into recession. On the other hand every time it wants to start tapering off it discovers it can't.

What did they used to call it in another context — the *jones*?

If Mr. Bernanke really is going to leave the chairmanship at the end of his second term — we have our doubts, but we're a minority of one on the point — he doesn't have much time to start doing what he once said he was 100% confident he could do. He would insist, of course, that there is no danger of inflation and that the Federal Open Market Committee just wants to make sure of things. Here it is, quoting today's Fed press release, in the micro-language known as Fedspeak:

"Taking into account the extent of federal fiscal retrenchment, the Committee sees the improvement in economic activity and labor market conditions since it began its asset purchase program a year ago as consistent with growing underlying strength in the broader economy. However, the Committee decided to await more evidence that progress will be sustained before adjusting the pace of its purchases. Accordingly, the Committee decided to continue purchasing additional agency mortgage-backed securities at a pace of $40 billion per month and longer-term Treasury securities at a pace of $45 billion per month."

One of the ways one can tell this was a surprise development is that value of the dollar started plunging almost immediately — and dramatically. Before the Fed trans-configured everyone's expectations, the value of the dollar was something like a 1,300th of an ounce of gold. By the mid-afternoon, it had plunged to but a 1,360th of an ounce of gold. We wouldn't want to make too much of minute-to-minute fluctuations in the value of the dollar, not in this age of fiat money. But we wouldn't want to make too little of it either, not in this age of fiat money.

The fact of the matter is that if Mr. Bernanke is nearing the end of his years as chairman of the Fed, he will be leaving his successor a dollar that is of less value than any other Fed chairman has ever left behind him. His defenders are going to spend the next generation trying to credit him with saving the country from another Great Depression. We would not want to suggest that monetary policy is never a tool that can be used in the face of a recession. And we don't blame Mr. Bernanke, or the Fed, so much as we blame the Congress.

But given the boastfulness with which Mr. Bernanke has advanced his aggressive expansion of his balance sheet, it's hard to put the today's action in anything but sharp relief. The derisiveness — the barely concealed contempt — with which Mr. Bernanke has testified before Congress in respect of measures that might have been recommended by, say, Presidents Harding or Coolidge, who so quickly turned around the near depression in which they made their accession to national leadership, well, let's just say it is off key. It puts a premium on the hearing that will be held in the senate in respect of the next Fed chairman.

— September 18, 2013

# What a Default Looks Like

What would happen if America defaults? Our prediction is that millions would be thrown out of work, housing prices would collapse, people's savings would be wiped out, and we would be forced to retreat in war. Congress would be deadlocked, foreign governments would be calling for the establishment of a new international reserve currency, the Middle East would be in flames, Communist China and Russia would be flexing their muscles, and the unemployment rate would soar and stay above 7% for four, five, or six years or even more, and the Federal Reserve would be looking irrelevant.

If that sounds a lot like the past six years, it's no coincidence. That's because we are living in the midst of a default. America defaulted on the dollar in the first decade of the 21st century, and we have been seeing what a default looks like ever since. On the day that President George W. Bush was sworn in as president, the value of the dollar stood at a 265th of an ounce of gold. Then, in the years of war that followed September 11, 2001, America defaulted. It allowed the value of the dollar it issues as its unit of account to collapse to less than, at the moment, a 1,300th of an ounce of gold and, at one point, to below a 1,800th of an ounce of gold.

That's a default. Oh, we understand that people don't call it a default. That's because we live in the age of fiat money. Under the law there is no definition of the dollar. If one takes a Federal Reserve note to the Treasury and asks for it to be redeemed, one gets another Federal Reserve note or metal slugs denominated in dollars or parts thereof and devoid of any specie, neither gold or silver. But the fact that people don't call it a default doesn't mean it isn't a default. We made this point before, in January 2011, when an aide to President Obama, Austan Goolsbee, asserted that a default would be "unprecedented."

There are serious observers who dispute that claim. Kenneth Rogoff and Carmen Reinhart, two distinguished economists, wrote a paper on defaults that has been widely quoted. They say it is possible to see America as a "sovereign default virgin." But that's only because they exclude "events such as the lowering of the gold content of the currency in 1933, or the suspension of convertibility in the nineteenth-century Civil War." James Grant, editor of the Interest Rate Observer, alerted us a while back to the fact that the phrase "American default " was current in the City of London after the gold devaluation of 1933. We would argue that America defaulted when, in 1971, President Nixon closed the gold window and ended the era of the Bretton Woods agreement.

In any event, there's no shortage of voices ridiculing how silly it would be for the government to leave the debt ceiling where it is and cut spending instead of borrowing more money. Warren Buffett predicted on CNBC today that on the question of default Washington would go right up to the point of "extreme idiocy." But in the age of default it's getting ever harder to see him as a sage. The value of a share of Berkshire Hathaway has plunged to 129.2 ounces of gold today from 197.8 ounces of gold a decade ago. Not that it hasn't invested in quality companies. But that's another feature of a default. In a default, even your great sages look less wise than they once did.

— October 3, 2013

# Wishing Mrs. Yellen Well

News that President Obama intends to nominate Janet Yellen to be the next chairman of the Federal Reserve sent us to see what we said about Ben Bernanke when, in October 2005, he was tapped to be the next chairman. "Mr. Bernanke is a cool customer," we wrote. "[H]e is not likely to be quite the relationship builder that Chairman Greenspan was. That's fine. A Fed with less personality and more predictability would spare us all some mortgage nightmares. America favors the rule of law over the rule of individual men. Let that doctrine hold for monetary policy as well."

As it would turn out, the Federal Reserve under Mr. Bernanke was about the rule of men — and women. The PhD standard is the phrase James Grant of the Interest Rate Observer likes to use. When Mr. Bernanke was put forward, the dollar was valued at a 495th of an ounce of gold. We hadn't yet issued our editorial called "The Bush Dollar," warning that the collapse of the greenback to below a 500th of an ounce of gold "is something Mr. Bush is going to have a hard time explaining to his grandchildren — not to mention the rest of us."

Our editorial expressed the hope that Mr. Bernanke would pay attention to the gold price. In the event, Mr. Bernanke paid little attention to the price of gold. He was derisive toward the notion that any attention should be paid to the price of gold. When he was asked about it by Congressman Paul Ryan, Mr. Bernanke allowed that he didn't "fully understand the movements in the price of gold" though he thought there was "a great deal of uncertainty and anxiety in financial markets right now and some people believe that holding gold will be a hedge . . . ."

A cool customer indeed, and we'll see in due course how Mrs. Yellen compares. We certainly wish her well. The hubbub that erupted over our editorial "The Female Dollar" obscured the fact that we made no endorsement, one way or another, between Mrs. Yellen and the other named contender,

President Summers. She is famously focused on jobs as much as any other measure. But in our view there was little difference between Mrs. Yellen and Mr. Summers, in the sense that they are both partisans of a fiat money system that, in our opinion, must be reformed — by which we mean abandoned — before real progress will come.

It is hard to see Mrs. Yellen pushing for the kind of reconsideration of the Federal Reserve that we would like to see the Congress under-take as the central bank begins its second century. The initiative for that, if it is to come at all, is going to have to come from the Congress or from a president of America who thinks the way the founding presidents of America thought. Meantime we can't help but note that Mrs. Yellen's famous speech warning of a housing bubble, for which she gets much credit for being the first of the Fed governors to issue such a warning, was made in 2006 — well after the value of the dollar had plunged to below a 500th of an ounce of gold.

— October 9, 2013

# Lagarde Lectures Her Owner

Of all the ironical elements of the debt crisis none quite matches the lecture delivered by the managing director of the International Monetary Fund, Christine Lagarde, to the Fund's largest owner.* Madame Lagarde went on "Meet the Press" to deliver the message that she and the Fund's smaller owners want America to borrow more money. She was fresh from the meeting in Washington where leaders of the World Bank and the IMF, as it was put by the New York Times, "pleaded, warned and cajoled" the United States to raise its debt ceiling. If America is drunk on debt, Madame Lagarde is lecturing on the virtues of Calvados.

There was a time when the cajoling of the IMF would have been aimed at convincing countries to live within their means. That was back in the days when there was a *raison d'etre* for the IMF, which is one of the Bretton Woods institutions. The Bretton Woods system "dissolved," to use the IMF's own choice of words, between 1968 and 1973. It's been hard to see a logic for the institution ever since, but never harder than in the current crisis when what the IMF ought to be doing, if it ought to be doing anything, is trying to get the heavily indebted countries to trans-control their spending.

David Gregory — we're actually a fan of the Meet the Press maestro — touched on this only glancingly. Not that he's alone. No doubt he was hearing little of this from his sources on the Hill or in the administration. It's like the debt crisis is being managed by people who were born yesterday. There is no one on duty who was present at the creation, to use a phrase made famous in a different context, because there was, in the wake of the collapse of Bretton Woods, nothing created. Unless one calls a system of fiat money something that was created. That would be, though, oxymoronic, wouldn't it? Like saying a vacuum was created. Or anarchy was created.

It's all enough to put us in mind of a new kind of grand bargain. Instead of a budget deal, America could step up to monetary reform. It could stop all the pretense that there'll be a default. What's needed is recognition that the default already happened. It happened in 1971. It happened again in the past decade. The value of the dollar, once regulated by the Congress by law at a 35th of an ounce of gold, has see-sawed wildly, eventually plunging to below a 1,900th of an ounce of gold. It is, at the moment, lurking under a 1,250th of an ounce of gold. The troubles we've been going through, in other words, are not the forerunner of default. They are the *consequences* of default. When that becomes clear, the road ahead will become clear, and America will be spared the hectoring of the IMF that it created.

— October 13, 2013

---

\* America owns a larger quota in the IMF than Japan, Germany, and France combined.

# Rand Paul v. Janet Yellen

News that Senator Rand Paul is threatening to block the promotion of Vice Chairman Yellen to be the next chairman of the Federal Reserve holds the promise of one of his patented filibusters. It is not our purpose here to oppose the elevation of Mrs. Yellen to the top job at the nation's central bank. Our view is that the monetary problem is much deeper than which Keynesian leads the system. If there is a chance through the use of parliamentary maneuvering within the Senate to put the issue of monetary reform before the American people, however, let us just say we're all for it.

That is, we favor Mr. Paul using every device that the long traditions of the Senate make available. What he wants, according to the Huffington Post quoting CNBC, is a vote on his Federal Reserve Transparency Act. The New York Sun was, so far as we are aware, the first newspaper to endorse this measure, which would require a full audit of the Fed of the kind for which Congressman Ron Paul, who is the senator's father and is now retired, started agitating years ago. The way the Huffington Post puts it is that the bill would "eliminate current audit restrictions placed on the Government Accountability Office and require the Fed to undergo a complete audit by a specific deadline."

An audit of the Fed of the kind for which the Pauls are asking is long overdue. It would involve not just an accounting of the institution's balance sheet and gold holdings but also an examination of how the Federal Reserve System operates, of its foreign entanglements, and of its monetary *philosophy*. The Fed's most private records and correspondence, one can imagine, would have to be opened to auditors, along with its un-redacted minutes. It strikes us that this is not too much to ask of the Senate as the Fed commences its second century.

The House, after all, has already spoken. It took a while. Congressman Paul started agitating for an audit of the Fed years ago. At first it seemed like a marginal quest. Then an audit measure was moved that wasn't the real deal. Dr. Paul actually opposed it. Then, in July of last year, the house passed an Audit the Fed Bill backed by Ron Paul and did so by an overwhelming bipartisan vote, 327 to 98. Reuters quoted Chairman Bernanke as calling it a "nightmare scenario."

Reuters, however, said the vote "showed bipartisan support in the House for greater scrutiny of the U.S. central bank's powers." Failure of the measure in the Senate can be laid at the feet of the majority leader, Senator Reid, who supposedly once supported an audit but changed his mind, throwing into sharp relief the question of what are the Democrats so all-fired afraid. Since then the logic of an audit, of transparency, has become only more and more clear.

This is particularly true in light of the failure of the Congress to enact the kind of centennial review of the Federal Reserve Act that has been sought by the chairman of the Joint Economic Committee, Kevin Brady of Texas. We are just at a junction at which it is time to look at the Fed, which Congress established a century ago on one over-riding condition — that nothing in the Federal Reserve Act would be construed as abandoning the convertibility of the dollar into gold.

At the time the value of a dollar was approximately a 20th of an ounce of gold. Today it's not worth a 67th of that, and the Drudge Report is headlining an editorial in the London Financial Times about how America is a superpower "at risk of slippage" and how in respect of the dollar "underlying confidence is shaken." All of which is to say, it's hard to imagine a more timely moment for Senator Paul to go to the mat for his Federal Reserve Transparency Act. If Vice Chairman Yellen turns out to be against a such an audit, the first question the Senate can ask her is what is she trying to hide.

— October 25, 2013

# Debt and Slavery

Governor Sarah Palin is in hot water again, this time for likening our national debt to slavery. She did this in a speech Saturday at Iowa. "Our free stuff today is being paid for by taking money from our children and borrowing from China," she was quoted by the Register in Des Moines as saying. "When that money comes due — and this isn't racist — but it'll be like slavery when that note is due."

This was greeted with a flurry of snide comments, including the Reverend Al Sharpton of MSNBC, who suggested that Mrs. Palin was racist, despite her attempt to deflect criticism anticipating that charge and denying it in advance. The Daily Beast suggested the ex-governor "must not have seen '12 Years a Slave' yet." And there was a comment by a writer named Jenny Kutner, who reckons that Mrs. Palin seems to be "confused about United States history."

Ms. Kutner's piece caught our eye because it appeared at Salon.com, which as recently as January ran out a long dispatch under this headline: "Has America become a slave to its own debt?" The piece, by Steve Fraser, editor at large of New Labor Forum magazine, ran to more than 4,000 words. A sub-headline summarized the piece this way: "For a small minority, it's a blessing; for others, a curse" and went on to refer to "Jekyll-and-Hyde relationship with debt."

"Credit has come to function as a 'plastic safety net' in a world of job insecurity, declining state support, and slow-motion economic growth, especially among the elderly, young adults, and low-income families," Mr. Fraser wrote. "More than half the pre-tax income of these three groups goes to servicing debt. Nowadays, however, the 'company store' is headquartered on Wall Street."

"Debt," he wrote, "is driving this system of auto-cannibalism which, by every measure of social wellbeing, is relentlessly turning a developed country into an underdeveloped one." Mr. Fraser writes for a journal whose Web site is published by the City University of New York and which is billed as a place for labor and its allies to test and debate new ideas. He concluded by posing the question: "Is a political resistance to debt servitude once again imaginable?"

We happen to think it's a good question, and it strikes us that one person Mr. Fraser could talk to about it would be a certain ex-governor of Alaska. Mrs. Palin, after all, is one of the few governors of our time who is a card-carrying union member and who has seemed to appreciate the role that organized labor can play in our battle of ideas. Our guess is that he would find Mrs. Palin a lot smarter than the Left likes to picture her as being.

— November 11, 2013

# Yellen Strikes Out

Vice Chairman Yellen's testimony before the Senate this morning moves us to oppose her confirmation to succeed Chairman Bernanke at the Federal Reserve. We don't mind saying it's an odd position for us, since we have great regard for her capacity as a forecaster, her character, and her comportment. She displays none of condescension that Mr. Bernanke so often allowed to show (we once expressed surprise that he wasn't held in contempt). What transports us into the opposition is Mrs. Yellen's truculence on the issue of auditing the Fed.

This came into view after a discussion of the central bank's regulatory role. Senator Vitter asked about what he called "true openness" at the Fed. He asked whether Mrs. Yellen would support Senate 209, a bill introduced by Senator Rand Paul and known as the "Federal Reserve Transparency Act of 2013." It is the Senate's companion to the audit-the-Fed measure offered in the House by Senator Paul's father, Congressman Ron Paul, and passed overwhelmingly on a bipartisan vote.

Mrs. Yellen insisted that she supports "transparency and openness on the part of the Fed." She claimed that in terms of the "range of information and the timeliness of that information, we are one of the most transparent central banks in the world." That's not only irrelevant but wan. She then declared that she would not support "a requirement — any requirement — that would diminish the independence of the Federal Reserve in implementing, and deciding on implementing, monetary policy."

"For 50 years," Mrs. Yellen averred, "Congress has recognized that there should be an exception to GAO ability to audit the Fed to avoid any political interference in monetary policy." She said she believes that "allowing a central bank to be independent in formulating monetary policy is critical to assuring markets and the public that we will achieve price stability, and I would be very concerned about legislation that would subject the Fed to short-term political pressures that could interfere with that independence."

Mrs. Yellen may be no different than Mr. Bernanke, nor than most, if not all, of the chairmen who have come before him. All the more maddening is the fact that the committee proceeded to drop the matter. Mr. Vitter surely gets the issue, or he wouldn't have raised it and co-sponsored Senate 209. But his colleagues made no follow-up about the Constitution of the United States. Not one senator who serves on the Banking Committee stood up for the prerogatives of the Congress. What is the Congress, chopped liver?

What needs to be confronted is the scandal of Federal Reserve independence. Where in the Constitution does it say that monetary policy is supposed — or permitted — to be independent of politics? If the Founders of America had wanted the monetary power to be given to a body independent of politics, they could have given it to the Army or the Navy or the Supreme Court. But they sat down in Philadelphia and gave the power to "coin money and regulate the value thereof and of foreign coin" to, in the Congress, the single most political institution in the entire constitutional system.

So where in the world does Mrs. Yellen come off lecturing the Congress on the need for independence? It's not as if independence and opacity have produced much in the way of results. The value of the dollar has collapsed to levels that would have appalled not only the Founders of America but the Congress that founded the Federal Reserve. Even after rising a bit in the past year or so, the value of the dollar is still, at a 1,250th of an ounce of gold, less than half of its value on the day Mr. Bernanke acceded to the chairmanship and a shadow of what it was when the Fed was founded.

Mr. Vitter speaks for a faction in the upper house that understands the need to open up the Fed to an audit. This isn't only about, say, what gold it holds in its vaults. It also involves how it works, what its un-redacted minutes say, and what it has been doing overseas. These are not questions on which it makes any kind of constitutional sense to keep Congress in doubt. There is legislation before the Congress —

introduced by the Joint Economic Committee — to review the record of the whole first century of the Fed. The right move for Mrs. Yellen would have been to welcome to this kind of inspection. The right move for the Senate would be to hold out for a chairman who is prepared welcome an audit.

— November 14, 2013

# Radioactive Yellen

It's starting to look like Janet Yellen's confirmation as chairman of the Federal Reserve may have to be pushed through under Harry Reid's "nuclear option." The outspoken fan of inflation comes up for a vote on Monday. Yet a cable from the American Principles Project, which is one of the tribunes of sound money, reports that in a test vote two weeks ago there were 34 "no" votes, "with at least two others not voting." So it may yet be that under traditional rules Mrs. Yellen couldn't win cloture.

This is no small thing as the Federal Reserve sets outs on its second century. There has never been a nominee facing this kind of resistance, and it's astounding in a Senate controlled by the party that holds the presidency. The liveliest opposition heretofore was to Chairman Bernanke, who was opposed by 30 senators (11 of them Democrats) when he was put up by President Obama for a second term as chairman. Mrs. Yellen is even more a friend of inflation than the chairman she'd succeed.

Feature the opposition she faces. The 34 "no" votes in American Principles's test included Ayotte of New Hampshire, Barrasso and Enzi of Wyoming, Blunt of Missouri, Boozman and McCain of Arizona, Burr of North Carolina, Crapo of Idaho, Coats of Indiana, Cochran and Wicker of Mississippi, Cornyn and Cruz of Texas, Fischer of Nebraska, Graham and Scott of South Carolina, Grassley of Iowa, Heller of Nevada, Hoeven of North Dakota, Inhofe of Oklahoma, and Johnson of Wisconsin.

Also included are Lee of Utah, McConnell and Paul of Kentucky, Moran of Kansas, Portman of Ohio, Risch of Idaho, Roberts of Kansas, Rubio of Florida, Sessions and Shelby of Alabama, Thune of South Dakota, Toomey of Pennsylvania, and Vitter of Louisiana. Not voting in the test but probably opposed were Senators Flake of Arizona and Johanns of Nebraska. Not voting and maybe against her were Senators Alexander of Tennessee and Chambliss and Isakson of Georgia. Senator Manchin of West Virginia voted for cloture but is understood to oppose confirmation.

If this holds up, it's possible that there could be 40 votes opposed to confirming Mrs. Yellen. This is against a history in which all confirmations of Fed chairmen save for the second of Bernanke and Volcker were passed by unanimous or near-unanimous Senates. If Senator Reid has to use the nuclear option to get Mrs. Yellen through, it would be, in essence, a measure of the radioactivity of the Fed. Even if the opposition is under 40 votes, it is shaping up as a sign that we are not at the end of the debate over monetary policy but at the beginning. One power yet to be heard is the bond market, a fact of which we were reminded in an important op-ed piece in this morning's Wall Street Journal. The piece is by the American Priniciples Project's chairman, Sean Fieler. He notes that it wasn't just Democrats' losses in the 1994 mid-term that doomed Hillarycare but the "power of the bond market." He argued the muscle of the bond market is going to be needed to roll back the federal over-reach of the Obama years.

The bond market's silence so far, he suggests, has been a product of bond-buying done by the Fed itself and championed by Mrs. Yellen. "So long as a threat of the Federal Reserve's bond buying looms, even rising bond yields are unlikely to produce discipline in Washington," Mr. Fieler writes in the Journal. He wants the Senate to condition its confirmation of Mrs. Yellen on a resolution for capping the Fed's balance sheet at $4.5 trillion cap and an unwinding of what he calls "the Fed's monetary adventurism."

Far-fetched? So was Congressman Ron Paul's bill calling for an audit of the Fed. For years it sagged in the House. Then, a year and a half ago, it suddenly passed the House by an over-whelming bi-partisan majority. It's a reminder that while the campaign for sound money may enjoy support of but a minority of the Senate, things can change. It will be something for Mrs. Yellen and the other governors of the Fed to remember no matter to what device Mr. Reid has to resort to get her confirmed as the chairman of our central bank.

— January 3, 2014

# The Senate Awakes

The decision of Senator Cornyn to get behind the idea of a Centennial Monetary Commission should put a bit of a spring in the step of the heroic band on the Hill that is nursing the idea of monetary reform. The legislation comes out of the Joint Economic Committee, which is chaired by Congressman Kevin Brady of Texas. The measure has something like 32 sponsors in the House, and they have been hoping for a serious figure to get behind it in the upper chamber. They've landed a terrific ally in Mr. Cornyn.

It happens that this newspaper was the first to endorse such a commission, which would undertake take a strategic review of the Federal Reserve as it begins its second century. Given the astonishing role the Fed has played in our national life, not to mention in the economy of the rest of the world, one would think that a centennial review would be a lead pipe cinch. Particularly because there has been such a radical expansion of the Fed's balance sheet in the current crisis.

Yet the sponsors of the Centennial Monetary Commission have found slow going, not only in the Congress but, save for the Wall Street Journal, in the big newspapers. It seems that the entire liberal establishment is determined to get through this current crisis without seriously exploring the idea of whether monetary policy — and even monetary structure — might be one of the culprits behind the fact that the Great Recession has consumed the first three quarters of the very presidency in which they'd invested so much of their hopes.

What is at the bottom of this blitheness? Is it the vested interest in inflation in a nation whose government owes so much money? Is it the heat that the Fed has taken away from a Congress to which the Constitution grants the enumerated power of coining money and regulating its value? Is it but partisan politics that makes the Democrats so skittish of monetary reform? Is it the failure of Governor Romney, who was given a platform calling for the establishment of a new gold commission, to use the plank in an imaginative and convincing way?

Whatever the worries, the Centennial Monetary Commission ought to be just the ticket. It was conceived by the Joint Economic Committee as what Mr. Brady once called a "brutally bipartisan" effort. It would have a broad brief, looking not only at the gold standard, rules-based policy making, and other issues, but also at the structure of the Federal Reserve. Yet it's not a project of radicals like, say, the Audit the Fed campaign of Ron Paul, a campaign we also endorsed. It is a project of honest, centrist, constitutionally-mindful reformers. It more than deserves a lively sponsorship in the Senate.

— January 9, 2014

# Fiat Wages

What a remarkable thing that President Obama delivered a state of the Union message on the 100th anniversary of the founding of the Federal Reserve and made not one mention of monetary policy. He certainly had an opportunity in respect of wages. "Today," said the President in his State of the Union message, "the federal minimum wage is worth about 20% less it was when Ronald Reagan first stood here." But wait, wasn't the minimum wage $3.35 an hour throughout Reagan's two terms? Isn't it now $7.25 an hour? How does *that* add up to a drop in value by 20%? The president glided right past that point.

By our lights, the president owed the country an explanation. The editor of The New York Sun, writing in the New York Post a column from which this editorial is adapted, noted that when the Federal Reserve Act was passed a century ago Congress refused to agree to a Federal Reserve until language was included that would mandate protecting the convertibility of the dollar into gold. That law unraveled in a series of defaults that started in the Great Depression and ended under President Richard Nixon. By the mid-1970s, America had moved to a fiat currency, meaning a dollar that is not redeemable by law in anything of value.

The minimum-wage crisis is a sign that fiat money is not working for working men and women. The sad fact is that they are being paid fiat wages. It's not, after all, that the *nominal* minimum wage has failed to go up (it's been raised seven times since Reagan). It's that the value of the dollar has collapsed. Even after strengthening somewhat in the past year, the greenback has today a value of barely a 1,250th of an ounce of gold, a staggering plunge from an 853rd of an ounce on the day Mr. Obama took office and a 265th of an ounce on the day George W. Bush acceded to the presidency. Gold isn't the only way to measure a dollar; Obama appears to be using the consumer price index to reckon the 20% decline in the value of the minimum wage since the Reagan years is serious.

Mr. Obama, in any event, endorsed a proposal by Senator Harkin and Congressman George Miller, Democrats of Iowa and California respectively, to raise the minimum wage by a staggering 39%, to $10.10 an hour. What's the point of raising the minimum wage if you're going to run down the value of the dollar? Today a person has to work 173 hours at the minimum wage to earn an ounce of gold; by the end of Reagan's presidency, it took only 125 hours. The Harkin-Miller bill would get closer to the Reagan years. But how long would that last? How is a person to know *what* his wages will be worth if the dollar is always jumping around? Banks and businesses are beset with the same problem. Wouldn't it be better to focus less on the minimum wage and more on stabilizing the dollar, just as Congress insisted when it set up the Fed?

It's five years now that Mr. Obama has been in office, and he has avoided the monetary question at every turn. His first Fed chairman, Ben Bernanke, is leaving us a dollar valued at less than half of what it was when he became chairman. Janet Yellen, who's set to succeed Mr. Bernanke, is promising policies that could drive the value of the dollar down further. We understand that it's not entirely their fault. In 1978, Congress passed the Humphrey-Hawkins law, which gave the Federal Reserve a dual mandate. The Fed must, on the one hand, protect the value of the dollar; on the other, it has to try to bring about full employment. It puts the Fed brass in a devil of a bind.

Even the liberals foresaw trouble. When the bill was passed, the New York Times warned that the law "would play a cruel hoax on the hard-core unemployed, holding before them the hope — but not the reality — of a job." At the time, unemployment was 6.1%. It has been above 8% for much of Mr. Obama's presidency and above 7% for almost all of it. Isn't it time Congress looked at Humphrey-Hawkins and other laws that govern the Fed to see whether they helped cause the Great Recession? That would have been a presidential-scale challenge for the Congress. The legislature's own Joint Economic Committee has proposed a bi-partisan Centennial Monetary Commission to review the first century of the Federal Reserve. Mr. Obama himself says that Americans are tired of "stale political arguments." If so, rescuing the dollar would be the place to start.

— January 30, 2014

# A Gift to Janet Yellen

As Ben Bernanke rides off into the sunset let us reflect on the dollar he has left his countrymen. The value of the greenback on the day he acceded to the chairmanship of the Federal Reserve was a 568th of an ounce of gold. The dollar he has left us was worth on his last day at office a 1,251st of an ounce of gold. If one accepts this as the best proxy measure of Mr. Bernanke's performance, it would make his record the second worst of any Fed chairman since the central bank came into being exactly a century ago.

We fully comprehend that there is no agreement that the value of the dollar is the right way to measure the performance of Mr. Bernanke or any other Fed chairman. We also have been made aware by Professor Krugman that there is no agreement that the value of the greenback is best measured in ounces of gold. But this editorial is appearing in The New York Sun, under whose flag an opinion has been sketched on this head going back to before the birth of Mr. Bernanke or, for that matter, the Fed, and it's our standard.

By this standard Mr. Bernanke's job performance was the second worst in the history of the central bank. The worst was that of Arthur Burns. It was the haplessness of the pipe-puffing professor to have been in office when, in 1971, President Nixon closed the so-called gold window, under which foreign governments were supposed to be able to redeem their dollars at a 35th of an ounce of gold. By the time he slipped from office, in 1978, the value of the dollar had needled more than 80% to less than a 175th of an ounce of gold.

That was under President Carter. But in one of the reminders that democracy is full of surprises, the weakest of presidents turned around and handed up one of the strongest Fed chairman, Paul Volcker, who, in a demonstration of political character, made it his business to wring consumer price index inflation out of the economy. He was blessed to have a partner in President Reagan, who led the fiscal and regulatory revolution that enabled Mr. Volcker's rescue of the dollar to succeed.

Rescue in the CPI sense, mind you. The actual and constitutional value of the dollar — that is, its value measured in gold — plunged 38.7% during Mr. Volcker's reign at the Fed, to less than a 461st of an ounce. It was the fourth worst record of any Fed governor. The third worst was that of Eugene Black, who was chairman during the depths of the Great Depression and on whose watch the value of the dollar nose-dived by more than 40%. The value of the dollar fell but 18.8% under the oft-over-maligned Alan Greenspan. Under all the other Fed chairmen, the value of the dollar plunged zero percent.

So let us confine this editorial to a simple point, which is that Mr. Bernanke's last dollar is a gift to his successor, Janet Yellen. She has inherited responsibility for a dollar that is in worse shape than any dollar ever handed to any holder of the chair of the Federal Reserve. It is a situation that would have left the Founders of America humiliated, just as they were by the collapse of the monetary scrip known as the continental dollar, by which they financed the Revolution. She has the chance to become the first Federal Reserve chairman in history under whom the value of the dollar increased.

— February 3, 2014

# Rand Paul's Next Filibuster?

The Centennial Monetary Commission, which a number of us reckon is the best vehicle for nursing the idea of monetary reform in the Congress, just picked up another sponsor in the Senate. Rand Paul of Kentucky has joined Senator Cornyn of Texas, who was the first senator to get behind the bill as a sponsor. The measure, which would set up a bipartisan group to take a look at what the Federal Reserve has wrought in its first century, was launched in the House by the chairman of the Joint Economic Committee, Kevin Brady, also of Texas, and has picked up more than two dozen sponsors there.

The accession of Dr. Paul to this campaign is good news, because the measure needs to be nursed in the Senate. Govtrack.us, a Web site that trans-scopes the prospects for legislation, puts the chances of the measure "getting past committee" at 1% and of being enacted at "0%." To which we can but say "no guts, no glory." In other words, it's a situation made for Rand Paul's capacity to focus on the pith of a political situation and to view things from the perspective of the United States Constitution. We are at the beginning of a long educational campaign to bring this issue to the fore.

Not that logic is lacking. What an extraordinary situation the Fed is in as it begins its second century. Its new chairman, Janet Yellen, is famous for attaching a priority to the second of the Fed's two mandates, namely the mandate to work toward full employment. We are approaching the three-quarters mark of a presidency, in that of Barack Obama, that has been ruined by the inability of either the Federal Reserve, the executive branch, or the Congress to bring down unemployment below what it was when the so-called "dual mandate" was established.

In that campaign, despite a multi-trillion-dollar expansion of the Fed's balance sheet, it's been six loooong years of zilch. With unemployment in a reduced work force now edging below 7% no doubt the administration is going to try to credit the Fed. But at what cost? And when will we know it? Chairman Bernanke's most famous utterance was his vow — in response to a question from Scott Pelley of CBS — that "We could raise interest rates in 15 minutes if we have to." We wish Mr. Bernanke a long and happy life, but predict that will be his epitaph. It seems that every time the Fed wants to end its quantitative easing, there's some new excuse. The latest is the confounded Europeans.

Out of this, we believe, will emerge the logic of monetary reform and the progressive nature of the idea of sound money. At the end of the day, this can only come through Congress. It created the Fed. It created the dual mandate. Congress is the only recipient of the grant of power to coin money and regulate the value thereof and of foreign coin. If reform can come only from Congress, the measure onto which Rand Paul has just signed is the likeliest vehicle. Not the only one but the likeliest one. One thing Dr. Paul has already shown is that he is a genius for putting an issue before the public.

— February 7, 2014

# Janet Yellen's Job

The question we will be listening for when Janet Yellen goes before Congress has to do with jobs. She is famous for her focus on the second part of the Fed's dual mandate. The first mandate is price stability and the second is jobs. How does she feel the Fed has done these five years? It has expanded its balance sheet into the trillions. It has picked up more than $2 trillion of the federal government's own debt. Yet the unemployment rate is still higher than it was when Congress put through the jobs mandate in the first place.

To us that's an amazing fact. We've mopped this floor several times, but just to run the buffer over it once more: The dual mandate was legislated in 1978 by the 95th Congress. It gave the measure the name Humphrey Hawkins, in honor of its sponsor in the House, Augustus Hawkins, and in the Senate, Vice President Humphrey. The short name of the bill is particularly useful not only because it reminds us of the illustrious liberals who concocted it but because the official "long-title" of the bill is:

"An Act to translate into practical reality the right of all Americans who are able, willing, and seeking to work to full opportunity for useful paid employment at fair rates of compensation; to assert the responsibility of the Federal Government to use all practicable programs and policies to promote full employment, production, and real income, balanced growth, adequate productivity growth, proper attention to national priorities, and reasonable price stability; to require the President each year to set forth explicit short-term and medium-term economic goals; to achieve a better integration of general and structural economic policies; and to improve the coordination of economic policymaking within the Federal Government."

It happens that the New York Sun ran that title through one of our niftiest contraptions, the "Long-Title Legislative Compar-o-Graf." It is an old vacuum tube model, but it still works. It turns out that the long-title of Humphrey Hawkins is one of the ten-most divorced from reality of all known pieces of modern legislation. Even, as we've noted before, the New York Times called it a "cruel hoax" on the American worker. It neglected to mention that it has made a fool of the Federal Reserve and the 95th United States Congress, both at the same time.

Now it may be that Mrs. Yellen is going to try to claim victory for Humphrey Hawkins and the Fed by pointing out that recent numbers have brought unemployment down below 7%. It is still above the 5.8% at which it stood when Humphrey Hawkins was passed. Even after all the trillions by which the Fed balance sheet was expanded, all the deficits Congress has run, all the columns Paul Krugman has written extolling Lord Keynes, even after all the speeches President Obama has made, the unemployment rate is still above what it was when the dual mandate was passed. What in the world will Janet Yellen say?

— February 11, 2014

# Yellen and De Gaulle

"Yellen Snubs emerging nation pleas" is the headline that catches our eye in the wake of the first testimony before Congress of the new chairman of the Federal Reserve. It was streamed across the top of the Financial Times. The pleas Mrs. Yellen was snubbing were over "effects of 'taper,'" meaning over the slowdown in the pace at which the Fed is pursuing its quantitative easing. The FT quotes India's central bank governor, Raghuram Rajan, as saying the Americans are "washing their hands" of emerging markets.

Far be it from us to worry about the rest of the world (we'd be happy, we sometimes joke, to see it run by an American colonel), but we happen to be sympathetic to this complaint. It's bad enough that we Americans have to make our economic decisions by triangulating off the "forward guidance" of a pyramid of PhDs at the Federal Reserve. Imagine how galling it must be to the editors of the Financial Times and the rest of the Europeans, Africans, Asians, and South Americans.

This is a moment to remember Charles de Gaulle. In February 1965, at the height of his stature, the president of the French Fifth Republic held a famous press conference in the Elysee Palace. He gathered 1,000 journalists in a room and sat them in gilded chairs. He himself sat, we noted when we first wrote about this moment, at a cloth-covered table in front of the newspapermen and women and warned that the dollar had lost its transcendent value and called for a return to the gold standard.

The virtue of the gold standard, in the eyes of De Gaulle, was that the system was not particular to any one country but imposed the same measure of value and thus of discipline on all of them. Time (magazine) stood still in amazement: "Perhaps never before had a chief of state launched such an open assault on the monetary power of a friendly nation," it said. Less than half a year later, President Lyndon Johnson signed the 1965 coinage act, beginning the formal debasement of American money.

Janet Yellen doesn't want to talk about De Gaulle's point. The political wise men and women fail to reference it (the FT itself often mocks the gold standard even though its editors front the very phenomenon that galled De Gaulle). Chairman Bernanke didn't want to talk about it. Congress is all too happy to delegate the power it was granted in the Constitution to regulate the value of our coin (and foreign coin). So the emerging nations are the losers, for now. When they finish emerging, though, watch out.

— February 13, 2014

# Will Europe Follow the Fed?

Suddenly all eyes are on Europe. The New York Times is out with an editorial today warning of deflation on the continent. The Sulzberger family wants the value of European money to fall rather than rise; weirdly, it wishes the same for American money. The Wall Street Journal is out with a much savvier piece, by the editor of Die Zeit, Josef Joffe. He focuses on the drama over whether the European Central Bank really has the power it has claimed — but hasn't yet used — to buy up government bonds on the open market through a maneuver called "Outright Monetary Transactions." The matter is now before the European Court of Justice. The Financial Times has been on the edge of a nervous breakdown over this for weeks.

Here at the Sun, we're rather enjoying the spectacle. It's another chapter in the epic experiment with fiat money. We're looking forward to seeing what the red-robed judges at Luxembourg decide in respect of whether the European Central Bank should be able to buy government debt this way. Wouldn't it be something if the Europeans struck a note of greater probity than what is permitted here in America? Supposedly, our central bank is prohibited from buying bonds from the United States Treasury. Yet its vast campaign of quantitative easing accomplished what Mario Draghi is claiming the authority to do. The Federal Reserve now holds more than $2 trillion of its own government's debt. No wonder Congress is in a rush to borrow yet more.

Is that the way the Europeans want to go? Mr. Joffe, whom the Sun switchboard reached by radio in the Alps, is confident the European court will give Mr. Draghi the authority he seeks. All the more we find ourselves reflecting on the fact that there was a time when Europe was the leader in the idea of honest money. There were the Austrian Economists. There were others in both Britain and France. There were political leaders with the vision to see the consequences for small and medium-sized countries of a profligate country holding the sole reserve power. DeGaulle, whom we wrote about the other day in our editorial "Yellen and DeGaulle," was the most blunt. He had Jacques Rueff, an economist who stood for both European integration *and* honest money. He also served, between 1952 and 1962, on the European Court of Justice. It — we all — could certainly use him now.

— February 18, 2014

# Rescuing the Stimulus

Paul Krugman has a column out about how President Obama's economic program was a political disaster because of the "perception that stimulus failed." It reminds us of Mark Twain's jibe about Wagner's music being "better than it sounds." At least Twain was aware of the circularity of his famous wise crack.* Professor Krugman seems oblivious to the fact that, in the stimulus racket, success is nothing if it's not perceived.

Mr. Krugman reckons the aim of the stimulus was to "provide a temporary boost" to the economy "both by having the government directly spend more and by using tax cuts and public aid to boost family incomes, inducing more private spending." That may have been *his* logic. But it wasn't the New York Sun's. We comprehend he wasn't addressing the Sun, but the stimulus we favored was tax cuts, deregulation, lowering restrictions on trade and immigration, and honest money.

Opponents of the stimulus, Mr. Krugman insists, "argued vociferously" that outlays in excess of revenues "would send interest rates skyrocketing, 'crowding out' private spending." If that argument was made, it wasn't made by conservatives of the ilk we favor. What we've been arguing for was a return to constitutional money. Then lenders would know what value they would get when loans were repaid.

We have, in any event, been opposed to lifting the debt ceiling at any stage of the current crisis, preferring instead that the government try as a strategy for staying within legislated debt limits the novel idea of reducing spending. It is not, by our lights, the government's moral responsibility to provide work. Its responsibility is to use logic in its tax policies, prudent in its outlays, and integrity — specie — in its monetary policy.

Mr. Krugman trans-supposes that the travail of the European austerity economies demolishes the case against the stimulus. He forgets to factor all the socialism in Europe. How can one have austerity in a socialist economy? Once you have socialism, spending cutbacks by the government merely ensure socialism's sadness. That's the problem in Greece and the other European regimes. And here all too much of late.

Which brings us back to the problem of perception. The problem of perception goes back to legal tender fiat money. Feature our favorite example, which was when the president gave his radio address on the high price of gasoline. The actual value of gasoline, measured in gold, was less than half of what it had been but four years earlier. It wasn't the gas that was up, but the dollar that was down.

There's Mr. Krugman's perception problem. We comprehend that our greenbacks have gained *something* in value in the past year or so, but the value of the dollar began sagging again within minutes of Chairman Yellen delivering her first testimony has head of the Federal Reserve, and, in any event, the value of the dollar is little more than half of what it was when the stimulus program began.

Mr. Krugman's column is but one of a raft of pieces we can expect trying to rescue the reputation of the stimulus program. The next day the Times issued a long editorial called "What the Stimulus Accomplished," ruing how "Republicans were successful in discrediting the very idea that federal spending can boost the economy and raise employment." It's tied to the release by the White House of the impact five years on of the American Recovery and Reinvestment Act. The basic idea is that it's better than it sounds.

— February 23, 2014

---

* Twain appropriated it from a humorist named Edgar Wilson Nye.

# God and Bitcoins

One of our favorite japes is about the group of scientists who figure out the secret to life — a way to make a human being from nothing but dirt. When they've worked it all out, they are so excited they go directly to God to announce their discovery that He is no longer necessary. He appears a bit surprised, but they offer to demonstrate. He nods. One of the scientists bends down and scoops up a fistful of dirt.

"Oh, no," God exclaims. "You've got to make your own dirt."

This is how we feel about bitcoins. The idea that one can make money — specie — out of thin air just strikes us as illogical. The *money* is gold and silver. Bitcoins, as we comprehend the whole business, could be a form of currency. But money is a different matter. It's not merely the scarcity of gold and silver that make them money. It's their innate qualities, which have endured over millennia.

What put us in mind of this today is Newsweek's scoop in tracking down the founder of bitcoins, Satoshi Nakamoto. It found him standing shoeless at the end of his "sunbaked driveway" looking "timorous" and "annoyed," it says. It describes Mr. Nakamoto as "tacitly acknowledging his role in the Bitcoin project" by looking down and "staring at the pavement" as he "categorically refuses" to answer its questions. "I am no longer involved in that and I cannot discuss it," Newsweek quotes him as saying.

If Newsweek asked him about gold, the story has no mention of it. Yet our own sense of bitcoins is that they are a commentary on — a phenomenon of — the age of fiat money. They are similar to the money being issued by the Federal Reserve, in that they are electronic files generated on and transmitted via computers. Federal Reserve notes are redeemable, as a matter of statute, in lawful money, meaning other electronic files or paper scrip or base metal slugs.

One of the big weaknesses of government money is that it is legal tender — that is, it must be accepted as payment for a debt, public or private. This is one of the features of government money that prevents the discovery of its value: One doesn't actually have any idea of what would be the value of a government dollar were one not forced to accept it as a matter of law. Can anyone imagine that were a Federal Reserve Note to lose legal tender status it would go *up* in value?

In this one sense, bitcoins are at a relative advantage over Federal Reserve Money, or what Lawrence Parks of the Foundation for the Advancement of Monetary Education calls "irredeemable electronic paper ticket currency." For the acceptance of Bitcoins is purely voluntary. They are not legal tender, and if someone tried to pay his taxes or mortgage with them, neither the government nor the bank would be required to accept.

Nor would they, incidentally, be *required* to accept gold or silver. This is one of the bizarre features of the fiat system. The irredeemable electronic paper ticket money is deemed superior under the law to the real thing, which is no longer legal tender. This, in a sense, is the one hope of bitcoins, that they, too, will emerge as superior to real money. It brings to mind the Founders of the American constitutional system.

How humiliated they were by the financial fallout of the Revolution. It was paid for with the electronic paper ticket money of their day — the continental dollar. It soon became irredeemable ("not worth a continental"). This is why the Founders, when they first exercised the monetary powers the Constitution granted to Congress, insisted that the first Coinage Act define a dollar as a fixed amount of silver or gold.

Whatever else can be said about them, the Founders had enough wisdom — humility — to understand that they couldn't create money any more than the group of scientists in the famous jape could create life. The bitcoin system may have, as it does, a process called "mining" in which coins are created. But using the word "mining" does not make it mining in the monetary sense. This may be — we can but speculate here — what accounts for Mr. Nakamoto's silence.

— March 10, 2014

# George Soros' Two Cents

The billionaire George Soros is warning Britons against pulling out of the European Union. He contrasts, as we did in "The American Option," the fact that Ukraine is agitating to get into the E.U. just as Britain is agitating to get out. But it's another matter when a warning of this kind is made by the man who famously shorted the British pound and, as the Guardian reminded its readers this morning, helped to force Britain's currency out of the European exchange rate mechanism. That was in 1992 on what is known as Black Wednesday. Nice little economy you have there, Mr. Soros seems to be saying today. It would be a shame if anything happened to it.

What gets us about this is Mr. Soros's harping on jobs. Here's what he is quoted by the Guardian as saying in respect of the political consequences of any British withdrawal from the E.U.: "I will leave it to the British business community, particularly the multinationals that set up factories here as an entry point into the common market, to explain to the public what they stand to lose. But in one word — jobs." He did this, the Guardian reports, after the Labor Party leader, Edward Miliband, "won plaudits from business groups" for suggesting that if Labor wins the next election, there won't be a referendum on Europe.

It's an incredible demarche by Mr. Soros, actually — irresponsible, demagogic, and detached from any reference to history. We don't mind saying that we are not Soros haters; we have a mixed view of the billionaire. He's done many great things, including in Eastern Europe. But if he wants to talk about the employment consequences of Britain pulling out of Europe, he also needs to talk about sound money. After all, British employment was perking along just fine after World War II. Unemployment never got above 3% even once between 1946 and 1970. That's a full, long generation of full employment.

Then, bang. All of a sudden, unemployment started rising. It went above 3%. It dipped a bit to 2.6% in 1973 and 1974, and then started soaring, hitting 14.8% in 1986. It hasn't been down to what it was prior to 1971 since then. It hasn't been close. So wouldn't it make sense for Mr. Soros to make at least some reference to what happened in 1971? Particularly since something big happened that year. It was that President Nixon closed the gold window. America defaulted on the dollar. The gold exchange standard that had been operated since Bretton Woods was abandoned.

Now a lot of people, including Mr. Soros, made a lot of money in the chaos that followed. We don't begrudge them a cent of it. We do not blame them in the least for the chaos. But we do blame them for suggesting that the way to get the jobs back, or to protect what jobs they do have, is to entangle one's economy with a European Union that issues a fiat currency like the Euro. What Mr. Soros and his fellow sages should be saying is that long-term full employment is not going to return to Britain until it restores itself to a system of sound and honest money.

By the way, we'd say the same thing to Ukraine and its striving millions. Their hunger for freedom and democracy is inspiring. But to scramble to get onto the European Union is to seek to clamber aboard a raft that is caught in a whirlpool. For Mr. Soros to argue that Britain should cling to the same raft, well, he should — he no doubt does — know better. It is a tragedy. He could play such a constructive role on this head. It looks, however, like this issue will have to wait until the Republicans turn, as they did in 1896, to a candidate who understands the centrality of sound money and makes it the center of a presidential campaign.

— March 12, 2014

# A Guidance Overhaul?

The "immediate challenge confronting" the new Federal Reserve chairman, Janet Yellen, who is for the first time leading the meeting of the central bank's policy-making committee, "is to overhaul the Fed's forward guidance for short-term interest rates." That's the sentence that jumps out at us from the New York Times dispatch on the meeting of the Open Market Committee, which started today and runs through tomorrow. It was, after all, only a year or so ago that the idea of "forward guidance" came into widespread use in the first place. It strikes us that the guidance system is at awfully low mileage to come up for an "overhaul." Unless, of course, it was a lemon to start with.

The idea of forward guidance seems to be part of what these columns have called the "verbal dollar." We first used that phrase when news broke that the previous chairman, Ben Bernanke, was going to start holding press conferences to explain the Fed's policies. It seems that there weren't enough words in the minutes of the Fed or in the statements of the various Fed presidents or in the shadow open market committee or in the chairman's testimony before the various committees of the Congress. Or his lectures to college students. On top of all that verbiage, the Fed chairman undertook to meet with the press on a quarterly basis.

This was the price of quantitative easing and ultra low interest rates. How long would it last? What kind of expectations were reasonable? These kinds of questions sprang up as the Fed expanded its balance sheet by trillions and loaded up on debt issued by its owner. The value of the dollar itself had plunged, to a 1,900th of an ounce of gold at one point, before recovering to the range of a 1,300th of an ounce. At some point the Fed put up on its Web site a statement under this headline: "How does forward guidance about the Federal Reserve's target for the federal funds rate support the economic recovery?"

"Clear communication is always important in central banking," it said. It noted that since December 2008, its target for the federal funds rate has been between 0.0% and 0.25%. "Through 'forward guidance,'" it said, "the Federal Open Market Committee provides an indication to households, businesses, and investors about the stance of monetary policy expected to prevail in the future. By providing information about how long the Committee expects to keep the target for the federal funds rate exceptionally low, the forward guidance language can put downward pressure on longer-term interest rates and thereby lower the cost of credit for households and businesses, and also help improve broader financial conditions."

Then the Fed said the aforementioned target range "will be appropriate at least as long as the unemployment rate remains above 6-1/2 percent, inflation between one and two years ahead is projected to be no more than 1/2 percentage point above the Committee's 2 percent longer-run goal, and longer-term inflation expectations continue to be well anchored." Then it noted that in December the Open Market Committee "indicated that, in determining how long to maintain a highly accommodative stance of monetary policy, it will consider other information including additional measures of labor market conditions, indicators of inflation pressures and inflation expectations, and readings on financial developments."

Then it said the committee "now anticipates, based on its assessment of these factors, that it likely will be appropriate to maintain the current target range for the federal funds rate well past the time that the unemployment rate declines below 6-1/2 percent, especially if projected inflation continues to run below the Committee's 2 percent longer-run goal." Then it insisted that the "formulation of the forward guidance based on thresholds helps to clarify policymakers' intention to maintain accommodation for as long as needed to promote a stronger economic recovery in a context of price stability."

"And," the Fed added, just to be clear, "by more clearly describing the connection between future monetary policy and economic conditions, forward guidance helps to make monetary policy more transparent and predictable to the public." To which one can but say, *no wonder* the Times' reporter, Binyamin Appelbaum, is underlining the immediacy of overhauling forward guidance. Back in the old days, we were stuck with having to look what people were doing with gold, and the only way one could tell if money was too loose or too tight was whether they were buying or selling. Now forward guidance turns out to be just as rickety, another confounded barbarous relic.

— March 18, 2014

# 'Driftwood'

Here's how the London Financial Times reacts to the first press conference of the new Fed chairwoman, Janet Yellen: "Within seconds of perhaps accidentally suggesting that interest rates would rise sooner than anticipated, the Dow Jones dropped almost one percent. The markets recovered a little of their lost ground later on. But her slip further muddied what has proved to be an almost meaninglessly vague revision of the Fed's forward guidance policy. Central bank communications ought to be clearer than this. When markets have so little to go on, they will seize on whatever driftwood passes by."

Well, *sic transit gloria mundi*, as is said. One minute you're the most powerful woman in the world, featured on the cover of Time magazine under the headline "The $16 Trillion Woman." The next minute your utterances are likened in the Financial Times to flotsam. Forgive us for sticking with the point, but this is just a feature of the era of the verbal dollar. Our money, once backed by gold and silver, is now backed with driftwood. It bobs up and down on the great ocean of finance. People remark on its interesting and ever-changing shape. It floats near shore. It drifts away, as the currents may carry it.

Let us say that we don't blame Mrs. Yellen for this. She may be chairwoman of the Fed, but she is not its architect and the Fed is not ultimately responsible for the dollar. That is the United States Congress, which, in the early 1970s, invested in the idea of fiat money to a degree that would have just shocked the Founders of America down to the ground. Our national malaise has dragged on now as long as the first years of the Great Depression. And what happened back then? The country did not recover. It plunged into the depression within a depression.

It's not our intention to predict the same fate here, though neither would we rule it out. What we do predict is that historians will conclude that fiat money was during the long travail of the Great Recession a drag on the American economy. We do not blame Mrs. Yellen and her colleagues. But neither do we look to them for the solution. We blame Congress, to which the constitutional monetary powers are granted. "It was," the FT insists, "always going to be difficult to find an exit." Not, it neglects to mention, according to Ben Bernanke, who famously declared "We could raise interest rates in 15 minutes if we have to." Those words turned out to have been but some of the driftwood that was passing by.

— March 21, 2014

# Lagarde's Waterloo

The failure today in the Senate the so-called "reform" of the International Monetary Fund is an encouraging moment. Senator Reid had tried to tie the scheme, a lunge for money, to the Ukraine rescue, but then retreated, saying the IMF part of it would not have been able to pass the House. His retreat will enable the $1 billion package for Ukraine to go through, but it bitterly disappointed President Obama, who — as Judy Shelton warned the other day in the Wall Street Journal — didn't want to let the Ukraine crisis go to waste. There is little doubt that Mr. Obama and the European Left will be back with a new attempt to get the "reform" through.

The dissembling of the Treasury Department and the IMF's leadership has been just shocking, even for Washington. The IMF managing director, Christine Lagarde, issued an op-ed piece in the Wall Street Journal this morning, saying, among other things: "The IMF reforms come at no additional cost or risk to the American taxpayer. Money that Congress already appropriated five years ago will simply be transferred from a temporary fund at the IMF into its permanent resources." Translated into plain English that means: "You know that temporary loan you made to the IMF? We're keeping it."

The fact is that the reform under discussion would move some money out of a facility called "New Arrangements To Borrow." NAB is money which America and others have lent to the IMF. Our share, which is north of $100 billion, is a loan. We are owed it back. What Mrs. Lagarde and her camarilla are talking about doing is removing from the NAB the money American taxpayers have lent them and making it part of the permanent quota of the IMF, which means we don't get it back. It's gone. This kind of switcheroo is usually played with three walnut shells and a pea.

It's worse than that, as Heritage has been pointing out. (Heritage has a lot of time-in-grade in battle with the IMF, going all the way back to the early 1980s, when we had, in

Ronald Reagan, a president who understood the IMF's game.) The Treasury Department has been creating a false sense of urgency to the IMF money grab. It disputes the notion that the "reform" will cost billions, when in fact it would double the American quota — "$63 billion more taxpayer dollars," is the way Heritage characterizes the damage.

President Obama's "reform" would also mean a reduction in our ability to control what is done with the money we advance. Once money goes out of the NAB and into IMF quota, use of it no longer requires specific American approval. Plus, the reforms being hatched would end America's ability as a matter of right to decide who will represent it on the IMF's board. Heritage has been emphatic on this head, warning that America's president "might not be able to name someone to the IMF who shared his or her political and economic philosophies."

All this aside, the real problem with the IMF is that it is spreading socialism at a time when the world needs more free-market capitalism. The countries that have been under IMF tutelage have been disasters; the IMF pushes for tax increases. It dispenses abroad the kind of advice that wouldn't get to first base in the Congress. We are coming up on the 70th anniversary of the IMF. That's a long time without a fundamental review of the whole enterprise. By our lights, its last logic disappeared in 1973, with the advent of fiat money. We wouldn't advance one fiat cent to the Fund absent a top to bottom review by Congress of whether there's any logic left in it.

— March 25, 2014

# Yellen's Missing Jobs

The new Federal Reserve chairman, Janet Yellen, gave a policy speech today at Chicago, where, in a startling gesture, she mentioned three working individuals by name — Jermaine Brownlee, Vicki Lira, and Doreen Poole. They lost their jobs in the Great Recession and have been struggling ever since. It was a refreshing, even affecting demarche by Mrs. Yellen, who has made a return to full employment a public priority. She underscored her sincerity by telephoning Mr. Brownlee and Ms. Lira and Ms. Poole before delivering her speech.

All the greater the sense that the three — and the millions of unemployed or underemployed Americans like them — deserve a more radical, more courageous initiative than the bromides they got. They deserve a look at whether the Federal Reserve itself is part of their problem. We are now in the sixth year of an employment crisis that has consumed an entire presidency. The month that Barack Obama acceded, January 2009, the unemployment rate was at 7.8%, according to the Bureau of Labor Statistics. It reached 10% in October of that year and, while it has slid down somewhat, it has yet to fall below 6.5%.

Yet this entire time the Fed has been busting a gusset to reduce unemployment. It has expanded its balance sheet by trillions. It has launched forward guidance, held press conferences aimed at jawboning the system, and undertaken its quantitative easing. With all this, the unemployment rate is still substantially above what it was in 1978. That was the year the Congress gave the Federal Reserve a second mandate — to work toward full employment — on top of its traditional mandate of price stability. The legislation was the Humphrey Hawkins Full Employment Act.

What a mockery it has been. The year Humphrey Hawkins was passed, the unemployment rate was 6.1%. Since then the unemployment rate has *averaged* 6.4%. Even the liberals at the time comprehended the law was a sham. The New York Times, in a famous editorial, warned it would "play a cruel hoax on the hard-core unemployed, holding before them the hope — but not the reality — of a job." Shouldn't this record of failure instill some humility in the new chairman of the Fed? Maybe its accommodative monetary policy isn't the right solution in the first place.

How about a look at the year 1971. That year stands as a divide. From 1947 to that year, unemployment averaged only 4.7%. Since 1971, unemployment has averaged 6.4%. If President Obama had been able to deliver that at pre-1971 rates, he'd be bound for glory. So what was it that happened in 1971? That turns out to be the year America defaulted on the dollar. President Nixon closed the gold window. The gold-exchange standard of the post-World War II Bretton Woods system was abandoned. America turned toward the system of fiat money over which Janet Yellen and her colleagues preside today.

Yet the mandarins of the Federal Reserve do not want to open up the question of what Lawrence Parks of the Foundation for the Advancement of Monetary Education calls "irredeemable, electronic, paper ticket money." No member of the Fed is, or can be expected to be, receptive to questioning the fiat system itself. But where does that leave individuals like Mr. Brownlee, a plumber by trade, and Ms. Lira, who worked for a printing company, or Ms. Poole, who used to process medical insurance forms for a living?

There was a time when labor's representatives understood the importance of sound money. If one looks at a graph of the declining share of the all American workers who are members of a union, the long plunge begins in the mid-1970s, when we moved to the fiat system. The figure was above 28% in 1971; now it's below 11.5%. It's not our purpose here to plump for union membership. It is our purpose to suggest that people like Jermaine Brownlee, Vicki Lira, and Doreen Poole — who are eager and able to work — are owed better than the talk they are getting from the United States Federal Reserve.

— March 31, 2014

# Fiat Art?

The prospect that Jeff Koons' rendering in steel of the cartoon character Popeye will fetch $25 million when it is put up for auction next month is the lead story in the latest number of the Interest Rate Observer. "The art of inflation" is the headline that has been put on the piece by the paper's famed editor, James Grant. It illuminates a question that has dogged us for some time, namely whether the age of fiat money has begat an age of fiat art.

We last wrote about this question in 2008, in an editorial called "Monet and Money." It was triggered by the sale the week before of "Water Lily Pond" for what we called 80 million copies made by the Federal Reserve of a small government etching of George Washington. It was an astonishing price increase from the earlier decade, when "Waterlily Pond and Path by Water" fetched but 32.9 million of the small government etchings of Washington.

Despite the price rise in fiat money, we noted, the actual value of the Monets (discounting for the fact that they were two different paintings) had plunged 24% to but 85,333 ounces of gold from the 112,286 ounces of gold that the earlier sale had established as the value of a Monet canvas of these luxuriant lilies. At the time, we suggested that the "the enduring qualities of a great painting are a mockery of the qualities of our monetary management in Washington."

Mr. Grant invites his readers to reflect on the fortunes of two painters. One is Oscar Murillo, who was born in 1986 and whose canvas of squiggles, "Untitled Burrito," fetched 10 times its low estimate when it went on auction in February. The other is Esteban Murillo, who was born in 1617 and one of whose renderings of Christ, "Ecce Homo," and another of Mary were withdrawn after failing to attract their low estimates.

Mr. Grant likens Oscar Murillo to "a kind of momentum stock" and Esteban Murillo to a "kind of value stock." Mr. Grant goes on to quote Carol Vogel of the Times, relating a meeting two years ago of Oscar Murillo and the collectors Mera Rubell and her husband. He'd stayed up overnight to make seven or eight paintings and later, in another creative burst, did yet more canvases. "It was so intense," Ms. Vogel quotes Ms. Rubell as saying. "I don't even think he was on drugs."

"Maybe the central bankers are on drugs," remarks Mr. Grant. He then goes on to quote that even the more classical paintings have had their ups and downs. He notes that in 1852, Esteban Murillo's "Immaculate Conception" brought — in today's "gold value" (please excuse the redundancy) — $6.6 million. But also notes that in subsequent years the value of a Murillo plunged sharply. If it can happen to Esteban Murillo, why couldn't it happen to Oscar? he asks.

"Tastes change, money cheapens — and cycles turn," he concludes. To which we would but add that ideas can have cycles, too. Count these columns as among those that haven't the slightest doubt that eventually the folly of fiat money will be discovered again in the Congress of the United States that has the only constitutional grant of power to coin money and regulate its value and to fix the standard of weights and measures. And we enjoy the possibility that it will be art that helps them to see.

— April 19, 2014

# Piketty's Gold?

With all that has been written in respect of Thomas Piketty's new book, "Capital," you would think that someone — Paul Krugman, say, or Jonathan Chait or David Brooks or Hendrik Hertzberg; we're not worried about who it might be so much as *someone* among the liberal intelligentsia — would have remarked on an odd coincidence of timing. We're speaking here of the timing of the rapid rise of the blasted inequality over which Professor Piketty is so upset. After all, this inequality has become the cause celebre of the season for President Obama and his entire political party. It's the issue of the hour. Yet when it comes to the timing at which this phenomenon presented itself, nada. Omerta.

Well, feature the chart that Professor Piketty publishes showing inequality in America. This appears in the book at figure 9.8. It's an illuminating chart. It shows the share of national income of the top decile of the population. It started the century at a bit above 40% and edged above 45% in the Roaring Twenties. It plunged during the Great Depression and edged down in World War II, and then steadied out, until we get to the 1970s. Something happened then that caused income inequality to start soaring. The top decile's share of income went from something like 33% in 1971 to above 47% by 2010.

Hmmm. What could account for that? Could it be the last broadcast of the "Lawrence Welk Show?" Or the blast off of the Apollo 14 mission to the Moon? Or could it have something to do with the mysterious D.B. Cooper, who bailed out of the plane he hijacked, never to be seen again? A timeline of 1971 offers so many possibilities. But, say, what about the possibility that it was in the middle of 1971, in August, that America closed the gold window at which it was supposed to redeem in specie dollars presented by foreign central banks. That was the default that ended the era of the Bretton Woods monetary system.

That's the default that opened the age of fiat money. Or the era that President Nixon summed up by echoing* Milton Friedman's immortal words, "We're all Keynesians now." This is an age that has seen a sharp change in unemployment patterns. Before this date, unemployment was, by today's standards, low. This was a pattern that held in Europe (these columns wrote about it in "George Soros' Two Cents") and in America ("Yellen's Missing Jobs"). From 1947 to 1971, unemployment in America ran at the average rate of 4.7%; since 1971 the average unemployment rate has averaged 6.4%. Could this have been a factor in the soaring income inequality that also emerged in the age of fiat money?

This is the question the liberals don't want to discuss, even acknowledge. They are never going to get it out of their heads that the gold standard is a barbarous relic. They have spent so much of their capital ridiculing the idea of honest money that they daren't open up the question. It doesn't take a PhD from MIT or Princeton, however, to imagine that in an age of fiat money, the top decile would have an easier time making hay than would the denizens of the other nine deciles, who aren't trained in the art of swaps and derivatives. We don't belittle the skills of the top decile. We tend to view them the way we view great baseball players or violinists — heroic figures. Neither do we make a totem out of economic equality; in inequality, after all, are found incentives.

In terms of public policy, though, we favor honest money. It works out better for more people. And there is a moral dimension to the question of honest money. This was a matter that was understood — and keenly felt — by the Founders of America, who almost to a man (Benjamin Franklin, a printer of paper notes, was a holdout), cringed with humiliation at the thought of fiat paper money. They'd tried it in the revolution, and it had been the one embarrassment of the struggle. They eventually gave us a Constitution that they hoped would bar us from ever making the same mistake.

There is an irony here for Monsieur Piketty. It was France who gave us Jacques Rueff, the economist who had the clearest comprehension of the importance of sound money based on gold specie. He was, among other things, an adviser of Charles De Gaulle. It was De Gaulle who in 1965, called a thousand newspapermen together and spoke of the importance of gold as the central element of an international monetary system that would put large and small, rich and poor nations on the same plane. We ran the complete text of Professor Piketty's book "Capital" through the Sun's own "Electrically-operated Savvy Sifter" and were unable to find, even once, the name of Rueff.

— April 21, 2014

---

* What Nixon actually said was, "I am now a Keynesian in economics."

# The Gail Collins Dollar

After issuing all those columns by Paul Krugman about how there is no inflation, the New York Times has finally brought in Gail Collins to tell the truth. The editor emeritus of the paper's opinion pages does so this morning in a marvelous column called "It's only a million."

"It's sad what a million dollars has fallen to," Ms. Collins begins. The comment was triggered by her discovery that when Jeb Bush left the governorship of Florida, he had net worth of "only," as Ms. Collins put it, "$1.3 million." She admits she was surprised. "He must have felt terrible at family gatherings."

Imagine how the rest of us feel at the debasement of the dollar that Ms. Collin's Nobel-prize-laureate colleague has been insisting is not being inflated. Ms. Collins is commiserating with the former Florida governor because of the paltriness of the million dollars a year he's now making for advising Barclays Bank.

"A million dollars used to be a magic number, a sign of permanent affluence. You'd made it!" Ms. Collins exclaims. "But now it won't buy you lunch with Warren Buffett." The Sage of the Times notes that at a charity auction, lunch with the Sage of Omaha went for $1,000,100.

No doubt there will be a tendency to discount what Ms. Collins says. She didn't intend her column to be about inflation, after all; she was swinging at Governor Bush. But the Times has run out not one but two columns by Mr. Krugman using the same, identical headline, "Not Enough Inflation."

Professor Krugman has made it a practice to deride anyone who worries about the value of the dollar. He once mocked Congressman Paul Ryan for warning Chairman Ben Bernanke of the Fed that it was a terrible thing to "debase" the dollar. Mr. Krugman is the one with the Prix Nobel.

Well, Ms. Collins may not have been summoned to Stockholm (at least not yet — more on this in a moment). But she rose to glory via classical newspaper work covering local and state level politics (in her case Connecticut's) before moving up to the national story. She's got the same kind of common sense as Sarah Palin.

It was Governor Palin who, on the eve of the G-20 Summit in 2010, confronted Chairman Bernanke over the collapse of the dollar about which Ms. Collins has just written. Mrs. Palin focused not on Governor Jeb Bush's consulting fees but on what Americans discover when they try to stretch at the grocery store the dollars issued by the Federal Reserve.

What Ms. Collins and Mrs. Palin are putting into sharp relief is the fact that the dollar has lost more than 98% of its value since the founding of the Federal Reserve. It was valued at a 20.67th of an ounce of gold back then. Today it is valued at less than a 1,200th of an ounce of gold. It has lost more than 34% of its value since President Obama was sworn to the presidency.

Ms. Collins views this through the prism of Marilyn Monroe's famous movie "How to Marry a Millionaire." That was in the 1950s, when, Ms. Collins writes, "nobody ever suggested that a million dollars would not be enough to keep a kept girl fed and sheltered." Now, Ms. Collins points out, the owner of the Los Angeles Clippers "spent $1.8 million just to buy his lady friend a duplex."

"It's not that money doesn't buy happiness," Ms. Collins writes. "It's that these days it requires a whole lot more than a million dollars." Well, none dare call it inflation, at least not at the Times. Maybe the Nobel Committee will rescind the prize it gave to Professor Krugman and give it to Ms. Collins. Professor Krugman won't mind. The $1.2 million that comes with it isn't worth what it used to be.

— May 6, 2014

# The Coolidge Dollar

What an event the Calvin Coolidge Presidential Foundation hosted in the city to mark the introduction by the United States Mint of the "Coolidge Dollar." The base-metal coin is the latest in the Mint's presidential series. The evening was cheerful and non-partisan; the dollar, after all, is a concern for all parties. The speaker, journalist James Grant, asked whether anyone knew the etymology of the phrase "sound money." He then held up the genuine article, a silver dollar, and dropped it on the podium. The ringing of *l'argent* filled the room with a merry reminder of the constitutional principles.

Our Second Congress, the first to use the Constitution's coinage power, defined the dollar as 371 ¼ grains of silver, or a 15th as much gold. This opened a century long debate over bimetallism. It was settled in the presidential election of 1896, when the Democrats put up William Jennings Bryan. He stood for free silver and vowed he would not be crucified on a cross of gold (he ended up hawking swamp land in Florida). The Republicans put up William McKinley, who stood for defining the dollar in gold. It proved it to be the winning formula.

The Gold Standard Act became the supreme law of the land in 1900. It defined the dollar as a 20.67th of an ounce of gold. That, for the record, is the dollar in the Coolidge years. It was the legal definition of the dollar when, a century ago, the Congress established the Federal Reserve. It happens that the House balked at the idea of a central bank, but it finally agreed to create one after language was put into the law saying that nothing in the act would authorize an end to the convertibility of the dollar into gold at the legislated rate.

War rattled the international gold standard, but it is to the great credit of America that it held fast — including in the 1920s, when others fell away. Coolidge enabled this triumph by cutting the budget, leaving it smaller than when he had entered office. The 30th president, we are reminded by the

Web site thegoldstandardnow.org, records in his autobiography that he came to an understanding of the gold standard in the very 1896 presidential campaign in which Bryan stood for inflation. Coolidge was in Northampton, and a Democrat had endorsed Bryan in a column in a local paper.

"This I answered in one of the city papers," Coolidge later wrote. "When I was home [in New Hampshire] that summer I took part in a small neighborhood debate in which I supported the gold standard." He said that "the study I put on this subject well repaid me." And, we'd add, the country. How wonderful that one of the programs of the foundation that now honors the 30th president — and is chaired by our own Amity Shlaes — gathers high school students at Coolidge's birthplace at Plymouth Notch, Vermont, for a series of debates of the kind in which our 30th president honed his understanding of political economy.

— May 6, 2014

# Elizabeth Warren's Chance

"**W**orse yet, *the number of bankrupt families was climbing. In the early 1980s, when my partners and I first started collecting data, the number of families annually filing for bankruptcy topped a quarter of a million. True, a recession had hobbled the nation's economy and squeezed a lot of families, but as the 1980s wore on and the economy recovered, the number of bankruptcies unexpectedly doubled. Suddenly, there was a lot of talk about how Americans had lost their sense of right and wrong, how people were buying piles of stuff they didn't actually need and then running away when the bills came due.*"

* * *

Those sentences are from Senator Elizabeth Warren's new memoir, "A Fighting Chance." It is full of insights into a brilliant woman. She strikes us as smarter, more earnest, better balanced, and less entitled than Secretary Clinton, against whom some reckon she should make an attempt for the Democratic presidential nomination in 2016. Her book makes us wonder whether at some point she could be enlisted in the long struggle for monetary reform.

The senator understands the future of which her parents dreamed is gone. The "game," in her view, is "rigged" for "those who have money and power." She argues that the "basic infrastructure" such as roads, bridges, and power grids has crumbled. "The scientific and medical research that has sparked miraculous cures and inventions from the Internet to nanotechnology is starved for funding, and the research pipeline is shrinking. The optimism that defines us as a people has been beaten and bruised."

What we find so arresting is that Ms. Warren entered the debate through bankruptcy law. Yet she fails to connect it with the event that coincided with the explosion in bankruptcy filings. They began to take off in the mid-1970s. This is plain to see in a chart issued by the St. Louis Federal Reserve Bank. For the first half of the century, bankruptcy filings were fewer than one per a thousand Americans. Suddenly, the rate soared, starting in the early- to mid-1970s

What was it that happened then? That was the period in which America closed the gold window at which, under the Bretton Woods system, foreign governments could redeem their dollar reserves in gold. Before then the bankruptcy rate had been steady for generations. Since then, our whole fiber as a nation seems to have been weakened, and the future seemed to evaporate. As we plunged ahead in Senator Warren's book, we kept hoping she would get to this point. The default, after all, took place under a Republican.

Yet the only occasions on which Senator Warren uses the word "gold" in her book are to describe some tiles in the headquarters of AFL-CIO, the "soft gold and pale colors" in the Oval Office, and a pin worn by Holly Petraeus, an advocate for protecting GIs from debt problems. The phrases "gold standard," "monetary reform," "fiat money," "sound money" "Bretton Woods" fail to appear. The solutions she proposes are regulatory. None is radical.

Could she seize this issue? We keep returning to the year 1971. It wasn't just bankruptcies that began soaring in the mid-1970s. Unemployment also soared after Bretton Woods was lost, a point we marked in the editorial "George Soros' Two Cents" and "Yellen's Missing Jobs." This ought to be a perfect issue for Senator Warren, who is on the banking committee and before she was a senator helped create an agency, the Consumer Financial Protection Bureau, that is seated within the Federal Reserve. Governor Romney had the issue of monetary reform in his platform, but he failed to run on it. The issue is just lying out there for Elizabeth Warren. Talk about a fighting chance.

— May 11, 2014

# The Dwindling Fed

The Federal Reserve, for the first time in its 100-year history, is on the verge of operating with just three governors, the New York Times is reporting this morning. It says that the "dwindling of its board" is "straining the Fed's ability to manage its complex responsibilities." That's the good news. The bad news is that it's not yet clear whether Congress will rise to the occasion and — oh, say — audit the Fed to see what is going on there. This is a crisis that Senator Rand Paul, for one, wants to avoid wasting.

What precipitated the Times story is the pending departure of Governor Stein, who chairs two committees at the Fed. "He is also the only remaining member of those committees," the Times' Binyamin Appelbaum notes dryly. He also notes that three nominees to the Fed board are awaiting Senate confirmation but adds that "so are scores of other nominees to other offices." He quotes Senate Democrats as saying there is a "real chance" that "no vote will be held before Mr. Stein departs at the end of this month."

This crisis highlights the wisdom of those who want expand the representation on the Fed's Open Market Committee of the presidents of the regional Federal Reserve banks. This has been one of the measures being advanced by Congressman Kevin Brady, the chairman of the Joint Economic Committee of the Congress and the leader of an effort to conduct a centennial review of the Fed. As it is, the Fed governors are joined on the Open Market Committee by the presidents of five of the 12 regional banks.

The March and April meetings of the Open Market Committee, the Times reports, "represented just the third and fourth times in history that a majority of the votes were cast by the regional presidents." Their five seats rotate among the regional banks. They are neither nominated by the President nor subject to Senate confirmation. The members of Open Market Committee who come from the board of governors are presidential appointees, who are to subject to Senate confirmation.

One of the reasons this is a hot issue is that the members of the Open Market Committee from the regional banks are often, though not always, more conservative and business-minded than the appointed governors. The Times characterizes the Fed's "predicament" as "particularly striking because there is no real opposition" to two nominees to the Fed board, Stanley Fischer, a former head of the Bank of Israel, and Lael Brainard, a former Treasury official. Confirmation to a new term is being awaited by an existing governor, Jerome H. Powell.

Enter the junior senator of Kentucky, Dr. Paul. He is warning the majority leader in the upper chamber, Harry Reid, that he will do his best to delay those votes unless the Democrats allow a vote on his Federal Reserve Transparency Act. The measure would redeem the campaign of Senator Paul's father, Congressman Ron Paul, to audit the Fed. The Sun was the first newspaper to endorse the measure, a version of which was passed by the House in 2012 by an overwhelming bi-partisan margin.

The Federal Reserve fears this audit. It fears the private businesses. It fears the Congress that is its creator. It claims that an audit of the kind the House wants would interfere with its "independence." What independence? The staff of the Sun dissolved the entire text of the United States Constitution in a chemical solvent and then put the solution through a Hamilton-brand high-speed, rotary separator. Yet we were unable to detect even a particle of a requirement that monetary policy be independent of the Congress of the United States.

On the contrary, Congress is granted the power to coin money and regulate its value, to borrow money on the credit of the United States, and to lay and collect taxes. So we have long felt it past time for Congress to pull rank on the Fed. It is overdue for a top to bottom audit. The Times points out that "depletion of the Fed's board" is "a relatively new phenomenon." It notes that President Franklin Roosevelt put up six nominees on a Monday in January 1936 and all six were confirmed by the following Thursday.

Of course, no sooner did the Senate succumb to the bum's rush and confirm FDR's six nominees than America plunged into the "depression within the depression," the collapse of 1937. Let it be a lesson to the current Congress. There is no need to rush to fill the board of the Fed. Better for Congress to look to the substance and see what share of the blame the Fed itself deserves for the Great Recession that destroyed the presidency of Barack Obama, stranded millions without work, and forced us into retreat overseas.

— May 21, 2014

# The Anti-Piketty

Steve Forbes is just out with the book we've been waiting for. It's titled "Money." It contains his treatise on the destruction of the dollar and the threat its collapse represents to the global economy. His prescription is for a return to sound money based on gold. He is learned, plain-spoken, and wise, with a fluent understanding of history rivaled by few editors of his generation. His book will stand for many of us as the first answer to the neo-Marxist Thomas Piketty, whose "Capital" is all the rage in the Obama administration.

Mr. Piketty, after all, is advancing the view that the growing share of our wealth held by the top decile is creating a kind of irreversible plutocracy, an era of inequality. This theme is being echoed by all the panjandrums of the Left, from Paul Krugman to Senator Warren to President Obama. No doubt Secretary Clinton will try to get in on the act, too. This theme is going to be at the center not only of the 2014 congressional election campaign but of the 2016 presidential campaign. This is the issue that is written in the stars, and it will rarely get an answer as apt as Mr. Forbes'.

What Mr. Forbes gets so clearly is that all this inequality, this is a function of the age of fiat money. We noted in an earlier editorial that the very chart that Professor Piketty uses to show the soaring inequality shows it taking off in the mid-1970s, just after the collapse of Bretton Woods. Mr. Forbes nails this point. "Much of the speculation that takes place in today's financial markets is a response to the volatility produced by the collapse of the Bretton Woods gold system," he writes at one point (and under a heading that says: "George Soros May Have to Find a New Job.").

One of the rhetorical delights of Mr. Forbes' book is the inclusion at the end of each chapter of a summary that he calls "the nugget." They include, to cite but three, "An unstable currency means an unstable economy and less prosperity"; "Money measures wealth, but it does not create it"; and "To paraphrase Ron Paul: if printing money created wealth, there'd be no poverty left on earth." The whole batch of these nuggets could be printed on palm cards for our politicians to take to the hustings.

When Mr. Forbes went out on the hustings himself, he got his head handed to him, a fact that will no doubt be lobbed at this book. But those were different times — 1996 and 2000, when we were still in or enjoying the fruits of the vast boom that began under President Reagan. That was a period, extending through the presidencies of George H.W. Bush and William Clinton, when the value of the dollar had stabilized in a range of around 350th of an ounce of gold. Even Mr. Forbes' flat tax, the best fiscal idea since Reagan, was failing to resonate.

Experience since then has moved the monetary question to the fore. It is at the heart of our troubles, including the crisis of 2008. Loose money policies of the early 2000s led to what Mr. Forbes calls the "worldwide panic and global recession in 2008." The Keynesians threw everything they had at it, including expanding the balance sheet of the Federal Reserve by *trillions* of dollars in an effort to create growth and, in line with Humphrey Hawkins mandate, jobs, too. So a recession was lengthened into what we now call the Great Recession.

We had hoped that Governor Romney would take this issue to the voters in 2012. The long Republican primaries had actually forced the party to adopt a monetary reform plank in its platform. It called for a monetary commission to be established to open up the question. Mr. Romney, in the biggest blunder of the campaign, failed to stand on the very plank his party gave him. The importance of Mr. Forbes's book is that it will be there for the next candidate. It gives better expression to such a plank than has ever been given and at just the right moment. It is the answer to Professor Piketty and whatever Democrat runs in his name.

— May 21, 2014

# Bernanke's Lunch Bill

Ben Bernanke is certainly raking in the big bucks — ah, make that small bucks. It turns out, according to the New York Times, that since he stepped down as chairman of the Federal Reserve, Mr. Bernanke has been raking in the dough making speeches. As Fed chairman, he pulled down about $200,000 a year. Now he earns that in an hour or so, the Times reckons. He does this by giving speeches to hedge fund billionaires, bankers, and others he used to regulate.

Nice work, if you can get it. We don't begrudge Mr. Bernanke, though if $200,000 over lunch is what a Fed chairman can fetch, we ought to let him give such speeches while he's in office and save ourselves the salary. Then again, the value of 200 grand isn't what it was when Mr. Bernanke acceded. It is less than *half* of the 568th of an ounce of gold it was worth when the Princeton professor was sworn in as head of our central bank.

Aye, there's the rub. Wouldn't it be nice to have a monetary system in which one didn't have to pay a Federal Reserve ex-chairman 200,000 spondulicks in order to gain a glimpse of what the value of the dollar might be? What, after all, would one do if Mr. Bernanke weren't, as one person quoted by the Times phrased it, "joined at the hip" with the current chairman, Janet Yellen? Maybe accrued millions in speaking fees will get people thinking about a law-based definition of a dollar.

— May 21, 2014

# Jeff Bell for Senate

The victory of Jeff Bell in the Republican primary in New Jersey sets up what could be one of the great Senate races of the generation. And let us be among the first to endorse the veteran of the long drive for political and economic liberty that came together in the 1970s and ignited what became the Reagan revolution. Mr. Bell will face Senator Booker, a Rhodes Scholar turned Democratic Party glad-hander who has been, since winning a special election last year, a disappointment even to his original backers.

Not that he'll be easy to beat, as the New York Post pointed out; he's running in a blue state where the seat that will be filled in November has long been held by a Democrat — indeed, since Mr. Bell defeated the moderate Republican, Clifford Case, in the Republican primary in 1978 only to lose the general election to Bill Bradley. The significance of that race was Mr. Bell's role in crafting and honing the free market, supply-side arguments that would, two years later, later be brought to triumph by Ronald Reagan.

The electrifying thing about Mr. Bell's candidacy is his nigh singular appreciation for the issue of monetary reform. Better than any candidate we can think of, he grasps the fact that fiat money — dollars that are pure scrip, backed with nothing and convertible by law into nothing but other dollars — is at the root of the long travail of recession or near-recession that has consumed the Obama presidency. Our politics needs a tribune for the idea of sound money, a tribune who can illuminate this issue for the voters.

Can Mr. Bell prevail in November? William Kristol, in a cable endorsing Mr. Bell within moments of the primary victory, noted that Mr. Booker starts out way ahead. But he noted that Mr. Bell is going to run as both an intelligent and aggressive "full-spectrum conservative" who emphasizes a "pro-growth, pro-Main Street agenda, with a focus on monetary policy, in particular a return to the gold standard" —

a message sure to "bewilder the elites." But not the middle class voters in New Jersey.

They understand that their dollars are not what they used to be. They understand the travail of the past six years. The fact is that the explosion in inequality everyone is talking about, this began to show up on the charts in the mid-1970s, when we were launched into the age of fiat money. So did the sharp rise in unemployment, which averaged 4.7% years between the end of World War II and 1970. Then, come fiat money, unemployment started soaring. So did bankruptcies.

The Great Recession that we're still feeling saw the value of our fiat dollars collapse, to, at the moment, less than a 1,200th of an ounce of gold. We haven't had a mainstream Republican politician take this issue to the hustings as the central campaign theme, though there are some far-sighted Republicans who plainly get it (Rand Paul, Mike Lee, Paul Ryan, among them). Governor Romney had a platform plank on monetary reform but failed to make it an issue. All the greater the importance of Mr. Bell's candidacy in New Jersey. It has the potential to make history.

— June 5, 2014

# Yellen's 15 Minutes

The clock is ticking, as they say. The Federal Reserve's last chairman, Ben Bernanke, famously said that "We've been very, very clear that we will not allow inflation to rise above 2 percent. We could raise interest rates in 15 minutes if we have to." Mr. Bernanke never got around to it, and Chairman Yellen is signaling she's in no great rush, either. The New York Times's story about what it calls "the most significant speech yet in her still-young Federal Reserve chairmanship" runs under the headline "Janet Yellen Signals She Won't Raise Rates to Fight Bubbles."

Well, Mr. Bernanke had to be referring to fifteen fiat minutes. What is 15 minutes, anyhow? Is it 900 seconds? Or 9,000 seconds or nine months. Our sense is that it's a kind of floating 15 minutes, to be cashed in whenever the market will bear it. That must have been what Mr. Bernanke meant. Mrs. Yellen, for her part, is described by the Times as believing that "it would most likely be a bad idea to raise interest rates to fight financial excesses. Her focus, crucially, is not on preventing Wall Street from having ups and downs, but on making sure that those ups and downs don't bring economic disaster."

The writer for the Times — we're quoting Neil Irwin here — reckons that Mrs. Yellen's "focus on resilience differs from much of the public discussion, which often concerns whether some particular asset class is experiencing a 'bubble,' and whether policy makers should attempt to pop the bubble. Because a resilient financial system can withstand unexpected developments, identification of bubbles is less critical. As global financial markets continue their five-years-and-counting rally, urged along by policy from the Fed and other central banks, worry has been rising that the seeds are being sown for the next crisis."

Mrs. Yellen was rolling her words at an event at the International Monetary Fund in Washington. She was also speaking in the wake of the release of a report by the Bank for

International Settlements that, as Mr. Irwin puts it, "essentially accuses its own members of fecklessness in their easy-money policies." The Wall Street Journal, in its editorial on the BIS report, got to the issue ahead of the Times and did it under a classic headline, which summed up what the bank for central bankers was saying as "Stop Us Before We Kill Again."

The new Fed chairman, the Times reports, "doesn't absolutely rule out using interest rate policy as a tool to combat financial excess." But she is "making clear it is a less than optimal option." It characterizes what Mrs. Yellen was doing as "putting banks and everyone else in the financial world on notice: The Fed is not going to protect you from making mistakes. It is just going to try to ensure that if you do make them, the rest of us won't pay the consequences." When she's going to do that she doesn't say. She wants her own 15 minutes of fame at a time of her own choosing.

— July 3, 2014

# Waiting for Warren

The report that President Obama has promised Senator Elizabeth Warren "complete support" if she runs for president has the ring of truth. We read it in the New York Post under the byline of Edward Klein, author of the number one New York Times bestseller "Blood Feud," about the relations between the Clintons and the Obamas. He calls the promise the President has made to Senator Warren "a stinging rebuke to his nemesis Hillary Clinton."

Our interest in a Warren campaign has to do with the opening it would present to address what we see as the most important issue facing America — the crisis of fiat money. We wrote about this in the editorial "Elizabeth Warren's Chance." She entered public life through the door of bankruptcy law, which she teaches at Harvard. It's hard to think of a door more likely to bring one face to face with the hardest truths.

Yet Mrs. Warren completely misses the story. She comprehends the importance of the explosion of the bankruptcy rate. Through much of our history it had perked along at under two, or even one, personal bankruptcy filing per one thousand Americans. Then it took off. It soared to something like six per thousand. For Mrs. Warren this is about the evil of rich people and the depredations of the big banks. But were that the problem, why did the rate suddenly take off?

After all, we've had rich people and banks for centuries. So there's got to be another explanation. The explosion in the bankruptcy rate, it turns out, began in the mid-1970s, coincident with America's default on the dollar — that is, with the end of the gold-exchange standard that was set up at Bretton Woods, New Hampshire, at the end of the World War II. Could the soaring bankruptcy rate that has so energized Elizabeth Warren's career be but a feature of the age of fiat money?

Or, to put it another way, could Senator Warren be failing to understand her own signature issue? Our point is simply that this question would make for a great campaign. It is an issue for her potential opponents to comprehend down to the ground. It is the great tragedy of John Boehner's speakership in the House and of Governor Romney's candidacy for president that neither of them has managed to bring this issue to the fore of the mainstream Republican campaign. A Warren candidacy would be a slow pitch.

The soaring personal bankruptcy rate isn't the only tragedy that has emerged in the age of fiat money. We've also written — in "Yellen's Missing Jobs" — of the soaring jobless rate. Between 1947 and 1971, unemployment averaged only 4.7%. Since 1971, unemployment has averaged 6.4%. "If President Obama had been able to deliver that at pre-1971 rates, he'd be bound for glory," we've written. Instead, the tragedy of unemployment has consumed his entire presidency.

Even the 6.1% to which the latest jobs report indicates unemployment has fallen is nothing to cheer about. It is the same rate that obtained in 1978, when the Federal Reserve was given its second mandate — in the Humphrey-Hawkins Act — to promote full employment. It was given the assignment because of an unemployment crisis and a generation later, an unemployment crisis has consumed an entire presidency, even while the Federal Reserve has been running a radical, low-interest rate policy.

All this is material in which it would repay the Republican candidates — and, for that matter, Secretary Clinton — to become fluent. Yet only a few Republicans seem focused on the fiat dollar that lies at the heart of this political story. According to Mr. Klein, after all, President Obama is being advised by the First Lady and aide Valerie Jarrett that Elizabeth Warren is his "Mini-Me." That is why, Mr. Klein reports, the president has promised Mrs. Warren his "complete support." Comprehending the crisis of fiat money is the way to beat her on her own issue.

— July 6, 2014

# Krugman's Last Hurrah?

'I'm a defender of the economic policies that we followed after World War II, that produced the best generation of economic growth that this country has ever experienced. . . . I like the America that my parents prospered in. I think we can restore a lot of that."

\* \* \*

Those words were uttered by Paul Krugman two years ago when Congressman Ron Paul, in a debate on Bloomberg television, had him on the ropes over inflation. Mr. Krugman had a whole list of things he liked about the 1950s and 1960s. But he forgot to mention one — the gold exchange standard that was set up at Bretton Woods, New Hampshire, in the closing days of World War II and undergirt the growth his parents enjoyed.

Oh, does Mr. Krugman have a blind spot about that. He's out this morning with a column that runs under the headline "Belief, Facts and Money." It's about what Krugman calls "conservative delusions about inflation." It seems to have been ignited by a cable in the Times from a political scientist, Brendan Nyhan, about how more Republicans and religious people doubt Darwin and ignore climate change.

Mr. Krugman suddenly thought about what he called "the similar state of affairs when it comes to economics, monetary economics in particular." Those who worry about inflation, he seems to suggest, are as dumb as he perceives religious people to be. He denounces the Wall Street Journal for pointing out, in a typically savvy editorial issued in 2009, that the bond vigilantes were on the prowl. Yields on the 10-year Treasury had just climbed above 3.7%, the Journal noted, as "investors are now calculating the risks of renewed dollar inflation."

The Nobel laureate also went after what he called "a virtual Who's Who of conservative economists and pundits,"\*

who published an open letter to the Federal Reserve chairman at the time, Ben Bernanke, warning that his policies risked "currency debasement and inflation." He neglected to mention that they doubted the Fed asset purchases would achieve the Fed's goal of promoting employment.

"Reality, however, declined to cooperate," writes Mr. Krugman. By reality he apparently means "core inflation," the element of the consumer price index that excludes items on which prices are rising. The actual debasement of the dollar — its collapse in value — did turn out to be breathtaking. Mr. Krugman doesn't mention it, but the value of the dollar fell at one point to less than an 1,800th of an ounce of gold from the 1,368th of an ounce of gold at which it was when the conservatives wrote their letter.

Unemployment, meantime, has proved way more stubborn than the Democrats expected. Even after millions have dropped from the work force, it has come down to only the level it was at when, in 1978, the Fed first got its mandate to deal with joblessness. The conservative letter-writers gently suggested that rather than more monetary stimulus, "improvements in tax, spending and regulatory policies" be given "precedence in a national growth program."

Had either the Fed or President Obama listened to the conservatives who wrote the open letter, Mr. Obama might have been spared the humiliation of his poll numbers. The wisest of the Democrats, meanwhile, are starting to ask serious questions. This is what Paul Volcker did in May in his speech to the Bretton Woods Committee in Washington. The former chairman of the Fed reprised the whole post-World War II monetary history under a title with three question marks: "A New Bretton Woods???"

It would be inaccurate to suggest that Mr. Volcker called for a return to a 1950s type gold exchange standard that framed the generation of growth that lifted up Mr. Krugman's parents and millions of others. Nor did Mr. Volcker put forward any other program. But, he said, "by now I think we can agree that the absence of an official, rules-based, cooperatively managed monetary system has not been a great success." There was more wisdom of experience in that speech than in the entire run of the Krugman column in the Times.

We don't yet know what America will do in November in respect of the Senate. But if voters break up the Democratic log-jam in the upper chamber, we could yet get reforms of the type for which Mr. Volcker hinted he, for one, is ready. The chairman of the Joint Economic Committee, Kevin Brady, has been nursing a formal review of the Fed's performance on its centennial and is starting to win sponsors in the Senate. Congressman Ron Paul may have retired, but his son, Senator Rand Paul, is keeping alive his father's bill to audit the Fed (it passed the House handily in 2012).

Another signature measure of Ron Paul's, the Free Competition in Currency Act, is also being nursed on the Hill. It would codify Friedrich Hayek's ideas of the denationalization of money. Plus an important new generation of economists — John Taylor of Stanford comes to mind — is pressing for the institution of a rules-based monetary system. It's hard to predict which of these these ideas will triumph in the years ahead. It's not hard to predict that it will fall to others than Mr. Krugman to design the new system. We'd like to think they will create something even better than the gold exchange standard in place when Mr. Krugmans parents prospered.

— July 7, 2014

---

• The two-dozen signers included two former owners of the Sun, Roger Hertog and Paul Singer, and journalist and historian Amity Shlaes, who is married to the editor of the Sun.

# A Rule for the Fed

A cable this morning from Professor John Taylor of Stanford alerts us to the introduction in Congress of the newest piece of legislation offered in respect of monetary reform. It is called the "Federal Reserve Accountability and Transparency Act of 2014." H.R. 5018 would, as Mr. Taylor describes it in his Web log, require the Fed to adopt a "rules-based policy." The Fed would make the rules. It would then have to submit them to Congress, and be transparent about whether it is following them. The Sun endorses the measure as a step in the right direction.

Not that we harbor illusions about easy passage of the bill, which was introduced by Congressman William Huizenga, a Michigan Republican. "Potentially important" is how Mr. Taylor described it to us. The measure is all the more significant for the fact that it is part of the wider ferment going in in the 113th Congress over monetary policy. This is happening primarily in the House, though the Senate could catch fire on this issue after the November election. Among measures we're watching:

**Centennial Monetary Commission Act, or H.R. 1176,** which is being nursed by the chairman of the House-Senate Joint Economic Committee, Congressman Kevin Brady, to examine monetary policy since the creation, a century ago, of the Federal Reserve;

**Sound Dollar Act, or H.R. 1174,** another Brady project, which would, among other things, including on the Open Market Committee more presidents of the regional Federal Reserve Banks, get tougher with the International Monetary Fund, and focus monetary policy on price stability;

**Free Competition in Currency Act, H.R. 77,** which was introduced by a Republican of Georgia, Paul Broun, and would codify Nobel laureate Friedrich Hayek's idea of the denationalization of money by ending legal tender status of United States fiat scrip and open the system to privately-issued competing currencies, and end any tax arising from the spending of gold or silver;

**Sound Money Promotion Act, S. 768,** offered by Senator Mike Lee of Utah, would exempt from taxation any gold and silver coins declared to be legal tender by either the federal government or any state government, extending nationally the most radical monetary measure to be enacted anywhere in recent years, the Utah Sound Money Act, which makes gold and silver coins legal tender in the Beehive State and removes state taxes arising from spending them.

**Federal Reserve Transparency Act, or S. 209,** offered by Senator Rand Paul, renews the drive to audit the Federal Reserve launched by the senator's father, Ron Paul, to audit the Federal Reserve. His father's measure passed the House by an overwhelming bipartisan vote in 2012 and is being offered by Mr. Broun in the lower chamber in the 113th Congress as H.R. 24.

Scant chance of passage is given to each one of these measures by Web sites that predict such things. One thing we learned in a long newspaper life, however, is a principle summed up by the long-time editor of the Wall Street Journal, Robert Bartley (he is now gone, alas): "Change happens on the margin." The legislation is marginal only in the sense that all this legislation faces an uphill slog. But the idea of John Taylor, that monetary policy should be subject to rules rather than discretion, is not marginal.

On the contrary, this is American bedrock. As is the idea that Congress ought to be involved. The coinage power — the power to coin money and regulate the value thereof and of foreign coin — is one of the powers most plainly enumerated in the Constitution and most clearly granted to Congress. As are the powers to borrow on the credit of the United States, to tax, and to regulate interstate commerce. Congress has a free hand to assert this power and to lay down the rules by which rules are set. A hearing is scheduled for Thursday, where we hope it will start to be made clear how overdue this measure is.

— July 8, 2014

# The Fed in Danger

It would surprise us if Chairman Janet Yellen of the Federal Reserve were not already huddling with lawyers about the danger ahead. That's our take-away from her testimony this week with the oversight committees in the House and Senate. We don't mean to suggest that Mrs. Yellen is in peril for any personal wrongdoing. We do, though, sense a whiff of danger for the Fed itself.

The danger stems from a growing sense in Congress that the Fed has, with its program of quantitative easing and ultra-low interest rates, lengthened the Great Recession. The House is now considering legislation to require the Fed to establish and follow certain rules. The bill, proposed by Congressmen Scott Garrett and William Huizenga, is called the Federal Reserve Accountability and Transparency Act of 2014.

The hazard came into focus as soon as Mrs. Yellen was finished sharing with the House her ruminations on the economy. "Chair Yellen," began the Financial Services chairman, Jeb Hensarling, "let's talk a little bit about independence." He read her a definition of central bank independence by Lawrence Summers, the former Treasury Secretary whom Mrs. Yellen edged aside for Fed chairman.

Mr. Summers wrote of the "institutional relationship between the central bank and the executive, the procedure to nominate and dismiss the head of the central bank, the role of government officials on the central bank board, and the frequency of contact between the executive and the bank." Mr. Hensarling, as cool a bicuspid as has ever questioned a Fed chairman, asked whether Mrs. Yellen agreed.

She started right off: "I see Federal Reserve independence . . ."

Suddenly, she seemed to sense danger. "Of course," she said, interrupting her own sentence, "I mean we are a creature of Congress. We have a responsibility to report to Congress.

And you used the term executive branch, I think, in the material . . ." Mr. Hensarling reminded her that he was quoting Mr. Summers. "So," Mrs. Yellen hemmed, "I see us as needing to report regularly to Congress about our conduct of monetary policy and the economy."

"Is it true," Mr. Hensarling asked, "that there is a weekly meeting between you and the Secretary of the Treasury?"

"Ah, many weeks, I mean it's not . . . every . . ." Mrs. Yellen hawed.

"Most weeks?" said Mr. Hensarling.

"Many weeks we get together and confer about matters of mutual concern, but we are completely independent from the executive branch in the conduct of monetary policy."

Mr. Hensarling then asked her whether she would be willing to report to his committee on the matters that were discussed in her meetings with the treasury secretary. Replied Mrs. Yellen: "I'm not willing to report on a regular basis on private conversations that I have, ah, but any agreement that we reached would certainly be in the public domain."

Any agreement?

That strikes us as a newsworthy statement in an era in which the Federal Reserve has just expanded its balance sheet by trillions of dollars. It is now holding trillions of Treasury notes and bonds that it ostensibly acquired on the open market but that represent, nonetheless, loans to the federal government from its own bank. These bonds were issued by the same Treasury Department with which Mrs. Yellen has been meeting with more or less weekly.

Just what agreements are there? What did they talk about? If she's not willing to share with Congress the details of her conversations, how will the constitutional custodian of the monetary powers know whether agreements were reached? How is the Fed going to ease out of these hyper low interest rates without bankrupting the Federal government that owes it all this money? If Congress has a right to know what agreements have been made, what about the rest of us?

We aren't suggesting a conspiracy. But a career covering monetary reform has left us with the opinion that the Fed is over-ripe for review. We endorsed the bill for a Fed audit that passed the House in 2012, and also the bill, still under consideration, for a Centennial Monetary Commission to see where the Fed stands at the beginning of its second century. We endorsed the Free Competition in Currency Act, and the Sound Dollar Act. Add to them the new Federal Reserve Accountability Act. These are serious measures, deserving of more than truculence from the Fed.

Feature, after all, the remarks in May by Paul Volcker, Mrs. Yellen's illustrious predecessor. He reprised the era of fiat money that has obtained since the collapse of Bretton Woods in the 1970s and declared: "By now I think we can agree that the absence of an official, rules-based, cooperatively managed monetary system has not been a great success." Surely Mrs. Yellen must know that there are millions of Americans who are coming to comprehend the truth of Mr. Volcker's words and are growing impatient with the Fed Congress created.

— July 17, 2014

# The Missing Data?

*'The crisis came from causes not captured by the new Keynesian models used at the Fed, such as excessive risk-taking in financial markets and failures of financial regulation and supervision. We had to figure out how to incorporate the effects of the crisis in our models."*

*"I'm sorry that light bulbs didn't go off in my head a couple of years before they really did, but there was no question. I was hearing stuff that was really scary. And I wouldn't have seen it in the data."*

\* \* \*

Those are the confessions of the ex-chairman of the Federal Reserve, Ben Bernanke, and his successor, Janet Yellen. They are contained in Nicholas Lemann's profile of Mrs. Yellen in the latest number of the New Yorker. It's a wonderful story, even if it adds up to a plea that Mrs. Yellen needs to be more of a politician. It's a reminder of, among other things, that they just didn't see the crisis coming. It just wasn't in the Fed's data. And no wonder. They weren't paying attention to Julie Satow.

Ms. Satow was the real estate reporter of The New York Sun.\* She broke the story that generated the most vituperous protests of any cable we printed during the first decade of the 21st century. She was writing about the latest report from the real estate industry in New York City, boasting that in the past six years the price of an apartment in Manhattan had nearly doubled to $1.4 million. Ms. Satow had taken the prices and refigured them in ounces of gold, resulting in a five-column headline at the top of page one: "Gold Value of Apartments Sinks."

What a cataract of complaints greeted the story, which was accompanied by a chart showing that the actual — meaning the gold — value of apartments was plunging even while prices in Federal Reserve scrip were soaring. Please mark the date: January 3, 2008. Within nine months, the real estate crisis, triggered by vast lending at inflated prices for dubious real estate, was upon us. In other words, we'd all have been better off had Ms. Satow been chairing the Fed. Ms. Yellen mightn't have seen it in the data. Mr. Bernanke's models mightn't have captured it. Gold, however, was onto it.

It was back in December 2005 that we issued the editorial called "The Bush Dollar." The editor of the Interest Rate Observer, James Grant, had just published in our pages a warning that the greenback's value in gold had so far plunged 46% over the course of George W. Bush's presidency. President Bush, we suggested, would be wise to spend less time worrying about the war than about the dollar. Since then we've issued more than 125 editorials stressing the primacy of this issue, largely in respect of constitutional first principles.

We are not so obsessed with specie and constitutional principles as to ignore the credit and regulatory questions confronting the Fed on any given day (for starters, we pore over the parchment of Grant's Interest Rate Observer every other week). All we're saying here is that it strikes us that there's something off for Mr. Bernanke and Mrs. Yellen to fetch up at this date blithely talking about how they didn't see trouble in the data and continuing to ignore the signals in gold. The fact is that a search always ends in the last place one looks.

— July 17, 2014

---

* Ms. Satow now writes a column on real estate for the New York times.

# Chinese Gold Standard?

Maybe the New York Times is a more worried about the prospect of inflation than Paul Krugman likes to let on. Maybe not. Either way it's out with a long op-ed piece raising the question of whether the Communist Chinese could eventually make the kind of move America made at Bretton Woods in 1944, when it established the dollar as a specified amount of gold and, as the Times op-ed piece put it, "confirmed the central position of the United States in the international monetary system."

The dispatch, under the headline "A Chinese Gold Standard?", is by Kwasi Kwarteng, a member of the British parliament who has a book just out on the 500 year history of empires and debt. The book, in the view of James Grant, writing in the Wall Street Journal, is exasperating in the author's refusal to "render historical judgment." That would be in the contest between real money — gold — and the fiat currencies on which the world has been relying, if that is the word, since the collapse of Bretton Woods under the strain of guns and butter.

Mr. Kwarteng's cable in the Times is a bit more forthcoming in its suggestion that the Red Chinese could, by expanding their gold holdings and international reserves, end up making their own currency an anchor of the international system. He suggests there is a possibility of the Chinese reds replacing the American dollar the way the dollar once replaced the British pound. It, after all, had been backed by gold and served as the world's reserve currency through most of 19th century.

Mr. Kwarteng notes that America is "$17.6 trillion in debt owed to the public, and large trade deficits are the norm." Yet, he reckons — wrongly in our estimation — that "there is no scope for revisiting the international monetary system, despite great dissatisfaction by countries like China and the Persian Gulf states, which hold large foreign currency reserves." He does concede that "Americans themselves question the security of the dollar when their country faces such large trade and budget deficits."

Instead, Mr. Kwarteng looks to the China, with its nearly $4 trillion in reserves "accumulated through its mercantilist trade policies" that "give it plenty of ammunition to claim leadership in the creation of a new monetary order." He asks: "Could China someday peg its currency to gold, as Britain did in 1821? China has the reserves to do this, and it could have the political will, if the dollar proved to be unreliable as a store of value in the future." He suggests that there could be a renminbi pegged to gold within a generation.

"With a balanced budget and a gold-backed currency, China's economy could be even more formidable than it is today," writes Mr. Kwarteng. "Such a move would truly mark its return as the 'Middle Kingdom.'" He also suggests that such a scenario "would, in many ways, be a more secure basis for an international monetary regime system than the system of floating exchange rates that Nixon inadvertently created in 1971, one that forever overturned the Bretton Woods order."

The piece in the Times marks the second time in recent weeks that we've heard recognition that we are being failed by our system of fiat money and floating rates. The more important was the speech in May by the former chairman of the Federal Reserve, Paul Volcker, to the Bretton Woods Committee in Washington. "By now," Mr. Volcker said, "I think we can agree that the absence of an official, rules-based, cooperatively managed monetary system has not been a great success." No doubt that history will render her judgment in her own good time.

— July 26, 2014

# Mystery of Jackson Hole

The panjandrums of our monetary system will be gathering over the weekend at Jackson Hole, Wyoming, for their annual retreat. Dissenters in the ranks of the central bank's governance are "increasingly vocal," as the New York Times put it in a headline, over their fears in respect of inflation. This adds some drama to a meeting at which, the Times reports, the theme is labor markets, which fits right in with Chairman Yellen's priority among the Fed's mandates, full employment.

We hope they get around to the pattern of unemployment that has come ever more clearly into focus with each passing season of the age of fiat money. Between 1947 and 1971 — that is, in the first generation of the Bretton Woods agreements, under which America defined the dollar as a 35th of an ounce of gold —the unemployment rate in America averaged but 4.7%. Since 1971 — that is, since America's abandoned Bretton Woods and opened the age of fiat money — unemployment has averaged 6.4%.

Now we understand that the above-described coincidence does not establish causality. But what a job for all the PhDs among those who manage what James Grant likes to call the PhD-backed dollar. Let them look, too, to whether the Humphrey Hawkins Full Employment Act of 1978 turns out to have been a good idea. It was the law that gave the Fed its jobs mandate. When President Carter signed that dog's breakfast, unemployment was 5.8%. It hasn't been that low in the entire Obama presidency.

Despite, of course, the trillions of dollars the Federal Reserve has added to its balance sheet. If we've been banging this drum for a while it's because of our conviction that the solution to this puzzles lies at the bottom of our economic woes. We are living in an age of illusion. We celebrate, say, the sages of Berkshire Hathaway. Yet the value of a share of Berkshire has plunged to something like 159 ounces of gold from the 269 ounces of gold a share was at, say, the day that George W. Bush acceded to the White House.

No wonder there is no joy in the land, even if the Dow Jones Industrial Average is bouncing in and out of record highs. The Obama presidency is nearing the final turn. Savers have been devastated. The market isn't what it seems. No one wants to lend and no one wants to borrow. Unemployment is still above where it was when Congress gave the Fed a mandate to bring it down. A new Fed chairman has made jobs her signature. But will anyone at Jackson Hole ask whether it is the fiat nature of our money that got us into this hole in the first place?

— August 21, 2014

# Krugman's Kryptonite

Paul Krugman is out with his latest column mocking conservatives for a fixation on inflation that he reckons has become an "obsession." He has been set off by the same dispatch in the Times that we wrote about in "Mystery of Jackson Hole." It reported on the "increasingly vocal minority" of officials at the Federal reserve who want the bank to "retreat more quickly" from its easy money policies. This owes to fear of inflation. The Nobel laureate thinks the persistence of the inflation obsession is the "more interesting and important story."

Let's stipulate for a moment that Mr. Krugman is right about this. Conservatives generally are worried about inflation. We share the worry, despite the consumer price index. But what about Mr. Krugman's own psychology? Here he is, a Nobel laureate in economics, who won't address the collapse of the value of the dollar. Its value at the moment is off more than eighty percent from the 250th of an ounce of gold at which it was valued in the middle of the year when Mr. Krugman became a columnist of the Times.

Yet he won't talk about it. President Obama can go on the radio and talk about how there is no "silver bullet" to the soaring price of gasoline. It turns out that at the time the value of gasoline in terms of silver was plunging. It was not the gasoline going up but the dollar going down. Silence from Mr. Krugman. He's obsessed with the Consumer Price Index, some versions of which exclude gasoline. He's worse than indifferent to specie. He's got a phobia. He's scared of it. To Mr. Krugman it's kryptonite.

That's the rock from Superman's home planet, Krypton. Put a piece of specie next to Mr. Krugman and he shrivels up like Superman on a slab from Krypton. It wouldn't surprise us were Mr. Krugman to keep his Nobel "gold medal" in a lead-lined case, lest he get woozy when he walks past it. He calls for analysis? Analyze this. During Bretton Woods, under which the dollar was fixed at a 35th of an ounce of gold, unemployment averaged 4.7%. Since then, it's averaged above 6%. Is that related to the fiat nature of money?

It's not just the jobless rate that has spiked in the age of fiat money. The bankruptcy rate also began its climb after the dollar was delinked from gold, which we wrote about in "Elizabeth Warren's Chance." So did the so-called inequality rate on which Thomas Piketty fixates and about which we wrote in "Piketty's Gold" and "The Anti-Piketty." Mr. Krugman says that those who have been warning about inflation should be ignored because of the CPI. What will be the fate of Mr. Krugman for failing to acknowledge the collapse of the dollar in specie?

— August 22, 2014

# William Jennings Krugman

Paul Krugman's latest column in his campaign for inflation turns out to be an endorsement of none other than William Jennings Bryan. He was the Nebraska Democrat who ran for president in 1896 on a campaign for the free coinage of silver, meaning for inflation. The Republicans put up William McKinley, who ran from his front porch a campaign for the gold standard and honest money. Mr. Krugman explains McKinley's landslide by saying that "the elite mobilized en masse" in the election with the highest campaign spending, as a percent of GDP, in history, and worries whether the wealthy are "similarly mobilized against easy-money policies today."

Mr. Krugman neglects to mention one feature of 1896. It was not only the campaign that demonstrated that the people were not so easy to convince of the virtues of inflation. It also showed that Americans weren't going to succumb to a campaign that blamed their troubles on the Jews. Early in his campaign for inflation, William Jennings Bryan had gone onto the floor of Congress and read into the record Shylock's bond. America, he asserted, could not afford "to put ourselves in the hands of the Rothschilds." He went on to demand that the Treasury "shall be administered on behalf of the American people and not on behalf of the Rothschilds and other foreign bankers."

Bryan's campaign was a repudiation of the faction of the Democrats, led by Grover Cleveland, that stood for honest money. The "Cassandra of the Plains," Mary Lease, had condemned Cleveland as the "agent of Jewish bankers and British gold." Bryan won the nomination with his vow, "you shall not crucify mankind on a cross of gold." The delegates were so transported that they didn't react until he'd left the stage. Then suddenly the hall erupted with an ovation of whoops and cheers. Some of the Democratic delegates, The New York Sun reported at the time, screamed "Down with gold! Down with the hook-nosed Shylocks of

Wall Street! Down with the Christ-killing gold bugs."

It's not our purpose here to suggest that Mr. Krugman is an anti-Semite; he is not. It is our purpose to suggest he's playing with fire. And that a credible columnist writing about Bryan would be more forthcoming about what 1896 was all about. Late in the campaign Bryan would deny that he, himself, was an anti-Semite. But the famed German anti-Semite at the time, Hermann Ahlwardt, campaigned for Bryan in New York. (When he feared for his life, the police commissioner, Teddy Roosevelt, mocked him by assigning him a retinue of bodyguards, all of them Jewish.) Ahlwardt backed Bryan in his newspaper, *Der Anti-Semit.*

Mr. Krugman's own paper, the New York Times, was appalled by Bryan. It noted that the Democrats in New York state "have always been for sound money." It called the platform put up for Bryan "a radical departure from Democratic doctrines" and Bryan's ticket one that "stands for Populism, not Democracy." It chastised the state party for getting behind the Bryan ticket with a "platform of repudiation and dishonor." So it endorsed John Palmer of a pro-gold faction called the National Democratic Party.

The Sun was among those that backed McKinley. His was one of the remarkable campaigns in all of American history, run from his front porch. He pressed the case for sound money, backed by gold, and warned of the consequences of repudiation. He won handily, and by the end of his first term, he'd won passage of the Gold Standard Act of 1900, which defined a dollar as a 20.67th of an ounce of gold, ending a century long debate over whether gold or silver was the more logical specie.

McKinley defeated Bryan again in the election of 1900. By then, Mr. Krugman's paper had swung into the McKinley camp. "No one will deny," it said, "that Mr. Bryan and his party were all wrong four years ago." It added: "We believe that the mere effect of the election of Mr. Bryan, representing the absurd and worn-out errors of finance which he does represent, would be in itself a disaster of a very serious nature." That's what the New York Times, at its apogee, thought of the ideas for which William Jennings Krugman is plumping today.

— September 8, 2014

# Audit the *New York* Fed

Could a political marriage of Rand Paul and Elizabeth Warren finally open up the question of the Federal Reserve? We ask because of the call this week by Senator Warren for hearings into the allegations aired on National Public Radio that the New York Fed has been treating the banks it supervises with kid gloves. Those allegations were the result of an investigation that NPR reported in league with another liberal news service, Propublica. It happens that Mrs. Warren's call came but ten days after the House passed the Federal Transparency Act.

Known as Audit the Fed, the measure would subject the Fed and its regional banks to a real audit, one that includes not only their books but their formation of monetary policy and their full range of operations. It just passed the House by the astonishing, bi-partisan margin of 333 to 92, wider than the margin the last time it was passed. In other words, passage wasn't just a tip of the hat as it was deemed to be two years ago to a departing Congressman Ron Paul, who was the originator of this demarche but has since left Congress. It turns out that the People's House wants this measure.

Yet Reuters reports that the legislation "is expected to meet a fate similar to its predecessor's: death in the Democratic-controlled Senate." Could that be turned around? The entry of Mrs. Warren into this fray makes us wonder whether there might be some hope that — as happened in the House, where the measure originally had tough sledding — Democrats and Republicans could come together. Particularly since a logical partner on this measure would be Ron Paul's son, Senator Rand Paul, who has had a companion measure to the House bill before the Senate for some time.

The gentlewoman from Massachusetts may be a socialist and the gentleman from Kentucky may be a libertarian. What that means is that they could make different uses of what would be turned up by a thorough audit of the Fed. Yet it strikes us at least they have a common interest in finding out what in Sam Hill is going on at the central banking system that the Congress created. The NPR/ProPublica report is shocking enough; it includes tape recordings made by a Federal Reserve bank examiner, Carmen Segarra, before she was fired by the Federal Bank of New York in 2012.

Ms. Segarra's surreptitious tapes seem to have recorded examiners from the Fed being "captured" by — meaning, going soft on — Goldman Sachs in the course of their work review of the big investment bank. And they also show her being cashiered when she declines to be captured herself. We're not so concerned one way or another whether the Fed has been captured by Goldman. The way to stop that racket is to end the era of fiat money and establish a constitutional system in which the dollar is defined as a set amount of specie, gold or silver.

That's the way to keep the Fed honest. It's the method to put some backbone in the New York Fed. It's the way to put Goldman Sachs in a situation that can be supervised. For if the money is not connected to anything real, what at the end of the day are the examiners the Fed sends out supposed to examine? No less a figure than the greatest of the modern Fed chairmen, Paul Volcker, has called for a New Bretton Woods. The chairman of the Joint Economic Committee of the Congress has called for a centennial review of where the Fed stands at the start of its second century. An audit of the Fed would be just the place to start, beginning with an audit of the New York Fed.

— September 27, 2014

# Janet Yellen's Halloween

*Mirror, mirror on the wall*
*Who makes us so un-equal?*
*Answer, thee, this white-haired head:*
*Could it be our very Fed?*

\* \* \*

Of that little ditty, which fetched up on our typewriter as Halloween approaches, we are put in mind by Janet Yellen's speech on inequality. The Fed's new chairwoman delivered her remarks earlier this month at a conference at Boston. She noted that the "past several decades have seen the most sustained rise in inequality since the 19th century after more than 40 years of narrowing inequality following the Great Depression."

The "extent of and continuing increase in inequality in the United States greatly concern me," Mrs. Yellen declared. "By some estimates," she noted at one point, "income and wealth inequality are near their highest levels in the past hundred years, much higher than the average during that time span and probably higher than for much of American history before then."

What's so striking about this speech is Mrs. Yellen's lack of self-awareness. There is no hint that she sees a possibility, imagined by the poet quoted above, that the Federal Reserve itself is the culprit. Yet it strikes us that by her own timeline, the rise in inequality of which she complains started showing up after America's default under the Bretton Woods Agreements and the enactment in the 1970s of a system of fiat money.

We have made this point several times, because it's so glaring and because no one else is pressing it. In "Yellen's Missing Jobs," we sketched the coincidence between the enactment of the system of fiat money and the soaring jobless rate. We marked the point in respect of Britain in "George

Soros' Two Cents." And in "The Anti-Piketty," about Steve Forbes' new book on money, we focused on the coincidence how inequality began rising in the age of fiat money.

One of our favorite newspapermen, Joseph Joffe of Die Zeit, looked at us across a dinner table not long after that editorial was issued and said, "Yes, but someone needs to determine whether fiat money is a cause or a coincidence." He's right as rain. But one doesn't have to be an economist to imagine how the advent of fiat money empowers the those who make their living in the financial markets over those who don't.

It's not just the employment picture, either. There's also bankruptcies. This is the focus of the work at Harvard Law School of Senator Warren. She wrote about it in her autobiography, "A Fighting Chance," and we wrote about it in "Elizabeth Warren's Chance." She is alarmed that the bankruptcy rate, which had been perking along for decades under the gold standard at under two per a thousand Americans, suddenly shot up in the 1970s.

Mrs. Warren doesn't mention it, but this trend begins right after the collapse of Bretton Woods. The left would like to deal with the rising unemployment, the rising inequality, and the rising bankruptcies by constructing ever more expensive programs to be run at taxpayers' expense out of Washington and ever more expensive regulatory regimes from the same quarter. There is going to be hell to pay when voters take account of the fact that these programs end up compounding the problem. It's a kind of monetary version of the old Halloween racket known as "trick or treat."

— October 28, 2014

# Beyond the Liberty Dollar

Congratulations are in order to United States District Judge Richard Voorhees of North Carolina for the judiciousness of his decision in the case of Bernard von NotHaus. We weren't personally present at the courthouse at Statesville, where von NotHaus had been ordered to appear Tuesday for sentencing on his conviction of uttering — introducing into circulation — his Liberty Dollars. But we were on tenterhooks, because von NotHaus, 70, was looking at the possibility of spending the rest of his life in prison.

The reason we've been watching the case is that von NotHaus' demarche is one of the few direct challenges to what the Foundation for the Advancement of Monetary Education likes to call "legal tender irredeemable electronic paper ticket money." That refers to the scrip being issued by the Federal Reserve. Von NotHaus had designed and circulated a medallion made of pure silver, the same specie that was fixed on by the Founders of America as the basis of the constitutional dollar.

A jury found, among other things, that von NotHaus' Liberty Dollar violated federal law against private coinage and was similar enough to American legal-tender coin that it constituted counterfeiting. "Attempts to undermine the legitimate currency of this country are simply a unique form of domestic terrorism," the prosecutor, Anne Tompkins, said after von NotHaus was convicted. She suggested that such schemes "represent a clear and present danger to the economic stability of this country."

In the three and a half years since the jury reached its decision, Judge Voorhees allowed constitutional and procedural objections to be heard but in the end supported the jury. The government on Tuesday asked for a prison sentence of at least 14 years and as much as 17 ½ years. The government was also seeking forfeiture of some 16,000 pounds of Liberty Dollar coins and specie, which in 2011 it had valued at nearly $7 million.

Then spake the judge, sentencing von NotHaus to but six months of home detention, to run concurrently with three years of probation. He departed from non-binding guidelines because, he suggested, von NotHaus had been motivated not by criminal intent but by an intention to make a philosophical point. That is what these columns have been reporting for more than four years, and, while the Sun's coverage played no part in the case, we are glad to discover that the judge is of a similar, if not identical, mind.

Von NotHaus is no doubt relieved that he doesn't have to go to jail, but he has put out no statement. Our guess is that it is sinking in on him that he has been marked now as a felon, and his own dream of a parallel form of money, composed of constitutional specie, is gone. There may yet be surprises, but the sagacity of Judge Voorhees's handling of this case lies in, among other elements, the fact that he has left no great incentive for either side to make an appeal.

Whatever happens, the logic now is for the issues raised in the von NotHaus case to be pursued in the political arena. We are coming up on the 50th anniversary of the Coinage Act of 1965, which stripped silver from our common coinage. President Lyndon Johnson, who signed the bill into law, called it "the first fundamental change in our coinage in 173 years." He noted that during that nearly two-century span our coinage of dimes, quarters, half dollars, and dollars have contained 90 percent silver."

"The new dimes and the new quarters will contain no silver," the president confessed. "They will be composites, with faces of the same alloy used in our five-cent piece that is bonded to a core of pure copper." That is how the debasement began, though LBJ did issue a warning. "If anybody has any idea of hoarding our silver coins, let me say this. Treasury has a lot of silver on hand, and it can be, and it will be used to keep the price of silver in line with its value in our present silver coin."

It was a vain boast. At the time, the value of the dollar was more than two-thirds of an ounce of silver, as it was in 1792. By January 1980, the value of a dollar plunged to less than a 49th of an ounce of silver and even today has regained nowhere near its historic value. It is a shocking abdication by the United States Congress, a point that von NotHaus has thrown into sharper relief than any monetary gadfly has managed to do in years. That is no small achievement.

— December 3, 2014

# Appendix

## Excerpts from the Coinage Act of 1792
## Act of 2 April 1792, 1 Statutes at Large 246
## CHAPTER XVI. – An Act establishing a Mint, and regulating the Coins of the United States.

SECTION 1. Be it enacted by the Senate and House of Representatives of the United States of America in Congress assembled, and it is hereby enacted and declared, That a mint for the purpose of a national coinage be, and the same is established, to be situated and carried on at the seat of the government of the United States, for the time being; and that for the well conducting of the business of the said mint, there shall be the following officers and persons, namely, — a Director, an Assayer, a Chief Coiner, an Engraver, a Treasurer.

\* \* \*

SECTION. 9. And be it further enacted, That there shall be from time to time struck and coined at the said mint, coins of gold, silver, and copper, of the following denominations, values and descriptions, viz.,

EAGLES – each to be of the value of ten dollars or units, and to contain two hundred and forty-seven grains and four eights of a grain of pure, or two hundred and seventy grains of standard gold.

HALF EAGLES – each to be of the value of five dollars, and to contain one hundred and twenty-three grains and six eights of a grain of pure, or one hundred and thirty five grains of standard gold.

QUARTER EAGLES – each of be of the value of two dollars and a half dollar, and to contain sixty-one grains and seven eights of a grain of pure, or sixty-seven grains and four eights of a grain of standard gold.

DOLLARS or UNITS – each to be of the value of a Spanish milled dollar as the same is now current, and to contain three hundred and seventy one grains and four sixteenth parts of a grain of pure, or four hundred and sixteen grains of standard silver.

HALF DOLLARS – each to be of half the value of the dollar or unit, and to contain one hundred and eighty-five grains and ten sixteenth parts of a grain of pure, or two hundred and eight grains of standard silver.

QUARTER DOLLAR – each to be of one fourth the value of the dollar or unit, and to contain ninety-two grains and thirteen sixteenth parts of a grain of pure, or one hundred and four grains of standard silver.

DISMES – each to be of the value of one tenth of a dollar or unit, and to contain thirty-seven grains and two sixteenth parts of a grain of pure, or forty-one grains and two sixteenth parts of a grain of standard silver.

HALF DISMES – each to be of the value of one twentieth of a dollar, and to contain eighteen grains and nine sixteenth parts of a grain of pure, or twenty grains and four fifth parts of a grain of standard silver.

CENTS – each to be of the value of the one hundredth part of a dollar, and to contain eleven penny-weights of copper.

HALF CENTS – each to be of the value of half a cent, and to contain five penny-weights and a half penny-weight of copper.

\* \* \*

SECTION 11. And be it further enacted, That the proportional value of gold to silver in all coins which shall by law be current as money within the United States, shall be as fifteen to one, according to quantity in weight, of pure gold or pure silver; that is to say, every fifteen pounds weight of pure silver shall be of equal value in all payments, with one pound weight of pure gold, and so in proportion as to any greater or less quantities of the respective metals.

SECTION 12. And be it further enacted, That the standard for all gold coins of the United States shall be eleven parts fine to one part alloy; and accordingly that eleven parts in twelve of the entire weight of each of the said coins shall consist of pure gold, and the remaining one twelfth part of alloy; and the said alloy shall be composed of silver and copper, in such proportions not exceeding one half silver as shall be found convenient; to be regulated by the director of the mint, for the time being, with the approbation of the President of the United States, until further provision shall be made by law.

SECTION 13. And be it further enacted, That the standard for all silver coins of the United States, shall be one thousand four hundred and eighty-five parts fine to one hundred and seventy-nine parts alloy; and accordingly that one thousand four hundred and eighty-five parts in one thousand six hundred and sixty-four parts of the entire weight of each of the said coins shall consist of pure silver, and the remaining one hundred and seventy- nine parts of alloy; which alloy shall be wholly of copper.

SECTION 14. And be it further enacted, That it shall be lawful for any person or persons to bring to the said mint gold and silver bullion, in order to their being coined; and that the bullion so brought shall be there assayed and coined as speedily as may be after the receipt thereof, and that free of expense to the person or persons by whom the same shall have been brought. And as soon as the said bullion shall have been coined, the person or persons by whom the same shall have been delivered, shall upon demand receive in lieu thereof coins of the same species of bullion which shall have been delivered, weight for weight, of the pure gold or pure silver therein contained: Provided nevertheless, That it shall be at the mutual option of the party or parties bringing such bullion, and of the director of the said mint, to make an immediate exchange of coins for standard bullion, with a deduction of one half per cent, from the weight of the pure gold, or pure silver contained in the said bullion, as an indemnification to the mint for the time which will necessarily be required for coining the said bullion, and for the advance which shall have been so made in coins.

* * *

SECTION 16. And be it further enacted, That all the gold and silver coins which shall have been struck at, and issued from the said mint, shall be a lawful tender in all payments whatsoever, those of full weight according to the respective values herein before described, and those of less than full weight at values proportional to their respective weights.

SECTION 17. And be it further enacted, That it shall be the duty of the respective officers of the said mint, carefully and faithfully to use their best endeavours that all the gold and silver coins which shall be struck at the said mint shall be, as nearly as may be, conformable to the several standards and weights aforesaid.

SECTION 19. And be it further enacted, That if any of the gold or silver coins which shall be struck or coined at the said mint shall be debased or made worse as to the proportion of fine gold or fine silver therein contained, or shall be of less weight or value than the same ought to be pursuant to the directions of this act, through the default or with the connivance of any of the officers or persons who shall be employed at the said mint, for the purpose of profit or gain, or otherwise with a fraudulent intent, every such officer or person who shall be guilty of any of the said offenses, shall be deemed guilty of felony, and shall suffer death.

# Acknowledgements

The publication of these 130 editorials in a single volume provides, among other things, the opportunity for me to express my appreciation of the reporters and editors who, on four newspapers over almost 50 years, helped shape my views on the United States Constitution and the dollar and helped me get them into print. They are not responsible for — and in many cases don't agree with — the opinions that emerged in the editorials of the Sun. The same can be said for the sources thanked below. All the more grateful am I to them.

My acquaintance with the subject of money began at the Berkshire Courier, a weekly in Great Barrington, Massachusetts, where I started my newspaper career in the summer of 1965. It was among my duties to operate the stapling machine in the basement when the paper's print shop was binding the newsletter of Colonel E.C. Harwood's American Institute for Economic Research. Harwood was an early and eloquent tribune of sound money, and I came to admire him for the integrity of his political economy.

In March 1971, just back from Vietnam and out of the Army, I joined the Detroit bureau of the Wall Street Journal. It turned out to be four months before President Nixon closed the gold window, brought an end to the Bretton Woods system, and opened the age of fiat money. Laurence O'Donnell, the Journal's Detroit bureau chief, encouraged his merry band of reporters to dig in as the federal government sought to impose wage and price controls.

From Detroit the Journal sent me to Asia, first for the Far Eastern Economic Review and then the Wall Street Journal's Asian edition, where similar encouragement came from its publisher and editor, Peter Kann, and its managing editor, Norman Pearlstine. These were the years when it became clear that even though America had lost in Vietnam, it was capitalism rather than communism that was emerging as victorious in the battle of ideas over which system would be the better engine for development in the Third World.

In 1980, the editor of the Wall Street Journal, Robert L. Bartley, brought me back to New York as an editorial writer. Among other assignments, Bartley sent me in 1981 to cover the hearings in Washington of the United States Gold Commission. Two of its members, Congressman Ron Paul and businessman-scholar Lewis Lehrman, were exceptionally generous in sharing their knowledge of the workings of the classical gold standard and of Austrian economics and, in the case of Mr. Lehrman, the French economist Jacques Rueff.

Later Bartley sent me to Europe to edit the Journal's overseas editorial pages. During those years I was given generous interviews by, among others, the president of the German Bundesbank, Karl Otto Poehl, the British chancellor of the Exchequer, Nigel Lawson, and the French minister of economy, Edouard Balladur. From there it was back to New York and my years at the Forward before founding — with its brilliant managing editor, Ira Stoll, and a group of investors — The New York Sun, in whose pages these editorials were issued.

In a long career, I have made a point to seek out those who offer a skeptical view. Few of my encounters with such sages have been as enjoyable as the several with Paul Volcker. When, after dinner one evening, I handed the former Fed chairman a copy of the first edition of this anthology, he put his arm on my shoulder and said, "Just remember, you can't go back." I'd edited the Forward, I reminded him. We both chuckled. Several months later, he gave a speech called "A New Bretton Woods?"

"I think we can agree that the absence of an official, rules-based, cooperatively managed monetary system has not been a great success," Mr. Volcker said. It would be inaccurate to suggest that these editorials played any role in the emergence on this issue of the central banker who conquered the inflation that erupted after the closure of the gold window. But it would not be inaccurate to say his words are a source of hope.

The Robert and Ardis James Foundation provided, via the Hudson Institute, financial support for my research on the Constitution and the dollar; the Lehrman Institute awarded me in 2012 a grant in the form of a Lifetime Achievement Award. Their support is gratefully acknowledged. David Pietrusza and Elliott Banfield assisted with editing and designing the book. For their encouragement and suggestions I am indebted to the editor of the Interest Rate Observer, James Grant, Lawrence Parks of the Foundation for the Advancement of Monetary Education, and George Melloan of the Wall Street Journal. And to the closest of all guides, my wife and friend Amity Shlaes, who has always kept the aspidistra flying.

— Seth Lipsky
New York City
December 2014

SETH LIPSKY, editor of The New York Sun, is a former member of the editorial board of the Wall Street Journal, for which he covered, in the early 1980s, the hearings of the United States Gold Commission. He is the author of *The Citizen's Constitution, An Annotated Guide*, which was published in 2009 by Basic Books.

JAMES GRANT is the editor of *Grant's Interest Rate Observer*. His books include *Mr. Speaker: The Life and Times of Thomas B. Reed, the Man Who Broke the Filibuster, Bernard Baruch: The Adventures of a Wall Street Legend, John Adams: Party of One, Mr. Market Miscalculates*, and, most recently, *The Forgotten Depression: 1921: The Crash That Cured Itself.*

THE NEW YORK SUN is a daily newspaper published at New York City. Between 2002 and 2008, it was issued in both print and digital formats and is now issued online at www.nysun.com. Its founders picked up the flag of The New York Sun that had been issued as a broadsheet between 1833 and 1950.

CPSIA information can be obtained at www.ICGtesting.com
Printed in the USA
LVOW04s0331180515

438860LV00025B/381/P